Praise for

BIG MAN

"The opening chapters, about Mr. Clemons's childhood in Virginia, have the clarity and resonance of a good Springsteen song."
— *New York Times*

"Legends have a way of growing every time they're told. This time, the tales of rock and roll history are brought to life by a legend himself, Clarence Clemons. BIG MAN relives Clemons's story in a unique personal narrative that's bound in both history and folklore. This is an essential read for any music lover." — President Bill Clinton

"Many fascinating stories...a great glimpse into the life, and the mind, of one of [the E Street Band's] key members...should keep Bruce fans thoroughly entertained." — *Newark Star-Ledger*

"Entertaining...His storytelling prowess is on display...Fans will be eager to savor every page." — *Publishers Weekly*

"The feeling I get watching Clarence walk to center stage to play his sax must be similar to the feeling a Yankee fan had watching Babe Ruth walk to home plate: You're sure a big man is about to do something that's gonna make you cheer louder than you ever have before. This great book makes that feeling even stronger. Now excuse me while I drive my sleek machine over the Jersey state line."
— Artie Lange, New Jersey native, E Street fanatic, and *New York Times* bestselling author of *Too Fat to Fish*

"Funny, entertaining, often profane...the E Street Band's larger-than-life sax player." — *Booklist*

"Entertaining."   —*Austin Chronicle*

"One of the greatest books about a big black man ever written. If you want to get really close to a big black man without getting punched in the face, this book's for you!"   —Chris Rock

"An appealing pseudo-memoir...offers an intimate look at the rapport among band members...The mystique is still intact."
                                        —Gannett News Service

"Clemons demonstrates that he might be every bit the raconteur that the Boss is in concert...Clemons imparts a warm, Indian summer feeling that deftly accompanies his rollicking reminiscences, making this a must for fans."   —*Kirkus Reviews*

"Clemons's elephant memory of the E Street Band, the early days, makes the book. And his breezy prose places the reader next to him at the counter of a local watering hole."   —*Palm Beach Post*

"An outrageous journey with one of the most charismatic, gracious, kind, and talented men of our time...This peek into the world of Clarence is full of fun and laughter, which is exactly what this guy is all about. He's a genuine soul worth his weight in gold."
                                —Pat Riley, NBA Hall of Fame coach

"Clemons's larger-than-life persona and love of storytelling shine. Essential reading."   —*Library Journal*

"Telling moments...What the reader gets, ultimately, is a story of friendship through music."   —*Oregonian*

"Too funny, soulful, outrageous, and wise to have been written by two people. I suspect Don Reo is an invented character. A mystical book, an oddly beautiful book, a wonderful book."   —Kinky Friedman

BIG MAN

REAL LIFE & TALL TALES

CLARENCE CLEMONS & DON REO

with a Foreword
by Bruce Springsteen

GRAND CENTRAL
PUBLISHING

NEW YORK   BOSTON

Grand Central Publishing
Hachette Book Group
237 Park Avenue
New York, NY 10017

www.HachetteBookGroup.com

Printed in the United States of America

Originally published in hardcover by Grand Central Publishing.

First Trade Edition: November 2010
10 9 8 7 6 5 4 3 2 1

Grand Central Publishing is a division of Hachette Book Group, Inc. The Grand Central Publishing name and logo is a trademark of Hachette Book Group, Inc.

The Library of Congress has cataloged the hardcover edition as follows:

Clemons, Clarence.
Big Man : real life & tall tales / Clarence Clemons and Don Reo. — 1st ed.
p. cm.
ISBN 978-0-446-54626-3
1. Clemons, Clarence.   2. Rock musicians—United States—
Biography   3. E Street Band.   I. Reo, Don.   II. Title.
ML420.C547A3 2009
782.42166092—dc22
[B]
2009017206

ISBN 978-0-446-54625-6 (pbk.)

To Danny, my teacher and my friend.
You always did things first.
"Chevy coma soma doma."

———

To Judith D. Allison,
who has made everything possible.

Foreword

This book gets as close to the "truth" about Clarence Clemons as I can imagine. Mere facts will never plumb the mysteries of the Big Man. That being said, there are only one or two stories in this book that I could swear are not true. All the rest are adventures that may and could have happened to my great friend.

Clarence has spent much of his life as a drifting spirit. Where he walks, the world conforms to his presence. For his size, "C" is an unassuming man. He does not impress himself upon you. He just brings it with him when he comes.

The story I have told throughout my work life I could not have told as well without Clarence. When you look at just the cover of *Born to Run*, you see a charming photo, a good album cover, but when you open it up and see Clarence and me together, the album begins to work its magic. Who are these guys? Where did they come from? What is the joke they are sharing? A friendship and a narrative steeped in the complicated history of America begin to form and there is music already in the air. Forty years later, I read this book with the same questions still running through my mind.

Enjoy.
Bruce Springsteen

A Note from Don Reo and Clarence Clemons

This is not a standard memoir. We are storytellers, and the sections labeled "Legend" are, quite simply, stories that we have told over the years in cars, bars, planes, trains, and rooms in hotels and hospitals. Most of them contain some fact and a lot of fiction, and so you should not take them literally. Conversations and situations have been constructed and imagined, swapped around in time and place, embellished, and invented. These legends are written in the third person because that's how legends are told.

Everything else you can take literally. It is all factual and reported just how it happened.

In the end, we wrote this book to shed light on the E Street story as well as share the truths, lies, recollections, and imaginings we've told each other over the course of thirty-plus years. The bottom line is this: we have amazing tales to tell, and they're all here. We had great fun living and writing these stories.

You should've been there.

Don and Clarence

From the Massive Desk of
Clarence Clemons

I'd like to add one other thing. As this book grew, one thing became clear—it's impossible to tell my story without telling at least part of Bruce's story. But so much of his story has been told elsewhere in so many different books and articles that the challenge became how to write about him in a new and different way. I wanted to give the reader a glimpse into the personal and private side of our relationship without getting too personal and private. I hope we accomplished that. My heart will always be filled with gratitude to Bruce for one simple reason: without Scooter, there is no Big Man.

BIG
MAN

Don

I'm not going to make it," said Clarence.

We were sitting in his hospital room overlooking the East River. He'd had his second knee-replacement surgery two days before. The other knee had been replaced two weeks ago.

"Don't talk like that," I said. "You're going to be fine."

"I mean the Super Bowl show," he said. "There's no way. You can't imagine the pain."

For him to say this, the pain must have been off the charts. I'd been with him through surgeries before, including three hip replacements, which are no walk in the park. But I had never seen him like this or heard him talk this way.

"It's too soon to say that," I replied. "Give it some time. Take the drugs and rest."

"They haven't made a drug that can touch this pain. I feel like I'm made of pain."

It was the first week of October, and the band was booked to play the half-time show at the Super Bowl in February. That was only four months away. In my heart I agreed with Clarence. I did not think there was any way on God's earth that he'd be able to make that show.

"Do you want to work on the book?" I asked. "Feel like telling me some stories?"

"Maybe," he said. "I've been having all these crazy dreams. Fever dreams about all the people in my life. My family, Bruce, music, writers I like..." He trailed off momentarily but soon picked up again. "Some truly bizarre stuff. These dreams—they're full of crazy conversations in weird places. I've been thinking about my mother and father a lot. I guess that's natural in this situation. They're gone and I feel like I'm moving toward them fast."

"This doesn't sound like you, Big Man," I said.

That was true. Clarence has always been one of the most positive people in the world.

"I know, Don," he said. "But I don't feel like me."

He turned his head away and looked out the window. It was early afternoon, and the FDR was already jammed with traffic. A big barge was being towed upriver just below us.

"I've never missed a show in my life," he said.

He didn't look at me when he said it, because he wasn't talking to me.

Clarence

My mother told me this story, and I love it with all my heart. —C.C.

The man was drinking Coca-Cola; the woman was drinking ginger ale. All the other people in the club were drinking alcohol in one form or another. Not that it was all that crowded. The small room was about one-third full. All eyes were on the stage and the man playing the horn. His name was Sill Austin and he was great. He played with a soft intensity that was mesmerizing. The man and woman had walked two miles from their home through the cold December evening to see him. They rarely went out these days. Babysitters were a luxury they couldn't afford. But when the man had seen the ad in the paper saying Sill Austin was booked at Frankie's Lounge, he knew they had to find a way to go. They'd listened to the recordings over and over.

"You're going to wear a hole right through that thing," she'd say to him every time he put one of them on the record player.

"Then I'll go buy a new one," he always said in return.

And now here they were in the same room with him, watching him play and create that magic.

Watching Sill Austin play pretty for the people. He reached out and took her hand. She squeezed his hand in response.

After the show they sat at the table for a while and finished their sodas. It felt like the old days when they'd first started going out. Before the war to end all wars.

"If World War Two was the war to end all wars," he said once, "how come they gave it a number?"

"I think that was World War One," she'd said, smiling.

"Even worse," he had replied.

"Did you like the show?" she asked him, even though she knew the answer.

"Yeah," he said. He was never a big talker.

She thought he looked handsome in his Sunday suit. The shirt was as white as his teeth.

"Why do you think you like him so much?" she asked. "There are plenty of other horn players out there."

"He plays the music that I hear in my head," he said.

It was very cold when they stepped outside. The wind had picked up. The weather forecast was calling for snow tomorrow. Christmas lights glowed in a lot of the shop windows. They both pulled up their collars and started to walk. She put her arm through his and they stepped in rhythm, shoulder to shoulder.

"I think that's him," she said.

He looked at Sill Austin putting his horn case into the front seat of a new DeSoto.

"Yeah, that's him, " he said.

"Wanna say hello?" she asked.

"No," he replied.

"Why not?"

"'Cause right now it's perfect," he said.

After the first mile she said, "Clarence wants a train set."

He didn't say anything.

"From Santa," she said. "Electric trains."

"Yeah," he said. "Then when he grows up he can become a Pullman porter."

"I don't think that's necessarily true," she said, smiling. The cold made it hard to feel her face.

"The boy's going to be nine years old," he said. "Time he grew up."

"Meaning what?" she said.

"I'm not getting him trains," he said.

"He'll be disappointed," she said.

"He'll get over it," he said.

"So what do you want to get him?" she asked.

He lifted his head and looked at her. He smiled.

"A saxophone," he said.

Clarence

I fell in love with Shirley.

Unfortunately, Shirley didn't know about it.

She was a cheerleader, and she was the most beautiful girl I'd ever seen. She was more beautiful than I could have imagined. She was tall, athletic, and the color of honey. Her smile made the world smile long before Mary Tyler Moore. I loved everything about her.

She didn't know I existed.

I was a sixteen-year-old defensive end on the football team. Not a glamour position. To the prettiest cheerleader in history, linemen were invisible.

But I forced myself to say hello to her when I passed by on my way to the field or the bench.

Just a "Hey, how ya doin'?" but at least it forced her to make eye contact with me. She'd smile in response and sometimes say "Hey" back at me.

I thought about her every night. I was obsessed with her. I could spend an hour just thinking about her lips and the way her teeth sparkled and how perfect everything about her seemed to be. I wouldn't have asked her to change anything. Usually I found fault with girls. Not that I could be selective; the fact was, I was thrilled to spend time with any girl who showed any interest in me at all. The horn helped. I was softer when I played the horn, and that made them feel safe. Otherwise I felt I was just big and black and scary. Some girls were pretty but had lousy personalities or strange voices or bizarre laughs or some fucking thing that just rubbed me the wrong way. Most of the time I'd just ignore those things and try whatever I could think of to get into their pants, but my heart wasn't in it—just my dick.

Shirley was different. I couldn't even think about fucking her. It seemed wrong, somehow. Sure, once we were married we would fuck all the time, but until then she was just too special, too fragile or something. I really just wanted to be near her. All the time. Alone. Just the two of us. If everybody else in the world died I didn't give a shit so long as Shirley survived and would talk to me. Would touch my hand and look into my eyes and smile. I wouldn't need food or water.

She lived in Woodlawn, a full twenty miles from my house. I'd hitch-hike over to her neighborhood and walk around. I liked treading the same sidewalk that she walked on. I liked going to the same supermarket and thinking how she probably stood right here in front of the cereal and took her time picking out Corn Flakes or Wheaties or Cheerios. Later I found out all she ate was oatmeal. That was after she started talking to me. That was after I'd spent several weeks walking past her house hoping to catch a glimpse of her through a window. After a while I'd determined that her room was on the second floor of the wood-frame house and her window looked out on the street.

"Oh, hi," she said. "What are you doing in this part of town?"

"You know," I said, looking at the ground.

"No, I don't know," she said. I stole a glance at her. She was smiling a little smile that made me think that she probably did know.

"Just hanging around," I said.

"Just hanging around," she repeated, lowering her voice and doing a fairly good impression of me. "Wanna come over to my house?"

"Yes," I said. I was thinking, *Hell yes,* and *Shit yes,* and *Fuck yes,* but all I said was "Yes."

"Well, c'mon then," she said, taking my hand and leading me away.

She was an orphan. Her parents had been killed in an accident when she was a baby, and she was being raised by her aunt Cara.

Cara was fine with us sitting on the couch in the living room or out on the porch, but she kept a fairly good eye on us. Not that there was anything to worry about. We were just getting to know each other and finding out what music we both liked, and film stars and food and colors and everything else there was to discover, and there was a lot.

We laughed easily. We both seemed to have the same sense of humor, and we both liked the "sick" jokes that had been going around recently like: "The murderer is dragging the little girl through the woods and says, 'What are *you* crying for? I have to walk back alone.'"

I made my way all the way over there every Sunday for the next two months. I didn't care how far it was, as long as she was there on the other side. I loved her with that deep and complete first love that knows no caution or fear, only joy. That's what I felt when I was with her, or when I looked at her in school or on the sidelines at a game, or even when I just thought of her or spoke her name: joy. She would be my wife as soon as we were old enough to get married, I was sure of that. If our first was a girl, we'd call her Joy.

After about a month of hand holding and flirting she finally let me kiss her. Actually, we were standing at the front door saying good-bye like we always did, and she kissed me. On the lips. She had to stand on tiptoes to do it, but she did it. Then she smiled up at me and said, "See you in school."

I didn't even look for a ride home that afternoon. I walked all the way. I floated home filled with a happiness I did not believe could have existed in this difficult world. We kissed again the next Sunday, this time on the couch when Cara wasn't looking. This time it was a grown-up kiss.

A movie kiss, and she slid her tiny tongue into my mouth. I thought I might elevate off the couch and slam into the ceiling. She giggled and kissed me again.

The following Sunday it was raining hard. I hitchhiked and was lucky enough to get a ride to within a block of her house. But even in that short block I got drenched before I got onto the front porch and knocked on the door. Aunt Cara opened it and looked at me.

"Afternoon, ma'am," I said. "Terrible rain today."

"Shirley's not here, Clarence," Cara said. "She's pregnant."

The smile was still on my face and didn't disappear right away. It would take some time for Cara's words to sink in and take on meaning.

"What?" I said in the meantime.

"I know it wasn't you, Clarence. You're a good boy. I'm sorry," she said.

I called my house to see if my father would pick me up.

"Where are you?" asked my mother. "As if I didn't know."

"At Shirley's," I said.

I heard my mother cover the phone and speak to my father.

"Clarence wants to know if you'll come pick him up over in Woodlawn."

"How'd he get over there?"

"How'd you get over there?" she said to me.

"I hitchhiked," I said.

"He hitchhiked," she said to him.

"Tell him to hitchhike back," said my father.

"Shirley's pregnant," I said. "But it's not my child. I had nothing to do with it."

My mother hung up.

I walked home in the rain. At least nobody could tell that I was crying.

When I got home my mother took my wet clothes and wrapped me up in a warm blanket. She gave me a mug of tea.

"Shirley's aunt called me and told me," she said. "I'm sorry, Clarence."

But I was inconsolable. It was a wound from which I never recovered.

*   *   *

It set the tone for all my relationships. I couldn't really trust anyone. Not completely. I've actually never been able to since that day. Turns out the father was another guy on the football team who didn't even know that I knew Shirley, too. It wasn't his fault. I don't know what happened to either of them. I never saw her again.

Clarence

It was like a tiny island in the middle of a shark-infested ocean. We were the only black people in the entire area. Not just the neighborhood—there were no niggers for miles and miles. It was like living in Canada or at the fucking North Pole or some shit like that.

One night in the winter of 1960 my car broke down, so I hitchhiked a ride part of the way home. I got dropped off about a mile from my house. A very long mile. I remember how dark it was. It was one of those moonless nights, and I swear to God it was pitch-black. Couldn't see your hand in front of your face. About halfway to my house lived these people who had these two dogs. Pit bulls. These motherfuckers hated me. They went nuts every time they saw me.

They were four-legged racists. So when I got near their house I was as quiet as I possibly could be. I walked directly into a garbage can, one of those big tin motherfuckers. It hit the sidewalk, and it sounded like the Fourth of July. The pit bulls went crazy. They started barking and snarling. I could hear them in the darkness. Then I heard their gate swing open. The barking stopped. Pit bulls don't bark when they're attacking. They're all business.

I don't know if the gate opened accidentally or if it had help. I knew I was in trouble, though. These two had been after me for years, and now they were getting a free shot in the dark. The next thing I remember hearing was their feet on the street. Just that sound of running dogs. The clicking of their claws on the pavement coming straight at me.

I realized that running wasn't going to do any good, so I took off my belt and started swinging it in the dark. I must've caught the lead dog in the head with the buckle 'cause he let out a yelp, which stopped the other one. Scared them both, and they ran back to their yard.

I never walked home again.

In fact, it was shortly after that night that I decided to start traveling. I felt there was something waiting for me there. Something more. I was afraid, but I was determined to find a better life for myself. To get a little something. I knew that if I didn't take a chance, I wouldn't have one.

Clarence

The first line of this story is similar to the first line of William Gold-
man's great novel Control. *In show business this is not stealing, it's*
homage. —C.C.

If there was one place in this world I never expected trouble, it was
Bloomingdale's. But I encountered weirdness on the third floor
that I never forgot.

I had come to the city to buy a new horn. It had taken years to save
the money. After many false starts I had finally made the decision to
leave Virginia permanently. I was determined to become a professional
musician, and this new instrument would take me there. The horn was
beautiful. When I picked it up for the first time I actually sighed in relief.
It was as if a part of me that had been missing was suddenly restored. For
the first time in my life I felt complete. It was waiting for me in its case
at Manny's. I didn't want to leave it in the car. I figured I'd pick it up in
about an hour and head south.

I'd spent the previous night in a cheap motel on the Jersey Shore. The
walls in the place were so thin you could tell what your neighbors were
saying by reading their lips. Just my luck the couple in the next room was

going for the longest fuck record. At first it was funny, even sexy, but it soon got tedious and then outright annoying. Finally I pounded on the wall and said, "Listen, motherfucker, you've got two choices—come or go!" After that it got quiet, and I fell asleep and dreamed about my first girlfriend, Shirley.

I drove over the bridge into the city in the morning, listening to the Drifters on the radio. They were singing "Sweets for My Sweet," and I loved it. I loved Manhattan. I felt at home there. I felt like it was a big treasure box and inside it was everything I'd ever wanted. Not only things but feelings, too. I knew my life would take me here somehow. It was just right.

After I bought the horn I figured I'd spend some time wandering around the city. I loved Grand Central Station, so I went there first and sat in the Grand Concourse and made up stories about the people passing by. From the outside I looked like a big black guy who was probably an athlete and probably dumb. That's the way most white people saw me. Most black people, too. But there was a world of colors and ideas and music inside my head that seemed limitless. My imagination was racing constantly with fragments of songs and pictures and a torrent of words. The horn was an instant window into my interior life. It was like a magic door in the wall that you could look through into the most beautiful garden in the world.

I had lunch at the counter at the Oyster Bar. I couldn't afford much. I had clam chowder and a beer. Both were fantastic. I wanted to eat there every day for the rest of my life. I put a package of oyster crackers in my shirt pocket, paid the bill, and reluctantly left.

Later I wandered up Lex to Bloomingdale's. I'd never been inside the famous store before, but I was on such a high from getting the horn I figured, fuck it, I can't buy anything in the place, but looking is free.

The store was like stepping into Christmas morning. I'd never been in the middle of such wealth. There had to be millions and millions of dollars' worth of stuff in here. I found it unbelievable. It was also filled with upscale white people. I wondered where all these people got enough money to shop in a place like this. The thought was overwhelming. Most of them were older women who all looked rich. Most wore suits with low heels, and some even wore hats. A lot of them smoked those long, elegant-looking cigarettes. They seemed to be creatures from some other universe. Shit, they *were* creatures from some other universe.

I walked around the store and looked at everything. The first floor smelled better than springtime. It was filled with powders and perfumes and shampoos. After a while I noticed a black guy in gray slacks and a dark blue blazer following me. I was not surprised. I was used to being followed in stores. The fact that I was being followed by the only other black guy in the building made me smile. After a while he seemed to lose interest, and when I made eye contact with him the guy gave me the "what's up" nod and drifted away.

I was looking at leather jackets on the third floor when I noticed her staring at me. Okay, lots of people stared at me, but not like this. She was sitting in a chair near the elevators. She wasn't looking around, she wasn't smoking, and she was hardly moving. What she was doing was staring at me the way a hawk would stare at a rabbit.

She was old—maybe eighty, it was hard to tell—but she was put together. Black suit, white blouse, white hair pulled back. Jesus, she was wearing gloves. White fucking gloves. Who wears gloves inside? She wore little makeup because she had great bones and didn't need it. She must have been incredibly beautiful when she was young. But now her eyes were framed by wrinkles and had a slightly haunted quality, as if the things they'd seen had wounded them.

I caught her eye a few times but quickly looked away. I'd learned early on that you didn't stare at white women. But every time I stole a glance she was following me. It was creepy. No, not really creepy; she didn't look scary or anything. It was just weird. She seemed to be looking through me. Into me.

I headed for the elevator. Fuck this. It was time to get out of here, anyway. Pick up the horn and get back on the road before the traffic got too heavy leaving town. Maybe go down to the Shore again and try to find a band that would let me sit in. There was an incredible music scene emerging down there, and it seemed like a new bar was opening up every day.

"Young man," she said.

I stopped. I looked over at her.

"Yes?" I said.

For a moment she didn't do anything. She just kept staring. I was about to just walk away when she stood up. She was tiny, just a little over five feet tall and rail thin. She crossed to me and put a gloved hand on my arm. She never took her eyes off mine. Up close her eyes were very dark, almost black, and her skin was as white as her hair. She practically shimmered.

"You're going to be a very important man," she said in a clear voice, which sounded like that of a much younger woman. "A big man," she said.

Then she smiled slightly, patted my arm, and walked away.

I ate the oyster crackers on the New Jersey Turnpike.

Jamesburg, New Jersey, 1969

Clarence

Iwalked out of the house, put my horn in the car, climbed in and started the engine. It was another Buick. I thought I'd never get into a Buick again after the accident, but I now saw that event as a blessing. It had been a mystical, deeply profound experience. Yes, it spelled the end of my career in football. My injuries stopped me from trying out for the Browns, but that's the way it goes. Charlie was more disappointed than I was.

"You had it all son," Choo-Choo Charlie said. They called him Choo-Choo 'cause on the ball field he'd run you over like a train.

Charlie had gotten me the job at the Jamesburg Reform School. I had been there for almost five years now, working with these boys everybody else had given up on. I loved helping them. Seeing even a little progress gave me joy. Most of these kids were mentally handicapped and never had a chance to begin with. Combine that with ignorance and poverty, and it spelled jail or death. I made them responsible for each other. Turned these separate groups into little families. On field trips I'd say, "If everybody doesn't get back safely we'll never be able to do this again, so watch out for each other."

It was rewarding work. And it had given me time to work on football.

I played offensive center and defensive end for a semipro football team in New Jersey. Charlie was my teammate and also my supervisor at the school. We were going to the pros together.

All that changed in 1968 when the accelerator jammed on that dark blue Riviera on the long, tree-lined driveway leading to the crowded square in front of the school. The car shot up to a hundred miles an hour in seconds. A motor mount had snapped, and there was no way to stop the car. I tried the emergency brake but nothing happened. Finally I took my eyes off the road and bent down to physically lift the gas pedal. It was a desperate move and it failed. When I got back up behind the wheel I was inches away from the tree.

There was no pain. No pain at all. I was floating up above my body watching the paramedics work on me. I heard one of them say I was gone. But I was there in this light. All I felt was euphoria. I felt like I should let go, but then I thought, *I'm not finished. I've got to go back.* So I did.

So now I was driving another Buick headed for Asbury Park. There were lots of clubs there and lots of people making music. The place felt alive. It felt like it was the center of the universe. You could be a musician here. That was all I wanted to do.

I had been playing the horn every chance I got for years. It was like a fever that kept rising. My connection with music just kept getting stronger until I couldn't deny it anymore. About that time I knew that if I couldn't make a living with my horn, I might as well be dead. It was that kind of passion. It still is.

For reasons I can't explain even to myself, I turned off at Englishtown. I drove down the street and hit a red light. It was a hot night so I had the windows open. There was a club on the right side of the street and I heard music. Country music. I turned into the parking lot, got my horn, and went inside.

The "band" was a country duo called the Bobs. Bob played guitar, and the other Bob played fiddle. I sat in. It was good. I found a common language with these guys who in other circumstances wouldn't even speak to me. I stayed for the night and kept playing. I came back the next night, and the night after that, and every night the Bobs played for the next two weeks. Yes, it was shitkicker music, but I didn't care. I was playing music and that was all that mattered.

The Legend of Puerto Rico, 1970

Here we combined and compressed several true stories into one. —D.R.

I still have the hat. —C.C.

The alarm clock wouldn't stop ringing.

Clarence rolled over and put the pillow over his head. His head hurt. He remembered drinking last night. He had started early.

The ringing continued.

He moaned, rolled over, and opened his eyes. He was in a hotel room. He didn't remember walking into it or getting undressed or into this bed at all. He turned quickly to find that he was mercifully alone. The movement made him dizzy. Slowly he turned his head back to locate the fucking clock. There wasn't any clock in the room. It was the phone ringing. It was on a table across the room. Clarence groaned and pulled himself out of bed. Noting that he was fully dressed, he stumbled across the room and picked up the phone.

"Hello?" he said. His voice was impossibly deep.

"Hi, Clarence," said a girl's voice.

"Hi," he said tentatively. He remembered that he was in Puerto Rico. He'd come down here to hang around, check out the clubs, and smoke some ganja. He did not recognize the girl's voice.

"It's Ginger," she said.

Nothing.

"From last night," she added, to fill the silence.

Nothing.

"From Danny's Hideaway?" she said, slight annoyance creeping into her tone.

Clarence knew that Danny's Hideaway was a club in San Juan he'd planned to visit. He had no recollection of going there. He decided to bluff.

"Oh, sure," he said. "How're you doing?"

"Great," she said. "Shall I come over?"

This was a question that raised more questions. Scary questions. Who was this chick? How did she know where he was when he wasn't sure himself? What if she was a fat pig?

"Uhhhh..." he said.

"Did I wake you?" she asked.

"No," he said. "I had to get up to answer the phone anyway."

She laughed. It didn't sound like a fat-girl laugh, but you could get fooled. "You were so funny last night," she said.

"I was?" he said.

"God," she said, "killer funny."

"Huh," he said. "What time is it?"

"Noon," she said. "I just got back from my run."

Maybe a pig but not fat. She sounded white. Clarence had never dated a white girl. White girls frightened him, which was good 'cause he seemed to frighten them, too.

"Tell you what," he began. "I've got some stuff to do. A couple of things, you know, so why don't we meet for a drink later?" The idea of having a drink made him feel like puking.

"Cool," she said. The way she said it made it sound like "Kul."

"How 'bout back at Danny's?" he said. "Say eight o'clock?"

"Think they'll let you back in?" she laughed.

Shit. What had he done?

"I wasn't that bad, was I?" he asked hopefully.

"No," she said. "But I guess you scratched up the piano when you climbed up on it."

Shit.

"Yeah," he said.

"You had the place rocking, though," she said. "Man, you can dance."

He never danced. He was a lousy dancer.

"That's me," he said. "I'm a dancer."

He got to the bar at seven thirty that night after spending the day sweating out the booze and filling in as many gaps as he could. He'd left the hotel the previous night right after checking in. His intention had been to have a few drinks, then head over to see Smooth Gary Walker and the Immortals, who were appearing at Johnny's Dreambar. One drink had led to another, as one bar led to another, and everybody was so nice and wanted to buy the big black guy a drink, and then things got a little fragmented in his memory. He had pieces: some faces, snippets of music, the feeling of heat around his head, and smoky rooms and lights and teeth and people on the sidewalk looking at him and getting out of his way and then... then just the blackout.

"You going to behave yourself tonight?" said a voice from behind him.

Clarence turned and came face-to-face with a big Puerto Rican guy wearing a nice suit and tie.

"Yeah man. Look, I apologize for what happened, whatever happened," he said.

"It's all right. You sold a lot of drinks. Turned this bar into a real party. It's usually dead out here late. Just stay off the piano, okay?" he said.

"I swear," said Clarence.

"Tommy, give the big man a drink on me," he said. "I'm Tony Desilva."

"Clarence Clemons."

"Yeah. You told me last night," said Tony. "You told me your entire life story. The football, the social work, the sax, the whole thing."

"Sorry," said Clarence.

"Be careful with Ginger. That chick is outrageous. I've never seen her go for anybody before, much less the way she went for you," he said.

"She's hot, isn't she?" Clarence asked.

"Molten hot," said Tony. "She's been in town a couple of weeks on the movie but nobody's been able to break the code till you showed up."

"I can't help it if I'm irresistible," said Clarence.

"Be good," said Tony, as he walked into the club's main room.

Later, when Ginger stepped through the front door, Clarence thought she was the most beautiful woman in the world. A tall, green-eyed redhead with milky-white skin and a sunburst smile.

"Clarence!" she said, as she crossed and hugged him. He was too stunned to move. There was no way in the world he would ever approach this woman, much less actually speak to her.

"Hey" was all he could manage.

"Are you okay?" she said, stepping back and looking at him closely.

"Yeah, I'm fine," he said.

"You sure?" she asked.

"Positive," he said. "Why do you ask?"

"I don't know," she said. "You seem so different from last night."

"I was drunk last night," he said.

"Hmmmmmm," she said.

They sat and talked for about ten minutes.

"You should stay drunk all the time," she concluded. "It really improves your personality."

He laughed. "You might be right."

"This is really how you are most of the time, right?" she asked, sipping the martini he had bought her. He was drinking club soda.

"Yeah," he said. "This is pretty much it."

"It's just as well," she said. He sensed she had made a decision. "We would've had major problems anyway."

"'Cause I'm black, right?" he offered.

"No," she answered. "'Cause I'm a dyke."

"Ahhh," he said. It seemed like a neutral sound designed to encourage her to continue.

"I'm really not interested in guys," she said. "But you were so much fun I thought, hey, what the hell…but…" She finished her drink. "It wouldn't have gone well."

"Probably not," he said. "I would've sobered up eventually."

"Yeah," she agreed. "Would you excuse me? I've gotta hit the head."

"Sure," he said, standing as she left the bar.

He didn't know whether to be relieved or offended. He felt a little of both. He sat back down and sipped his club soda. He laughed out loud at the absurdity of the whole thing. It was funny. You could cry or you could laugh, so he laughed.

Moments later a guy who had been sitting across the bar stood and approached. Clarence had noticed him when he came in because the guy was black and was wearing a very cool Panama hat.

"My brother." The guy extended his hand, poised for that month's soul shake.

"Wassup?" said Clarence. They faked their way through the handshake. They were the only black people in sight.

"I'm Smooth Gary Walker," the guy said.

"God damn! No shit?" said Clarence, shaking his hand again. This time he used the old-fashioned method.

Gary smiled.

"No shit?" said Clarence again. "I was going to see you tonight."

"We're off tonight," said Gary. "Sorry."

"You working tomorrow?"

"Oh, yeah," said Gary. "Two shows. Eight and ten, which are actually nine and eleven or eleven thirty."

"I play sax, too," said Clarence.

"Cool," said Smooth Gary, who was clearly not paying attention. He was looking past Clarence.

"I loved that song you did, 'Dreamboy,'" said Clarence.

"Good," said Gary. "Listen, the lady you were talking to…is she…I mean, are you and her…?" He let it hang.

Clarence had noticed that Gary had no interest in him, and it stung a little. It was better to never actually meet your heroes. "Well," he said, "could be."

"That's one fine-looking woman," said Gary. "I noticed her right away. I think I've seen her at the club."

"Yeah, she's hot, all right," said Clarence.

"But, it looks like you got there first, and that's just my bad luck, right?" said Gary.

"Well…"

"Well? Well what?"

"Well, maybe we could reach an accommodation," said Clarence, doubting that this clown had ever heard the word *accommodation* used like that before. Clarence wasn't really sure the usage was proper, but fuck it. "I could be gone when she gets back."

"Would you do that, man?" said Gary.

"I might," said Clarence. Now it was his turn to let it hang.

Gary reached into his pocket. He knew a proposition when he heard one. "What would it take?" he said.

"Your hat," said Clarence.

Gary touched the brim of the hat. "This is a Monte Cristi fini," he said. "Some dude in Panama spent a month weaving this motherfucker."

"She seems to like brothers," said Clarence.

Gary thought for a moment then took the hat off and looked at it. Clarence prayed that Ginger would stay in the bathroom for just another minute.

"Wanna try it on?" asked Gary.

Clarence did, and it fit perfectly.

"Deal?" Clarence asked.

"Deal," said Gary.

Clarence stood. "Good luck," he said. "And have a martini on me."

"I don't touch alcohol," said Gary. "But thanks anyway."

Clarence smiled, tipped his new hat, and walked out into the sultry night.

Clarence

I was driving home with the Entertainers, the band I was playing with at the time. We had just played a successful gig at the N.C.O. club at Fort Monmouth. We were a tight group who did soul covers, and I had been with them on and off for six months.

The "off" part happened after they fired me for being late for a rehearsal, but they hired me back when I explained how one of my kids at Jamesburg had gotten cut in a fight and I had to get him to the hospital. I loved playing so much that when the Entertainers didn't have a booking I gigged with Bluesman Phillips, but now the job with the group was solid.

I had spent a few months with Lloyd Sims and the Untouchables before joining these guys here in Neptune. I knew the bartender at the club where Lloyd was playing, a woman named Candy Brown. Candy introduced me to Lloyd, and I got to sit in. Lloyd was looking to see if I had anything. I came back the following night and sat in again. I did that for the next two months, playing for free, making it hard for Lloyd to play without me. I knew that eventually the money would come. I knew for certain that this was what I wanted to do with my life. I wanted to play music.

I still had the job at the reform school, and to play with Lloyd I drove for hours in a Volkswagen bus with no clutch. I'd sold the last Buick to get a new horn because the old horn had been crushed in the accident and had never fully recovered. I thought a lot about the accident while I was on the road from work to the club and back. I felt I'd been touched by God's hand and that nothing would ever be the same.

I remembered waking up in the hospital as the male nurse, a guy from India, sewed my left ear together. It had been nearly ripped off my head in the crash. I thought about how a nurse had stitched it together, not a doctor. A man of color had fixed me. The doctors were busy elsewhere.

It was while I was playing with Lloyd, eventually for money, that I got the offer from the Entertainers.

So, like I said, I was driving home with the Entertainers, and the car died.

It was out of gas or out of time. In either event, we cruised to a stop in the parking lot of a club called the White Elephant.

One of the guys was going to find a pay phone to call his uncle to come and pick us up. I got out of the car, stood in the parking lot and, once again, heard the music. It was coming from inside the club. It wasn't R & B. It was rock and roll. There was something powerful in it and I loved it. Rock and roll spoke to me of something beyond.

I grabbed my case from the trunk and walked into the club. There was a girl singing Joplin tunes and she was good. The tall white guy with the red Afro was the leader. A lobby card said they were called Norman Seldin and the Joyful Noyze. The band featured a stand-up drummer named Barry Thompson and a terrific guitar player named Hal Hollender.

Between sets I approached Norman, who sat at the bar drinking a beer. We talked a while about people and places we had in common. Norman saw that I had my horn and asked me if I'd like to sit in. Just like that. It was a story that seemed to keep repeating. One amazing opportunity after another kept occurring. Sometimes I felt I was living a life in a book that had already been written.

Norman offered me a job that night. He loved what the horn added to the songs. He loved the soul of it.

But this was a white band. You had your black bands and you had your white bands and if you mixed the two, you found less places to play.

"You sure about this?" I asked him.

"Positive," said Norman.

I felt badly about leaving the Entertainers, but that was the way the game went in those days; the good players flitted around like bees looking for the sweetest flower. But first there was another issue to be talked about with Norman.

"You have noticed that I'm not exactly white, haven't you?" I said.

"No, I hadn't," said Norman.

When he hired me, Norman did in fact lose some bookings. A few club owners were fearful that my presence would attract a Negro crowd and scare the white kids away. Norman didn't care. He felt the music was so much better with me in the band that he didn't give a shit. He didn't even care when they called us Seldom Normal and the Jerk Off Noise.

Norman Seldin was a soulful Jewish kid who still worked part time in his father's jewelry store. But the music was in him. He played organ and was the first guy on the Shore to get a Moog synthesizer. And now with me on board, he finally had the band he wanted.

We worked all the places we could, like the Crossing Inn up in Princeton, and the White Elephant and the Wonder Bar and other clubs in and around Seaside Heights.

I was with Norman for almost three years. The girl singer in the band was named Karen Cassidy, and during that time her best friend started dating a guy named Bruce.

Don

The following is a conversation Clarence and I had out on the water about the legendary night he walked from the club where he was working to the one where Bruce was playing. —D.R.

Before you went to the Student Prince that night and sat in with Bruce for the first time, what did you know about him?"

"I kept hearing how great he was from this girl in our band," said Clarence.

"Who was that?"

"Her name was Karen Cassidy," he said. "Her roommate was going out with Bruce and Karen kept telling me, 'You've got to see this guy! He's fantastic.' I think I went over there just to shut her up."

"But you brought your horn."

"In those days I always had my horn with me. If I left it somewhere and it got stolen, I couldn't afford another one."

"Were you working at the time?"

"Yeah, I was still playing with Norman. We were at the Wonder Bar in Asbury Park. But I had the night off. I think it was a Wednesday," he said.

"And it was a dark and stormy night?" I asked.

"I know it sounds like bullshit but it really was. There was a nor'easter blowing. It was raining and thundering like a motherfucker. When I opened the door it blew off the hinges and flew down the street."

"Really?"

"I shit you not, my brother. Everybody in the room looks at the door and I'm silhouetted in it, this giant black guy. David said he turned to Bruce and said, "Boss, a change is afoot.""

"David Sancious?"

"Yeah. David read a lot."

"Who else was in the band that night?"

"Danny, Vinnie Lopez, I don't remember who was playing bass but it wasn't Garry. There were a couple of black girls singing backup. One was Delores Holmes, but I can't think of the other girl's name."

"Was there much of an audience?" I asked.

"Yeah. But it wasn't crowded 'cause it was raining so fucking hard," he said.

"So what happened?"

"Somebody introduced me to Bruce, everybody knew everybody, and he asked me if I wanted to sit in. So I said, 'Sure.'"

"Do you remember what song you played first?"

"It was an early version of 'Spirits in the Night.' See, the thing with Bruce was he didn't do covers. I mean, he'd play some classic shit he liked, but for the most part he only played his own songs. A lot of places wouldn't hire him."

"What did you see in him?"

"His passion. He was so passionate about the music. And I loved the music. I'll tell you something, when we started to play that night we looked into each other's eyes and it was like ... total magic," he said. "My girlfriend said we were queer for each other. But it was so solid. We used to go out and get drunk and talk about music and all kinds of shit. We both knew we were friends for life."

"But you didn't join the band right away, did you?"

"No. We needed that 'get to know you' time. I had a gig, and Bruce didn't hear horns in his music yet, I guess."

The Legend from Under the Boardwalk, Early '70s

In the early days, Bruce and I used to talk for hours and hours at a time. The next story is a compilation of some of those conversations. The words may not be exactly what we said; it's impossible to remember, but the feelings are true. There were many, many nights when this is exactly what it was like. —C.C.

Bruce and Clarence were sitting in the sand under the boardwalk in Asbury Park.

It was one of those warm summer nights along the Shore. Anything seemed possible.

It was now early evening, and the light over the ocean was turning to a blue/gray before slipping into darkness. Only a few stars were visible.

They had a six-pack of beer in a paper bag, and had just popped open their first. The beer was cold and tasted like July.

Above them they could hear all the sounds of the Boardwalk. The gorgeous smell of cheap fried food hung in the air all around them.

They were both wearing shorts and T-shirts and flip-flops, which they had kicked off to stick their feet into the sand. The sand was cooler just below the surface and felt good.

They were meeting two girls later at the Wonder Bar and thought they'd get a little buzz going to make conversation easier.

They hadn't yet formalized their professional relationship, but music had already given them a connection that felt good. They both knew that they would be best friends for a long, long time. Not that they talked about it; it was just there. It was obvious because they had that rare feeling of comfort with each other that some people never get to experience.

"You remember their names?" asked Bruce.

"Ann, and I think the blonde is Janie, but I'm not sure about that," said Clarence. He took a pull on the beer and felt it slide down his throat. It had been in the 90s all day, and the weatherman was saying it wasn't going to cool off anytime soon.

"I love this weather," said Bruce.

"Yeah, me, too," said Clarence.

They sat for a while listening to the footsteps above them moving in both directions. It was the sound of human percussion played in random patterns. Tinny carnival music floated behind the shouts and screams of children who had been suddenly frightened or delighted by something. The combined sounds were so rich, so intense, that they seemed to take on color. The whole night glowed as if the northern lights had descended on this stretch of New Jersey and wrapped themselves around everybody and everything.

"If you could have any car in the world, what would you pick?" asked Bruce.

"A 'Vette," said Clarence. "A yellow 'Vette."

"Mine's black," Bruce laughed. "Someday..."

They finished their first beers without speaking. The lights of offshore boats dotted the water. Clarence wondered about the people on those boats. Were they fishermen or people who'd been out sailing all day?

"I wonder who's on those boats," said Bruce.

Clarence laughed. "I was just thinking the same thing."

"Some lawyer from the City out on his cabin cruiser all day with his secretary," said Bruce. "But the engine blows up and he has to call the Coast Guard to come and save him, and he forgets that his wife's brother is in the Coast Guard...." Bruce let the story hang in the air.

Clarence was getting used to the fact that this was how Bruce talked.

This was how the guy thought…in stories. And there was no end to them. He could go on and on and on, and the stories were actually fucking good. He'd throw in little insights and nuances that made the characters come to life. He gave them dimension. They all had secrets.

"You've got a way with words," Clarence said. But even as he said it, he knew it didn't convey his admiration for the way Bruce created things out of nothing.

"You've got a gift," he added.

"Nah," said Bruce. "I'm just good at bullshitting."

"Real good," said Clarence. "You could write a book or something."

"That's what my mother says," Bruce replied. "But that's not for me. At least not now. Maybe when I'm done with music."

Clarence laughed again, and this time Bruce joined in as they both acknowledged the absurdity of the thought.

"When we're dead," said Clarence. "That's when we're done with music."

"Yeah," said Bruce. "Before music I could hardly communicate at all. I never said shit in school, you know? It was like they were talking another fucking language or something. I spent the first part of my life inside my own head."

"That's probably where you got the story thing," Clarence speculated.

"Yeah, maybe I should be grateful," said Bruce. "Maybe it's good that I got ignored."

"Let's just hope we don't get ignored tonight."

"Yeah, well…who knows? Maybe we'll sit in with whoever's playing there. That always helps," said Bruce.

They drank, crushed the cans, and put them into the bag along with the fresh ones. They opened two more. It was nearly full dark now, and the evening stretched out in front of them like a highway that led everywhere in the world.

And they were not afraid.

"I want to make a living with the horn," said Clarence. "I don't ever want to have a straight job again."

"I hear you," said Bruce. "Me, too. It's going to happen."

"I think so, too," said Clarence. "I think something big is coming. I think someday we'll get a hit record and everything will change. That's all it takes, you know, one fucking hit. It doesn't even have to be a big hit. Just a fucking hit and then nobody can stop you."

"Yeah," said Bruce. "Then we get 'Vettes, right?"

"Right," said Clarence. "We'll race 'em down this fucking Boardwalk." They laughed and toasted each other.

As they watched the blinking lights of planes high above them, they wondered where they were coming from or going to, and they both thought that there might be at least one person they knew flying in one of those planes tonight. But neither of them said anything about that.

"How many people do you think are in the air at any given time?" said Bruce.

"Shit, I don't know. Must be tens of thousands if you're counting all the planes in the air all over the world," said Clarence.

"That's an amazing thought, isn't it?" asked Bruce. "There's like maybe the population of Rhode Island up in the sky all the time. They're not on Earth."

"Yeah," said Clarence. "Which means they can't buy tickets to see us and we can't fuck them. The women in the sky."

Bruce laughed. "The women in the sky," he said.

You could almost hear him thinking, rolling the phrase around in his head and then filing it for possible use later. But he didn't say anything out loud, and the moment passed.

"What do you think is going to happen when you die?" he asked.

"All over the world girls will break down and cry," said Clarence.

"Yeah, yeah," said Bruce. "But you believe in life after death, right? The whole heaven thing?"

"Of course," said Clarence. "I come from a very religious family. I have faith. Don't you?"

"This stuff is hard," said Bruce. "Bottom line? I think that after you die is exactly like before you were born. You know, you try to remember the first thing you can remember, right?"

"Right," said Clarence.

"And what do you remember before that?"

"Nothing."

"That's what death is like," said Bruce. A full thirty seconds passed before he spoke again.

"I think," he said.

A woman holding a little boy by the hand came walking up the beach from the water's edge. They were stragglers who didn't want the day to end. The boy was about seven years old and had a blue and white tube around his waist. It had seahorses on it, and he was struggling to hold it up with his free hand while he walked in the deep beach sand. He wore a Garden State T-shirt.

The woman sensed Bruce and Clarence sitting there in the dark and instinctively started to veer away from them.

"It's okay," said Bruce. "We're harmless."

She looked closely, shielding her eyes from the pier lights above.

"Is that you, Bruce?" she said.

"Yeah," he replied. "Who's there?"

"I recognized your voice," she said, walking toward them. "I'm Vinnie Testa's mother."

"Hey," said Bruce.

"I'm Marie Testa," she said. "And this is Vinnie's little brother, Carl."

"How you doing, Carl?" said Bruce.

"Fine," said the boy, looking down at his tube.

"Bruce is a singer," she said to Carl. "He's got a band. Vinnie turned me on to you guys. He said, 'Mom you've gotta see this guy.'"

"How's Vinnie doing?" asked Bruce.

"Oh, you know," she said. She was wearing a frayed man-cut white shirt over a damp one-piece bathing suit, and Carl tugged at the hem of the shirt as she spoke. "He's doing much better since he got into that trouble back in May."

"Right," said Bruce, nodding.

"He's in the union now," she continued. "And people will always need plumbers, right?"

"Oh, yeah," said Bruce with one of his little laughs. "This is my friend Clarence Clemons."

"I know you, too," she said. "You play with Norman Seldin."

"Guilty," said Clarence.

"He's good, too," she said. "I used to wait tables at the Student Prince, so I got to hear everybody. That was a while ago, but still...it was before my accident. I'm on disability now."

Neither guy could discern any kind of disability, so they didn't say anything. They knew a lot of able-bodied people on disability. She looked like a typical Jersey Mom. She had light brown hair that she wore big and teased. She was about forty-five years old and maybe twenty pounds overweight. In one way or another she was like almost everybody they knew.

"Tell Vinnie I said hello," said Clarence.

"I will," she said with a big smile. "He'll be thrilled I ran into you guys. He talks about you all the time and the stuff you've done together. You've got to promise to keep him out of trouble."

"He won't get into trouble with us," said Clarence. "I promise."

"Me, too," said Bruce. "We're law-abiding citizens."

"Right," said Clarence.

"Want a beer?" asked Bruce.

"No thanks," she said. "I've got to get home and start dinner. Anyways I gave it up for Lent and never went back to it."

"Probably just as well," said Clarence. "I mean not that you were a lush or anything."

She laughed. When she did Carl looked up at her and smiled.

"No, I know what you meant," she said. "I was a lush, but that's a whole 'nother story."

"I hear you," said Clarence, for lack of anything better to say.

"Well," she said. "You guys take care."

"Okay," said Bruce. "Bye, Carl."

"Bye," said the kid. He waved and dropped his tube. He picked it up without letting go of his mother's hand and slid it back up to his waist, where he balanced it on his hip. They headed off toward the stairs.

"Tell Vinnie to call me," said Clarence.

"I will," she called back.

They went up to the boardwalk.

Bruce sipped his beer, then turned to Clarence.

"I have no idea who Vinnie Testa is," he said. "Do you?"

"Not a fucking clue," said Clarence.

Don

So when did you and Bruce finally get together?"

"When he was recording *Greetings from Asbury Park*," said Clarence. "I think the record company was pushing him to spice it up...thought it needed something more."

"It needed you," I said.

"I'm glad it did."

"And the rest is history."

"Yeah, but not right away. I think our first gig was opening for Cheech and Chong, and whoever the promoter was, he was expecting a folksinger. He thought he was getting just Bruce and his guitar, and we go out there with this entire band. They pulled the plug on us halfway through the first song."

"And how long was it before you knew this would be big?"

"Moneywise?"

"Yeah," I said. "Money and fame."

"A long time. I always knew it was good. Better than that. I mean the music was always fantastic. But I spent a lot of time riding around in vans and sharing rooms for fifteen dollars a week. It gives truth to the phrase, 'I play music for free, I get paid for the bullshit.'"

The Legend of Daphne, 1972

The girl in this story is a compilation of all the girls who ever used me. It's a sad story of love and betrayal. The names have been changed to protect the guilty. It's set on the day that a phone call changed my life. —C.C.

"How you doing, jelly-snack?" said Clarence to Daphne.

He was driving through the New England countryside. It was a beautiful place he'd never been to before. It was also very white. They were in the fucking White Mountains, and he had a white girl in the car. It was disconcerting. Daphne was writing in her leather journal with her fancy blue pen. She seemed to spend all her time writing.

"Jelly-snack," she said. "That's cute."

"I could call you the wonder waif," he said. God damn, she looked young. And it didn't help that she dressed even younger. Today she was in one of those shift dresses with big pockets that had little ducks appliquéd on them. And her shoes were those Mary Janes. She looked about twelve.

"Turn left up here," she said, as she finally closed the cover and clipped the pen to it.

"You sure you know where we're going? Lots of woods up here."

"I know this part of the world pretty well," she said. "Just follow the signs for Cornish. There's a coffee shop there with the best apple pie in the Northeast."

"Left up ahead," he said. "Lights on, flaps up, visors down."

"You say things I couldn't think of in a hundred years," she said. She opened the book and began to write again.

"You're keeping track of what I'm saying?" he asked.

"Clarence, I'm a writer," she said. "I'm just gathering things that go into the big writing stew that's in my head. Someday when I'm hungry for a certain word or phrase, I'll dip into the stew and see what I come up with." She closed the cover again and clipped the pen to it.

"I liked your book," he said.

"I'm glad," she replied. "It came out...okay."

"Quite an accomplishment to get published at nineteen," said Clarence.

"How old are you?" she asked.

"Old," he replied.

He made the turn and pointed the car toward Cornish. He wondered if that was where the game hens came from.

He had met her at a wedding in Boston. He and Hal Hollander played it for Hal's cousin, who was the groom. Daphne was a friend of the bride and had flown up from New York where she lived. One thing led to another, and this trip to upper New England resulted.

"My mother is a painter," she said.

"Houses?" he asked.

"No," she laughed. "She's an artist."

"What kind of stuff does she paint?" he said.

"All kinds of things: landscapes, seascapes, street scenes. It runs the gamut. But somewhere in everyone of them is a screaming woman," she said. "It's her signature."

"Wow," he said.

She wrote for a while.

"How long are you going to keep traveling around?" she asked, turning toward him.

"I don't know," he said. "I'm sort of in a state of flux. I might be joining a new band. I'm not sure yet. At the moment I'm a razor in the wind."

She laughed and opened her journal again.

When the tall guy in the jumpsuit walked into the restaurant, something in Daphne's face changed. Not in a big way, but there was a shift of some kind. Her eyes seemed to widen and get a little brighter. The guy looked at her and Clarence seated in the booth along the back wall. He hesitated a moment, looked at his watch, then took a seat at the counter.

"You know that guy?" said Clarence.

"He looks familiar," she said. "I know so many people in this neck of the woods. I'm pretty sure..."

"What?" asked Clarence, when she trailed off.

"I'm pretty sure I've seen a picture of him, but it was taken a long time ago," she said.

Before Clarence could respond she put her fork down next to her half-eaten pie and wiped her lips with the napkin. "Excuse me," she said. "I'll be right back."

She got up and started toward the man in the jumpsuit, who had swiveled his stool around to watch her approach.

"You gonna finish that pie?" asked Clarence, as she walked away.

But Daphne didn't answer.

A few hours later, and they were in the guy's house. His name was Jerry. Clarence thought he was weird and that his house was weird. It was a modified A-frame kind of structure filled with books and a lot of Asian statues and artwork. You couldn't even see it from the road. Jerry himself was kind of hawklike, and he stared at Clarence in an unnerving way.

Daphne had come back to the table and said that he was indeed someone she knew, and would Clarence mind if they went by his place? Why the fuck not? The guy looked to be about sixty years old or something, so it was unlikely he'd be hitting on Daphne. Although there was that look on her face when the dude walked into the place that was so strange.

Now, sitting in his living room, Clarence noticed that she was still staring at the guy like he was the next big thing.

"May I get you something to drink?" asked Jerry.

"I'm fine," said Daphne.

Jerry looked at Clarence and raised his eyebrows.

"Beer?" said Clarence.

"I have ginger beer," said Jerry.

"Nah, that's okay," said Clarence. "We've got to get going anyway. We've gotta find some place to stay tonight."

"I'd love a ginger beer," said Daphne.

"Coming up," said Jerry. He smiled at Clarence and stood. "Sure you don't want one? They're quite tangy."

"I'm sure," said Clarence.

Jerry shrugged and walked off to the kitchen. Clarence spoke to Daphne in a stage whisper.

"What the fuck are we doing here?" he said.

"He's a writer," she said, as if that explained every mystery in the fucking universe.

"So what?" said Clarence. "He's weird and I don't like being here. I can tell he wants me out of his house."

"That's not true," she said.

"It's true," he replied. "It's a vibration that only registers on black skin."

"Nonsense," she said.

He could tell she was nervous. She was acting like a schoolgirl, which fit with the way she looked.

"So he's a writer. Why are we staying?" he asked.

"Well, I'm a writer, too. We have a lot in common," she said.

Jerry came back with two bottles of bubbly brown liquid with what looked like Japanese writing on them.

"I figured we'd forego glasses," he said.

"Fine with me," she said.

They sipped their ginger beers, looking at each other the whole time like they were sharing some kind of ginger-beer-drinking secret.

"So Daphne tells me you're a writer, Jerry," said Clarence. "What kind of stuff do you write?"

Daphne looked down at her Mary Janes. Her body language seemed to suggest an apology.

"What a good question," said Jerry. "What kind of stuff do I write? Well, let's see. I would say that I write subversive things. My work involves a lot of oblique angles."

Daphne coughed, but she might have been stifling laughter. It was hard to tell.

"And what do you do, Clarence?" asked Jerry.

"I'm a musician," said Clarence. "I play the saxophone."

"You don't say," said Jerry.

"No, I do say," said Clarence.

Jerry smiled then looked at Daphne who was sipping her ginger beer.

"Delightful," he said.

Later:

Standing by the car. Daphne was looking down at her little-girl shoes, with her hands in the pockets of her little-girl dress.

"So this whole thing was planned?" said Clarence. "This meeting was calculated? Set up?"

"We've been writing each other for months," she said. "But we had never met."

"And my part in this was what, taxi driver?" he asked.

"No," she said. "I had planned to come up here on my own, but then we met in Boston, and you were so sweet, and I thought it might be fun to drive up here with you."

"And let Jerry see you with a big black guy?"

"Jerry is neither jealous nor prejudiced, I can assure you," she said.

"Daphne, that guy is old enough to be your grandfather," he said.

"He's my hero," she said. Then she stood on tiptoes and kissed his cheek. "You'll be fine," she said.

He was in a phone booth an hour later talking to his friend Terry Magovern, who was back in Jersey. Terry became his assistant and later worked in the same job for Bruce.

"Where are you?" asked Terry.

"Nowhere," said Clarence.

"Springsteen is looking for you," he said. "He called like ten times already. He's in some studio. Said he needs to talk to you."

"Have you got a number for him?" asked Clarence.

"Yeah, right here," said Terry. "You got a pen?"

Clarence took the fancy blue pen out of his shirt pocket.

"I sure do," he said.

Clarence

For reasons I don't understand, I've always been aware of the song playing in the minor keys, the dark melody that runs counterpoint to life's sweeter song. The one that says time is short.

That thought was in my mind when I made the decision to go down to Seldin's Jewelry store to talk to Norman.

When I walked in Norman was with a customer. The customer was a small woman with gray hair holding a big purse under her arm. They both looked up when I came in. The woman grabbed her purse tighter. Norman smiled and held up a finger.

The air-conditioning in the store felt good to me. It was only ten thirty but it was already hot outside. Summertime in New Jersey.

I looked at the display cases filled with rings and watches. I looked at the big silver Rolex. *Someday,* I thought.

After a few minutes Norman finished his business with the woman. She kept her eye on me as she left.

"Big Man," said Norman. "What are you doing here?"

Norman was smiling, but I could see the look in his eyes. Norman knew what was coming.

I also noticed that he had brought the red Afro down an inch or two more. He started to change his look about six months ago, at about the same time that Karen had left the band.

"I wanted to talk to you in person," I began.

"Uh-oh," said Norman. "I don't like the sound of that." He laughed nervously. He had one of those jackhammer laughs that was equal parts infectious and annoying.

"Yeah," I said. "I got an offer from Bruce and I've decided to take it. He's in the studio right now with his album."

Norman looked down and then out the windows to the street. There weren't a lot of people walking around on account of the heat. Finally he looked back at me.

"Clarence," he said. "I love you, man, but I've got to be honest with you. You're making a huge mistake."

I had considered that possibility. Maybe it *was* a huge mistake. There was really no way to predict what would happen. I just knew that when I played with Bruce it felt right. Exactly right. It was like the hat I'd gotten in Puerto Rico. The second I put it on it fit perfectly.

"Maybe so," I said. "But like the man said, if you don't take a chance you haven't got one."

"We've been together what, two, two and a half years?" asked Norman.

This was worse than breaking up with a chick. Norman seemed set on doing the entire dance.

"'Bout that," I said.

"It's been pretty good, right?"

"Oh, yeah," I said. "This isn't about you, Norman, you've been great. I know you took some heat putting me in the band and I'm grateful. I've just gotta give this a shot."

"I think the Noyze is right on the edge, Clarence," said Norman. "I think we could be big."

"I hear you," I said.

Outside a fire truck roared past, sirens wailing.

"But I don't think that's what's in the cards for Bruce," Norman said. "Record deal or no record deal. I've heard his stuff, Clarence. He thinks he's the next Bob Dylan or something. He uses too many words."

I thought that was an accurate assessment. Bruce did use a lot of words. A torrent of words. I sometimes thought of cloudbursts when I heard Bruce singing. An impossible amount of rain crammed into too little time. "Madman drummers bummers and Indians in the summer with a teenage diplomat / In the dumps with the mumps as the adolescent pumps his way into his hat," Bruce sang on one of the new songs. I had no fucking idea what any of it meant, but it had that Chuck Berry syncopation, using vowels and consonants like musical notes. Instead of "School Days" or "Memphis," Bruce was singing about finding the keys to the universe in the engine of an old parked car.

He was like Dylan. But I thought he was like Elvis, too. And he was like Jerry Lee Lewis and even a little Hank Williams.

And musically Bruce was an adventure. The guy would try anything. There was an amazing amount of stuff going on in Bruce's head all the time.

But there was no point in trying to explain any of this to Norman.

"I know," I said instead.

"You know how many 'new Dylans' there have been who are out of the business now?" asked Norman.

I thought of pointing out the fact that we were having this conversation in a fucking jewelry store, but I didn't.

"I know all that, Norman," I said. "What can I say, man? I've decided to give it a shot."

"What's he paying you?" asked Norman.

This was an issue. I was going to be making next to nothing. Twenty, maybe twenty-five bucks a week. We were all going to starve for a while. Maybe a long while. Bruce's insistence on not doing covers cost us a lot of gigs. But if the record hit, the jobs would come and the money would go up fast.

"We haven't talked about money yet," I lied.

"Federici told me he's only getting fifteen bucks a week when you average it out," said Norman. "I can guarantee you thirty-five and on some gigs, like the Wonder Bar, I'll give you fifty."

"You're not making this easy," I said.

"I don't want it to be easy, C. I care about you, and I don't want to see you do something that you're going to regret for the rest of your life. You could end up being a sideman for Helena Troy, 'cause when you close this door it's going to stay closed."

"I understand that," I said.

Norman had finally gotten to it. It wasn't really a threat—he was too nice a guy for that—but it was clear that this bridge was going to burn.

"I'm sorry," I said. "But I've made up my mind."

Norman stood up straight and let out a big sigh. He looked out to the street again, then just stood there and nodded his head for a while.

"All right then," he said. "If that's the way it is, all I can do is wish you good luck."

He extended his hand. I shook it. I felt simultaneously exhilarated and terrified. I knew that I had just stepped off the edge of something high. "I appreciate that," I said.

"You're going to need it," said Norman.

The Legend of the Phone Call, Beverly Hills, 1972

I was only on half of the phone call in this next story so I can't swear that it's true, I've filled in the blanks on the other end of the line the way I imagine that it happened. —C.C.

The phone rang.

It was in an empty phone booth located on Rodeo Drive in Beverly Hills. It was one o'clock on a Wednesday afternoon. It was October 26, 1972.

Groucho Marx was walking down the street with Erin Fleming. Groucho wore glasses and a black beret. Erin was in a pantsuit and held his arm to support him. Groucho heard the phone ringing, looked at Erin, and smiled. She rolled her eyes.

"Go ahead," she said.

Groucho stepped into the phone booth and picked up the receiver.

"Dewey, Cheetem, and Howe," he said.

"I'm looking for Lovey," said Clarence.

"Good lucky," said Groucho.

"Is this the right number for Lovey Dexter?"

"It could be," said Groucho. "Who's calling?"

Erin gave a theatrical sigh and indicated through hand signals that she'd be going into the store behind her. It was Gucci. Groucho waved *okay* to her and she left.

"This is Clarence Clemons."

"And Clarence, pray tell, how do you know Lovey?"

"Is this her dad?" Clarence asked.

"That's a possibility," said Groucho. "But I doubt it."

"I met her in a club in Jersey about a week ago. I was in a different band than the one I'm in now. She gave me this number and I wanted to invite her to come and see the new show."

"That's a lot to absorb," said Groucho. "Fortunately I've got a mind like a sponge. First of all, am I to assume that you're in Jersey?"

"Yeah. You're in Los Angeles, right?"

"Beverly Hills, actually," said Groucho. "A much nicer class of losers here."

"I was going to send her a plane ticket."

"Lovey must be quite a girl," said Groucho. "And no, I'm not related to her."

"Is she there?" asked Clarence.

"'Fraid not. Either you dialed the wrong number or she gave you the wrong number."

Clarence repeated the number.

"That's it," said Groucho, reading it off the phone.

"Shit," said Clarence.

"Well said," said Groucho. "But I'm intrigued by random encounters; you're a musician?"

"I play the saxophone."

"That qualifies you. Had you been a drummer..." Groucho trailed off.

"This new band is great," said Clarence. "I wanted Lovey to check it out."

"This girl, and I regret to tell you that I don't know her, made quite an impression on you and, I would guess, your couch."

"Best sex I ever had," said Clarence.

"I remember my first sexual encounter," said Groucho. "I still have the receipt."

Clarence laughed. "You're funny, man," he said. "What's your name?"

"Julius," said Groucho.

"What do you do, Julius?"

"Currently I'm involved in making a comeback," said Groucho.

"You a show biz dude?" asked Clarence.

"Yes, but I'm not one of those phony Hollywood assholes," said Groucho. "I'm the real thing."

"You an actor?" asked Clarence.

"Among other things," said Groucho.

"I met Mickey Rooney once," said Clarence.

"I've had it to here with Mickey Rooney," said Groucho, indicating his knees.

"Hang on a sec," said Clarence.

There was the sound of a receiver being placed on a hard surface and distant voices. Groucho looked through the front window of the Gucci store, where he saw Erin looking at purses. A pigeon walked by on the sidewalk just outside the phone booth. Groucho looked down at it.

"Any messages?" he said.

Clarence came back on the line. "That was the Boss. We start rehearsal in five minutes."

"The boss?" said Groucho. "Do you mean the bandleader?"

"Yeah, but everybody calls him the Boss. His name is Bruce Springsteen."

"Sounds Jewish," said Groucho.

"German, I think," said Clarence.

"One drives the truck, one rides on the truck...same truck," said Groucho. "I've said that before but I was misquoted, and you can quote me on that."

"You're on fire, man. When we get to LA come see us. We're called the Bruce Springsteen Band."

"And you play the sax?" said Groucho.

"Yeah," said Clarence. "I'm the big black guy."

"I'm not prejudiced," said Groucho. "I hate everybody."

"What's your last name, Julius?"

"Marx," said Groucho.

"Like Groucho Marx?" asked Clarence.

"Yes," said Groucho.

"Give me your number, man, I'll call you when I get out there."

"You can reach me at this number every Wednesday," said Groucho. Inside the store Erin was buying a purse. She was paying with a credit card.

"Cool. Do you know Cheech and Chong?" asked Clarence. "We're doing a show with them Friday night."

"I know who they are. The potheads, right?" asked Groucho.

"Right," said Clarence.

"I'm a little too old for their stuff. Course, a man is only as old as the woman he feels."

Clarence laughed again. "I'm looking forward to meeting you, Julius."

"I don't blame you," said Groucho.

"I've gotta run. Nice talking to you," said Clarence.

"I had a perfectly wonderful time," said Groucho. "But this wasn't it."

Clarence

On Friday night we were going to open for Cheech and Chong. Bruce wanted to rehearse in the afternoon, so we all piled into Danny Federici's van and drove over to pick up David Sancious. We always picked David up last because he was never ready, and the theory was that if we got to him last he'd have more time to get his shit together and we wouldn't have to wait so long for him. It was a good theory, a fine theory, but it didn't happen. He was never ready. He lived in his mother's house in Belmar, and we'd park outside and just shoot the shit until he emerged.

When he did finally come out he always had some bullshit excuse, like his alarm clock was broken or he had to go to the store to pick up medicine or something. You know, the kind of stuff you couldn't really fault somebody for doing. After a while we started making bets on what the excuse would be this time.

But it wasn't so bad because we would pass the time talking nonsense. We'd talk about girls and music and girls. We told a lot of entertaining lies. Danny would always have these unbelievable stories about having sex with all these chicks, but none of us had ever seen him with any of them. On the other hand he was so charming, so good with women, that we really didn't know what to believe. But if he was telling the truth he was getting laid constantly. Danny was a ladies' man even before he got famous. After he got famous...well, that's a whole other book. Maybe I'll write a book that has all the sex-and-drugs stories from the early years and publish it after all of us are dead. (Nah, I can't do that either, 'cause now all of us have kids and grandkids.) But I think it's safe to say that for a while there some of us did not set a good example. I'll leave it at that.

Anyway, Danny would tell these sex stories and we'd all tell him he was full of shit, and that would go on for a while until some song one of us liked came on the radio. First we'd listen to it and sing along, but then we'd start to break it down into chords and meter and stuff. Steve Van Zandt was great at that. That guy has the most incredible ear. He sees music with his ears. It just appears to him in his head and he can tell you everything about it. He's a great, great talent. He also happens to be the nicest human being on the planet Earth. If you don't like Steven, you just don't like anybody. I would do anything for that guy. But back to the story.

Then Garry Tallent would start with his trivia questions. Garry knows everything about early rock and roll. I have never been able to stump him. I remember one day we were out there in the van waiting for David, and I turned to Garry and said, "Bluebirds over the Mountain," and without hesitating he says, "Ersel Hickey, 1958. It was the shortest song to ever appear on *Billboard*'s top one hundred. It was a minute and twenty-eight seconds long. Got as high as number seventy-five. Ersel is also the only guy named Ersel that anybody has ever heard of living or dead." He had that kind of information on the tip of his tongue.

But I think we all would've gone crazy in that van waiting for David if it hadn't been for Bruce. Bruce is the most amazing storyteller. He would see somebody walking down the street with a limp or something, and he would spin this incredible tale about how the guy had broken his leg in a bobsled race in Austria three years ago because the driver of the sled was screwing the limping guy's wife, and so halfway down the mountain the limping guy starts to strangle the driver and they go off the track and into the trees at like a thousand miles an hour or something, and the guy breaks his leg in three places but the driver is dead and the authorities never suspected it was murder. Shit like that right off the top of his head. I wish I could remember some of them exactly, but I was laughing so hard most of the time they went in one ear and out the other. He used to tell those long stories on stage sometimes. A lot of them were during my intro, where he'd make up all these tales about ghosts and visions and the heavens opening up and a light coming down at me standing on a hill with my horn held up over my head. Crazy, wild shit. Somebody once collected all of them on a bootleg and sent it to me. There was some very funny stuff. I swear to God that if he didn't have music, Bruce would be a comedy writer or some shit like that. Comedy novels, probably.

Actually, I do remember one of his stories. This girl is going skiing and she has a couple of cups of coffee in the lodge and then takes the lift up to the top of the mountain. But it's a long ride and it's cold and windy and when she gets off she's got to pee like a racehorse.

She can't hold it so she skis over into this bunch of trees. She sticks her ski poles in the snow and unzips her suit. Fortunately she's wearing one of those one-piece deals so she slips it down around her legs and squats down and starts to go, right? No problem. Except her skis start to slide. She doesn't realize it for the first few seconds but she's moving down the hill. She grabs for the poles but she misses and she starts to pick up speed. And remember she can't move, 'cause she's got her entire ski suit wrapped around her legs and she's actually in the perfect tuck position.

So she comes screaming out of the trees, naked, unable to turn or to slow down. She goes flying down the hill straight at the lodge. A waiter sees her coming and opens the front door and then the back door. She sails across the deck, right through the dining room, still screaming, still naked, and out the back door and into the parking lot, where she finally comes to a stop. She stands up, zips up the suit, steps out of the skis, gets into her car and drives away.

I'm pretty sure that's one of Bruce's.

Anyway, on this Friday afternoon we're sitting here and we're doing all the stuff I just told you about. Killing time. Now, we also do not have a name for the band yet. We were sort of "Bruce Springsteen and the Bruce Springsteen Band," which was a little redundant, and Bruce never had that kind of ego. So this "What do we call the band?" question is hanging in the air. We're starting to work a little steadier and things are happening, and the music is getting really good, so we've got to settle on something pretty soon.

"Should I go knock on the door?" said Danny.

"Blow the horn again," I said.

So he blows the horn. It's starting to get twilight now. The lights are on in the house. The curtain gets pulled aside and there's David holding up one finger. Course we all hold up one finger back at him.

Then Bruce sighs and gives that little laugh of his. He turns around in the seat.

"This band has spent so much time parked on this fucking street we should call it the E Street Band," he said. That's how it happened. Just like that.

Sing Sing Prison, December 7, 1972

Clarence

It was 1972. Mike Appel had booked us in Sing Sing, which is a maximum-security prison in New York. He thought it would be a good way to get some free publicity, but only one reporter showed up. It was a guy from a music magazine called *Crawdaddy*. It turned out to be one of the scariest gigs that I have ever played. Make that *the* scariest. It was going to be a daytime show. We weren't used to being awake in the daytime, so that was unusual, too. We drove up to the gate. We were all looking at each other because we did not know what to expect.

I remember the guards being very stern and hostile. I could feel that they did not want us there. After getting through the gate we were escorted to this building, where we were roughly searched.

It was the most sterile place I had ever seen. It was what I imagined a Nazi prison camp to be like.

We were then hustled into the place. All the time I felt like my throat could be slashed by some disgruntled inmate at any time. These were some of the hardest-looking individuals I have ever seen, even on TV. As we made our way to the prison chapel where we were to play, I avoided eye contact with anyone on the way. When we got there, there was no time for a sound check. We set up our equipment as the room filled up with killers and thieves. Men who didn't give a shit about their own lives, and I knew they gave less than a shit about mine. All I could think was *Let's start playing, get this thing over, and get the fuck out of here.*

Our roadie that afternoon was named Albee Talon. He was with us a lot in the early days. He plugged in the organ, the amps, and the mikes, and they all blew up. A stream of white smoke streamed from each of them. The prison had direct current instead of alternating current. All our mikes and electric instruments were dead. I suspected that we would be dead soon ourselves.

By now the audience of murderers and other very bad men were getting restless and we were getting scared. We were a rock-and-roll band with no guitars or organ or bass or vocal. The crowd started do get more like a mob, and the tension on the stage began to grow into panic. What could we do? Bruce looked at me with one of those "What the fuck do we do now?" looks, and I picked up my horn and began to play "Them Changes," which was a Buddy Miles song. Just the sound of the music, any music, calmed the crowd down a little bit, but we weren't out of the woods yet.

Vinnie picked up the beat, and pretty soon we had a groove going on. The audience started to get into it and before long we were rocking. Just sax and drums, but it was funky. Then I saw this guy in the middle of the audience holding an alto sax. He was a little guy. He got up and started to wail along with me. Now the audience of prisoners was really going nuts. Bruce was clapping his hands and dancing around. What else could he do? The crowd was cheering 'cause one of their own was now in the band. It seemed as if he was lifted up by their adulation and transported to the stage, 'cause the next thing I know the guy is standing next to me. He is the lost member of the E Street Band. We played that song for over an hour in every arrangement possible. The same song. It turned out to be the greatest one-song gig in the history of man.

I remember at one point, maybe an hour into this monster jam, Bruce runs up to the edge of the stage and yells something to the crowd that almost brought the house down literally.

"When this is over," he said, "you can all go home."

Don

O ver the years a lot of the shows have gone past curfew. In the early days Bruce pretty much ignored curfews, if there were any, and kept playing until either he or the audience couldn't take it any-more. Many shows went past midnight, and a few didn't end until closer to one o'clock.

I saw a show that didn't *start* until two a.m.

I was in the early years of my career as a television writer and pro-ducer, and I was always on the lookout for new talent to exploit. That's the way the business works. And because I was getting shows on the air, agents and managers always wanted me to see their clients. That's what brought me to the Troubadour nightclub on Santa Monica Boulevard at about eight o'clock that night. A friend of mine at Columbia Records had invited me down to see a few of their artists. The record company was trying to get more exposure for these acts in the media, so they had decided to throw what amounted to a private party with music.

Rumors around town that week were that Dylan would be perform-ing at the show. This was a complete lie but it did generate a lot of inter-est, and by the night of the show it was impossible to get into the club. That week, that night, this was the hottest ticket in town.

I snagged a seat right in front of the stage at one of the long tables and ordered a beer. It shaped up to be a long night, and I needed to pace myself.

At nine o'clock the show started with the Hawaiian duo Cecilo and Kapono. I have never been a big fan of Hawaiian music outside of Hawaii. It's sort of like buying a cowboy hat while visiting Texas. The hat looks good and you look good wearing it—as long as you remain in Texas. But get on a plane and fly to New York, and your hat will look and feel stupid. Anyway, Cecilo and Kapono were good, but not many people in the room were interested. I guess they couldn't sense that onstage 'cause they played their ukuleles for about an hour and a half. By the time they finished I had stopped pacing myself.

There was a delay while the stage was cleared and then set up for a band. There was a lot of excitement in the crowd. Almost everyone was there to see either Dylan or Bruce Springsteen and the E Street Band. I was still buzzing from the show a week earlier at the Santa Monica Civic Auditorium, where they opened for Dr. John.

The folks from the record company still had some reservations about just how commercial Bruce and the band were. A year before, they performed at a similar event and the night was less than successful. They had to follow Edgar Winter's blistering set, which had brought the house down, and Bruce ignored the fifteen-minutes-per-act rule and played some pretty obscure stuff for closer to forty minutes. The businessmen were not yet convinced.

At eleven thirty Roger McGuinn took the stage. The ex-Byrd was in fine form that night with a great backing band. He sang "We did it for the stories we could tell," and everybody loved him. I just wanted him to stop because I was starting to fade and I hadn't seen Bruce yet. Roger also played for an hour and a half. By that time I had gone past drunk and was well on my way back to sobriety. Since the bars in LA closed at two o'clock I had to make a decision. Do I really tank up and try to cruise through Bruce's set or switch to coffee now? I switched to coffee.

It would have been very difficult to imagine it that night, but I would be in another, bigger room watching Roger and Bruce perform together again in thirty-four years. It was inconceivable. That night at the Troubadour we hadn't even been alive for thirty-four years.

Roger's set finally finished about one o'clock, and the next hour was a kind of slow torture as his band cleared the stage and the roadies took over. First they tore down Roger's band's equipment and then set up Bruce's.

The lights went down and Bruce and the band took the stage at two.

It was worth the wait.

The first notes of the set were played by David Sancious, who stood at the side of the open baby grand piano and played its strings like a guitar, signaling the beginning of "Incident on 57th Street," and they were off. The East Coast bias in the room became evident when a huge cheer greeted the lines, "It's midnight in Manhattan, this is no time to get cute / It's a mad dog's promenade."

It was an incredible show. The hour and the circumstances were certainly contributing factors but the band also kicked ass. They played "Spirit" and "Sandy," and then the man who was to become my best friend took the spotlight and played his sax on an early version of "Jungleland." The night finally came to an end about three-thirty in the morning with a marathon version of "Rosalita."

Leaving the club that night I felt like my life had been changed. I had never experienced that kind of connection with an artist and his music. I didn't want to go home. Nobody did. I remember standing on the sidewalk talking to an equally jazzed James Taylor and his new wife, Carly Simon. We all felt it. We all knew that Bruce and the E Street Band were going to change the face of music forever.

Clarence

The first mistake was letting Bruce drive.

He wasn't used to driving and had a tendency to go either way too fast or way too slow. And he would alternate between the two depending upon what was on the radio or on his mind.

He was driving too slow when the cop pulled us over.

I was riding shotgun. Garry Tallent was in the backseat. The car belonged to our drummer, Vinnie "Mad Dog" Lopez, who was in the van with Danny and all the equipment. We were all on our way from Bryn Mawr, Pennsylvania, where we'd played the Main Point, to Boston, where we would do seven nights in a row at Paul's Mall.

I wasn't looking forward to it because we'd be bunking together in the attic of one of our managers' mother's. Ahh, the glamour of show business.

But right then it was the joint in my shirt pocket I was worried about. I didn't want to get busted. But two longhaired white boys and a big black guy in a car at night said *DRUGS* in capital letters to every cop in the world.

I went looking for the joint under my poncho but couldn't find it.

"Shit," said Bruce, as he pulled over and rolled the window down.

It was freezing cold outside and the car had no heater. My teeth were starting to chatter already.

"I hope Mad Dog doesn't have any shit in this car," said Garry.

"Shit," said Bruce again.

"Shit," I said, unable to find the joint.

The cop approached the car holding a big flashlight. He walked around the back and then the passenger's side, checking us out. Then he went back to his own car and got into it.

"Maybe he's leaving," I said.

"He's calling for backup," said Bruce.

Bruce was correct. A few minutes later another cop car pulled up with flashing lights and sirens. The cops got together, compared notes, and approached the car from both sides. The one on the driver's side shined the bright light directly in Bruce's face.

"Know how fast you were going?" said the cop.

The light was so fucking bright we couldn't see the guy's face.

Bruce shrugged. "Seventy?" he guessed.

"Seventeen," said the cop. "Let's see some ID."

Minutes passed. Very, very cold minutes.

"I wish they'd just take us to jail so I could get warm," said Garry.

I still couldn't find the joint. Could it have fallen on the floor? Was it in the folds of my shirt? Where the fuck was the thing?

The cops returned. Two flashlights, two hands on guns.

"Everybody out of the car," said the first cop.

"Officer, I don't understand—," Bruce began.

"Out of the car now!" the cop interrupted.

We got out.

We got patted down.

We got searched.

We had to take our jackets off.

Then our shirts.

Then our shoes and socks.

It was twenty-two degrees. The ground was covered with ice.

We unpacked all our bags and laid our clothes on the ground.

The cops harassed us for more than half an hour before allowing us to get dressed.

"You hang around with the Federici kid, don't you?" asked the other cop at one point.

"He's in the band," said Bruce.

"We've had problems with him," said the cop.

No shit.

Everybody in New Jersey had had some kind of problem with Danny at one time or another. He was a wild man. And yet the wild man and the guy named Mad Dog were peacefully on their way to Boston.

I was in a state of near panic, 'cause now I knew for sure the joint must be in the car, and the cops were about to start their search. Shit.

They had been pulling out seats and looking under the threadbare carpet for twenty minutes or so when one of them spoke.

"Got something," he said.

He had been rooting around in the glove compartment on the passenger's side.

I knew I was dead. Bruce had a strict "no drugs" policy, and this could ruin everything.

"What did you find?" said the other cop.

The first cop extended his hand to show four black capsules.

"Pills," he said. "Looks like black beauties."

"They're dog vitamins," said Bruce.

"What?" said the first cop.

"The guy whose car this is, Mr. Lopez, has an old dog named Mabel. A bulldog. She takes a lot of supplements on account of her bad hips. Those are her vitamins. The cap must've come off the bottle. It's in there someplace. Check it out."

They did, and Bruce was again correct. Which pissed the cops off even more.

After an hour and a half of physical and verbal abuse, they finally had to let us go.

We got back on the road and headed north. Garry was driving. Bruce sat in the passenger's seat and I was in the back.

"Assholes," I said.

"Let's get some coffee," said Bruce. "I'm freezing my ass off."

"Me, too," said Garry.

Almost unconsciously I reached under my poncho and patted my shirt pocket.

The joint was there.

It was some kind of miracle. I know the fucking thing wasn't there, and then it was. I can't explain it. But as soon as we got to the restaurant I went out back and set fire to the evidence.

Don

I first met Clarence in 1975. I've spent most of my life writing and producing television shows. That year I inherited Cher after her split with Sonny and embarked on my first big-time producing job, *The Cher Show*. This turned out to be more difficult than I had anticipated. For one thing, Cher herself really didn't want to do the show. Oh sure, she had agreed to do it and had made a great pilot for the series with Bette Midler and Elton John as guests, but when it came time to do the first new episode she was nowhere to be found.

I was sitting in my office on Beverly Boulevard with Tom and Dick Smothers, who had managed to arrive at ten a.m. even though they had started their day in San Francisco, and Bill Cosby.

A word about Bill Cosby: sometimes Mr. Cosby is not the friendliest guy in the world. He can be somewhat remote, somewhat cold. He was both of those things that morning, sitting across the room from me and staring with a malevolence usually reserved for Teutonic dictators. In his defense, however, Cher was not there and he was.

"Where is she?" asked Mr. Cosby.

"Let me call the house," I replied. Moments later I was talking to

Cher's housekeeper, who was telling me something I didn't want to hear. "She's on the way to the airport," she said. "She's going to New York to have her face peeled."

I couldn't make sense out of what I was hearing. Cher couldn't be going to New York; this was my first show. Tom and Dick were here, smiling and ready to go. Bill Cosby was going to kill me. And what the hell did it mean to have your face peeled? I took the only course of action that I could think of at the time. "Oh, my God," I said. "Was anyone hurt in the accident?" Bill Cosby stood up and walked out.

Eventually Cher did return, and after her face healed so did Mr. Cosby and the Smothers Brothers. The rest of that story will be left for another time. As a young producer ready to change the way things were being done in the business, I wanted to book different kinds of guests on that show. Specifically, I wanted hipper musical guests. I wanted David Bowie instead of Pat Boone (I ended up with both of them), but most of all I wanted Bruce Springsteen and the E Street Band.

I had seen them open for Dr. John at the Santa Monica Civic Auditorium the previous year and had been blown away. As an encore that night, they did the ballad "New York City Serenade." I'd never seen anybody do a slow song to start an encore, especially one that opened with a virtually classical piano riff by David Sancious and a beautiful sax solo by the giant horn player Clarence Clemons. Then I saw them at the Troubadour, and I was convinced that Bruce was the most important artist of the age.

I wanted them on *The Cher Show*. Columbia Records was supportive and even sent me an advance copy of the new album, called *Born to Run*. I thought it was pretty good. I had a feeling that it might even become a minor hit.

Mike Appel was managing Bruce and the band at the time, but he wasn't interested in me or Cher or television itself. At the time, I was stunned by this lack of vision. I thought I was the center of the universe and that *The Cher Show* was ground zero for what was happening now. To be dismissed was unacceptable. This guy just needed to be shown the true path to big-time show business.

Later that season Bruce and the boys were booked to play the Roxy. I arranged to see them and to talk to Mike and convince him that he needed me. My case wasn't helped much by the fact that about the same time of the Roxy shows, Bruce was on the cover of both *Time* and *Newsweek* magazines. Somehow the power of *The Cher Show* had been diminished. They turned me down. But I did get to hang around the club that week, see all those now-legendary shows, and meet Clarence, who is still my best friend to this day. That week in 1975 was noteworthy in more ways than one.

In addition to hanging out at the Roxy, I was still producing *The Cher Show*. Our guests that week were the aforementioned Pat Boone, Frankie Valli, and Dion DiMucci from Dion and the Belmonts. It was our "salute to the '60s" episode. As I said, we were ground zero for what was happening now.

Dion was also recording an album while he was in town, and he had invited me to a session at the famous Gold Star Studios in Hollywood. My wife and I arrived at about eight o'clock that night and were directed to the control booth door. When I walked in, I saw several things. Zack Glickman, Dion's manager, was sitting on a couch directly in front of me. To my left was a big glass window overlooking the studio, which was filled with the great musicians known as the Wrecking Crew, and Dion, who sat on a stool behind some baffles and was about to sing.

From off to my right I heard a voice say, "Who the fuck are you?" I turned and looked at the riser where the board was located, and I saw a small man in a white jumpsuit and a matching white Afro wig pointing a .357 Magnum at my head. This was my introduction to Phil Spector. Against the wall behind him sat Bruce, Steve Van Zandt, and Robert Hilburn, the music critic for the *Los Angeles Times*.

Zack jumped to his feet and said, "It's okay, Phil. He's with Dion."

"All right, then," said Phil. "Sit down and shut up while I show Mr. Springsteen how to make a fucking record."

Over the very strange next few hours, Dion and the Wall of Sound Orchestra recorded a song called "Baby Let's Stick Together." Many,

many years later, about the time that Phil was charged with murder, Clarence and I ran into Bruce in a hotel lobby in Ireland. He and Patti were returning from dinner, and Clarence and I were just leaving the bar. That night with Spector came up. I asked Bruce if he remembered it like I did. "I thought he was going to shoot you," he said.

Clarence

When I woke up I had no idea where I was.

I knew I was in a tent but I couldn't remember why. I'm not much of a camper. This must've been in 1973. I don't remember exactly, but it was around then sometime. Anyway, I hear this awful sound and I roll to my left side, and there's Danny, fast asleep as usual, sawing logs, his mouth open. Then I remembered. We set up the tent out behind the 914 Studio in Blauvelt, New York, so we didn't have to drive all the way back to Jersey to sleep. Mike Appel found that studio and thought it would be right for us. Plus it was cheap. We were working on *The Wild, the Innocent & the E Street Shuffle,* and Mad Dog was still playing drums at that time. In fact I'm pretty sure it was his tent. He took it with him when he left the band in early 1974.

Vinnie "Mad Dog" Lopez had trouble keeping time. It was fucking everything up, but Bruce is such a loyal guy that he couldn't bring himself to fire him. It was becoming a real problem. And Vinnie didn't like me at all. He saw that Bruce and I were tight, and I guess it pissed him off 'cause all he would do was give me shit. And I took it for a long time.

I was living in this little house with Vinnie, Danny, and three snakes. Boa constrictors. I hate snakes. I was deathly afraid of those motherfuckers. Every night before I went to sleep I'd count them. Know where each one was. Anyway, one day Vinnie did something that pushed me over the edge. I don't remember what it was. It could've been something small, but I had been putting up with his bullshit for so long that on that particular day I just snapped. I went off on that motherfucker. I didn't hit him but I put him up against the wall, I threw shit all over the apartment, I think I broke down the front door. At one point he was lying on the floor and I picked up one of his speakers and smashed it right next to his head. I was in a total rage. And I was big and strong and black. I must have scared the living shit out of him, because he ran from Neptune to Belmar where Bruce lived and said, "It's either him or me."

Turned out to be the best day of Max Weinberg's life.

But Max didn't join us right away. He and our piano player, Roy Bittan, came in toward the end of that summer. Mad Dog left in February 1974 and Ernest "Boom" Carter replaced him. I remember we auditioned him at Garry's parents' house. Boom was with us when we recorded the title track "Born to Run." That was the last song we recorded at 914. Then a whole bunch of big changes happened in a short amount of time.

That was when Bruce and his future producer and manager, Jon Landau, got together. Jon thought 914 was a little less than top of the line, so we moved our sessions to the Record Plant in Manhattan. Boom and David Sancious left, and Max and Roy came in. David wanted to pursue jazz, and we were strictly rock and roll. We spent the next forever recording the rest of that album. It felt like it would never get done. I remember thinking we'd be making that album for the rest of our lives.

The stakes were so high. The first two albums tanked, so the feeling was that this was our last shot. There was tremendous pressure on Bruce to deliver not just a hit but a masterpiece. And the more time we spent in the studio, the greater the pressure got.

In the beginning, I think Bruce was going for a rock opera kind of thing about this character called the Magic Rat. He had lots of songs and themes that were built around this narrative he had in his head. Eventually he let that go, but I know it frustrated him, and we've all heard the stories about how dissatisfied he was with the final product.

Of course, it all worked out in the end. But that year was a huge musical struggle for all of us. It was like some giant jigsaw puzzle with a lot of key pieces missing. Steve Van Zandt was a big help. He did the horn arrangement on "Tenth Avenue Freeze-Out" and background vocals on "Thunder Road." Plus, he was a good sounding board for Bruce. Steve is a great guy to bounce ideas off of.

That was also the time we had the first woman in the band. Her name was Suki Lahav. She played the violin on "Jungleland" and did some background vocals on "Sandy," I think. Interesting woman. Her husband Louis was an engineer we worked with, so Suki was always around. She was Israeli and had just gotten out of the army. She used to play kibbutz harvest songs on that fiddle. We thought she was an angel. We all loved her, especially Bruce. She had this kind of mystical aura. She used to wear these flowing white dresses onstage. We were sad to see her go when she and Louis got divorced and she moved back to Israel, but she has had a great career over there. Max told me she even wrote a couple of novels in Hebrew.

She was with us about six months. She was with us in the studio and out on the road for a while. If you listen to a live recording of "Incident on 57th Street" from that time you can hear the opening violin and piano intro that morphed into the opening of "Jungleland." That's the way things happened. When we got to that song in the studio Bruce told them to use what they'd been playing live. Turned out to be a perfect fit.

That was also the first time I heard the term *CD*. We used it all the time while we were making *Born to Run*. But it didn't mean the same thing it came to mean later. At first it stood for the Carnegie Deli, because we got takeout from there every day. But then it came to stand for Chicken Dinner. It included half a roasted chicken, stuffing, candied yam, and a veggie. I had a lot of CDs.

After a while, Bruce would only call us when he needed us for something specific. He still works that way. So I would commute back and forth from Jersey with Max throughout that winter. Max was the proud owner of an American Motors car called the Gremlin. It was an ugly yellow color—I used to call it baby-shit yellow. The damn thing was falling apart when he got it. The windshield wipers had a mind of their own. Anyway, one day we get a call from Bruce to come over. Max picked me up and we started out into a blizzard that had begun the day before. It was tough going, and the car was coughing and spitting. It sounded like everything inside that engine was trying to get out. Anyway, we were just past the first tollbooth on the Garden State Parkway when the son of a bitch finally quit. Cars dying on me was a theme in my life for a long while. Not anymore.

Anyway, Old Yellow was done, and Max glided her over to the side of the highway into the snow. And I'm talking a lot of snow. So there we were, stranded on the side of the road, and it was still coming down like shit. We sat there for a while trying to figure out if we should stay put and wait for help to come or get out and walk back to the tollbooth. We needed to get to a phone because Bruce didn't tolerate anybody being late. He was the Boss even back then. He had only two rules: no drugs and be on time. Since I regularly violated the first rule, it was important to me to follow the second.

So we were sitting there trying to figure that out, when I looked at the side mirror and I let out a scream. Scared the shit out of Max. There was a gigantic snowplow barreling down on us. It was shooting up this huge plume of snow and ice. We jumped out of the car and dove into the snowbank on the other side. The driver of the plow saw Old Yellow at the last second and swerved to avoid it, but he buried her under a ton of snow. I'm not shitting you...the entire car was gone. I never saw the Gremlin again. We hitched a ride into the city and got there on time.

I've often been asked to talk about the wild times on the road in the early days and I've always declined until now. The truth is this: the women on the road in the early days were incredible.

It was the most amazing thing. Everything got turned around. I'd spent my life chasing women, mostly in vain, and now they were chasing me. It was unbelievable. It was possible to have a different woman every five minutes. It was actually too much. I know that sounds stupid, but it was over the top. I mean, at first I took full advantage of this unbelievable position. Who wouldn't? But later I started to get more selective. Then I got *way* more selective. Then I started to fall in love with one woman at a time. I married a bunch of them. But I don't regret anything. I've known some amazing women, and I still love all of them.

We were doing a show in Indianapolis in 1978. So after sound check, Danny tells me there's a club right across the street called the Red Garter Lounge. Leave it to Danny. So we grab a couple of the other guys, I think Steve came with us, and we go over there. In those days, I had a fondness for strippers, and strippers had a fondness for me. It was a perfectly balanced relationship. We got friendly with a bunch of them and invited them to the show that night. So they show up backstage all dressed up and looking good. We all sat around in my dressing room, which was called the Temple of Soul, and before you know it it was showtime.

We went out and started the show, and the girls were right there in the wings, watching. Now, these women were uninhibited by nature, and they'd had a few drinks backstage. We were doing "Tenth Avenue Freeze-Out," and Bruce was up front doing his thing, and the crowd started to go crazy. Bruce thought he must have been especially good that night, and he was smiling and singing, and I turned to my left and there were the girls dancing around on the stage and taking their clothes off. This was a first for us. Bruce turned around and saw them and started laughing. These were classy strippers. They just got down to their underwear and danced around until the song ended. Not many people wanted the song to end, band included.

Then later in Houston, we had a three-hundred-pound stripper come out onstage and start taking off her clothes. And she was hot. This woman could dance her considerable ass off. She was great and the crowd loved her. After that we started to get a little more serious about security.

Thinking about those early times makes me miss Danny. He was the one who always started all those high jinks. People thought he was just the quiet guy on the organ, but he was insane. He would do the craziest shit.

One time, I was in my hotel room someplace on the road, and there was a knock at the door. I opened it and Danny was standing there in the hall completely naked. He stepped into the room, giggling like a kid, and said, "You've got to try this, C. It's an incredible rush to run down the corridor naked. I'm going to run back to my room. Take off all your clothes and run down. You won't believe what a buzz you'll get from it. C'mon, do it, man. I'll see you down there." And he ran back to his room.

I was already a little high and it sounded like fun. So I took off all my clothes. I was totally naked, right? I opened my door and looked down the corridor. It was empty. Danny's room was all the way down the other end by the elevators. So I stepped out into the hall, closed the door behind me, and took off down the corridor as fast as I could. And he was right. I got this incredible, silly rush. I mean, I was running down the corridor of a nice hotel butt naked.

I got down to his room, and his door was closed. So I knocked on the door. My room was locked, and I had forgotten to bring the key. And I heard him in there laughing. "Gotcha," he said. He had planned the whole thing. I was left out there in the wind. It was just about then the elevator doors opened, and I turned around to see the nuns.

The Legend of the Highway, 2008

Bruce and I have driven thousands of miles together in all kinds of cars and vans and trucks. If you've ever taken a road trip with somebody, you know that after a while boredom sets in and you look for ways to entertain yourselves. It's impossible to accurately re-create specific conversations we've had, but the following story contains a good approximation of what it's like when we're together. —C.C.

The car was a fucking beast. It was a '69 Chevy with some humongous souped-up racing engine putting out over 800 horsepower. The car was painted with black/gray primer paint, which seemed to absorb light like a black hole. The thing had an event horizon. It may have been the definition of dark energy.

Bruce was driving. Clarence was sitting in the other bucket seat. A man who might have been Hideki Matsui was in the backseat. He hadn't spoken at all since he'd gotten into the car two hours ago.

Astral Weeks was playing. They had listened to the whole album twice already.

It was raining.

Hideki was wearing running shoes, jeans, and a soft black leather jacket over a green T-shirt. On the T-shirt in red was the word RELAX.

Under that in white letters were the words, GOD IS IN CONTROLL. Hideki was looking out the window at the dark, wet night.

They were driving west on the Connecticut Turnpike, headed for the City. Bruce couldn't wait to get there. Sometimes the City looked and felt like Oz to him. This would be one of those times.

A wedge of black swans flew by.

"What the fuck happened to Marshall Crenshaw?" said Clarence. "That song of his, 'Someway Somehow,' was fucking great. I loved that motherfucking song."

"'Someday, Someway,'" said Bruce.

"That's what I said," said Clarence.

"Good song," said Bruce. "No 'Madame George,' but good."

Clarence half-turned and spoke to Hideki. "How you doing back there?"

Hideki just smiled and gave the thumbs-up signal.

"You think he speaks English?" Clarence asked Bruce.

"I don't know," said Bruce. "Why don't you ask him?"

Clarence turned again. "You speak English?" he said.

Again Hideki smiled and lifted his thumbs.

"Jury's still out," said Clarence.

"His T-shirt is cool," said Bruce.

"*Control* is misspelled," said Clarence.

"I think that's irony," said Bruce. "If it isn't, it is anyway."

After the game at Fenway the night before, the man who might have been Hideki Matsui went to Harvard. He loved Harvard. Everybody looked smart. It was as if all the people there were doctors. His friends were professors who specialized in quantum physics. Kevin Rooney, Chuck Sklar, and the brilliant Frank Sebastiano. These were the best minds on the planet, all trying to find an explanation for the force greater than gravity. The solution to the problem of an expanding universe. Hideki found magic in math. It spoke to him in the same way that music spoke to Bruce and Clarence. Hideki spent all his free time doing equations. Sure, it was a cliché to be an Asian math whiz, but how many of them could hit a ninety-five-mile-an-hour fastball? At least he didn't play the violin. Numbers were his true love. Somewhere deep within mathematics was the secret of space and time. The search for that secret was thrilling.

He had followed Brian Schmidt's High-Z Supernova Search Team the way other people followed the pennant race.

The evening at Frank's place was filled with dense conversation and good wine. But to Hideki the conversation was intoxicating enough.

He lost track of time and crashed on the couch. He woke too late to make the plane back to the city. He would make other arrangements to get home.

He took his time during the day and hung around the campus. He visited the library and sat on the steps outside listening to an a cappella group sing '50s songs. Nobody recognized him.

He made his way back into the city and checked out of the hotel near nightfall.

When he saw Clarence in the lobby he thought it was David Ortiz. He started to say, "Big Papi," but then he noticed the hair. No, it wasn't David. It was another big black guy who was with a smaller white guy in a leather jacket with a scarf wrapped around his neck in a stylish manner. The white guy wore a bunch of earrings. They were leaving the hotel. Outside sat a very cool black car that all the valet guys had gathered around. Then the big guy spoke.

"Hideki?" he said.

Hideki smiled and nodded.

"I'm Clarence Clemons," he said. "This is Bruce Springsteen."

Hideki smiled and bowed and shook hands.

The desk clerk then spoke to Hideki in Japanese. "They played a concert at Gillette Stadium last night," he said.

Hideki nodded.

"Is he headed to New York?" said Bruce to the clerk.

Hideki nodded that he was.

"So are we," said Bruce. "Ask him if he wants to ride along with us."

*   *   *

They were about a half hour outside of New Haven. The car made a deep-throated feline sound. Its rumble was the sound of pure power. Bruce rested his hand on the big Hearst shifter.

"You know how people are holding up signs with what song they want to hear?" said Clarence.

"Yeah," said Bruce. "It's kind of fun."

"They try to out-obscure each other," said Clarence.

Bruce laughed his reflexive laugh. "Eventually we'll do them all."

"I've got my own list," said Clarence. "Shit I'd like to hear you sing."

"Now that's interesting," said Bruce. "The Big Man's list. Don't make me wait. Tell me quick, man, I've got to run."

"That's not one of them," said Clarence. "Besides, Dylan did that one with us at Shea. Not that anybody knew what he was singing, but nevertheless..."

"Okay, so tell me your list," said Bruce.

"It's not a long list."

"Fine."

"You may not have heard of all of them."

"Would you just tell me the fucking list already?" said Bruce.

In the backseat Hideki laughed.

"Okay, first is 'I've Got Dreams to Remember' by Otis Redding," said Clarence.

"Great, great song," said Bruce. "I think Joe Rock cowrote that with Otis and Zelma."

Clarence turned and looked at him. "You know a lot of shit," he said.

"It's difficult to stand under the weight of all I know," said Bruce. "What else?"

"'Cadillac Walk,'" said Clarence.

"Willy DeVille had a hit with that," said Bruce. "Written by Moon Martin, not to be confused with Moon Mullican, who wrote 'Seven Nights to Rock.'"

"Sure," said Clarence.

"I love that song," said Bruce. "So far your list is great."

"Thanks," said Clarence.

"You're welcome," said Bruce.

"'Haley's Comet,'" said Clarence.

"Brilliant," said Bruce. "I wish I wrote that one. Dave Alvin." Then he sang, "'He closed his eyes and hit the stage in 1955 / As the screams of the children filled the hall.'"

"That doesn't count as singing it," said Clarence. "You've got to do it onstage for it to count."

"Great fucking song," said Bruce. "'The waitress said, "I don't know you from Diddley"'...Jesus Christ, that's good."

"Yeah," said Clarence.

"What else?"

"I'd like to hear your song 'Lift Me Up,' just to see if you could do it." Clarence laughed.

"I can do it," said Bruce.

"Uh-huh," said Clarence.

"I can," said Bruce. "You wanna hear it?"

"Onstage," said Clarence.

"Might have to work on my falsetto a little," said Bruce.

"Does this car have a phone?" asked Clarence.

"Is that a song?"

"No, it's a question. I thought of something else."

"Of course it's got a phone," said Bruce.

"Wanna have some fun?"

"Be stupid to say no to that," said Bruce.

"Let's call Caesars Palace in Vegas and page Mike Hunt," said Clarence.

Bruce laughed. "What the fuck are you talking about?" he said. "We're grown men. We can't be doing shit like that."

Clarence smiled. "Yeah," he said. "I know."

Two minutes later an operator at Caesars Palace answered the phone. Bruce had it on speaker.

"How may I direct your call?" she said.

"Would you please page the casino for Mike Hunt?" said Bruce.

"Could you spell that, please?"

Bruce spelled it.

"Just a moment," she said, and music came on. It was Celine Dion.

"The Queen of Hollywood High," said Clarence.

"Oh wow," said Bruce. "I haven't thought of that song for years. The guy who did it died this year. Stewart. John Stewart. Wrote 'California Bloodlines.'"

"Love to hear you do that one," said Clarence.

"'Saturday night,'" Bruce sang. "'Wheels along the boulevard…'"

"That's it," said Clarence.

"Hello?" said a guy's voice.

"Hello?" said Bruce.

"Who's this?"

"Mike?" said Bruce. "Is this Mike Hunt?"

Bruce looked at Clarence. Both of them looked amazed. Hideki didn't say anything.

"Yeah, this is Mike. Who's this?"

"Bruce Springsteen," said Bruce.

"Vinnie?" said Mike.

"No, it's Bruce Springsteen. I'm driving down the turnpike with Clarence Clemons and Hideki Matsui," said Bruce. "We called the hotel and asked for Mike Hunt as a joke. I didn't expect there to be a real Mike Hunt. You must get a lot of ribbing, Mike."

"I'll bet he goes by 'Michael Hunt,'" said Clarence.

"Bruce Springsteen?" said Mike.

"And Clarence Clemons," said Clarence.

"The Big Man," said Bruce.

"And the Boss," said Clarence.

"And Hideki Matsui from the Yankees," said Bruce.

"Cut the shit, Vinnie, I was winning," said Mike.

"No, Mike, this isn't Vinnie," said Bruce. "It's really us."

"No it's not," said Mike.

"Yes, it is," said Bruce. It's the three of us. Honest, Mike."

"And you're all in a car on a turnpike?" said Mike.

"The Connecticut Turnpike," said Bruce. "We're in a souped-up sixty-nine Chevy."

"Does it have a three ninety-six?" said Mike.

"Hey, Mike's a fan," said Clarence to Bruce.

"It's actually a little bigger than that," said Bruce. "More like a five fifty."

"But it does have a Hearst on the floor," said Clarence.

"Fuck you," said Mike, and he hung up.

Bruce and Clarence got into a laughing jag, and Bruce had to pull off the turnpike.

Hideki smiled throughout.

Finally they calmed down.

"Let's get something to eat," said Bruce.

They found an empty pizza place called DeLorio's a couple of blocks from the exit. They went in and sat in a booth. A waitress came over. She was a teenager with bad skin but pretty blue eyes. Her name tag read TAMMI. An older guy stood behind the counter near the pizza oven. It was one of the coal-burning types you don't see that much anymore. Clarence guessed the guy was the girl's father.

"Hi, guys," she said. "You need menus?"

"Nah," said Bruce. "We need pizza."

Hideki nodded and smiled.

"What do you want on it?" she said.

Bruce looked at Clarence and Hideki.

"Just cheese?" he said.

"Yes," said Clarence.

Hideki nodded yes. It was difficult to tell if he knew what he was agreeing to. But he looked happy.

"And to drink?" she said.

"Diet Coke," said Bruce.

"Two," said Clarence.

Hideki held up three fingers.

"Coming up," she said.

"Thanks, Tammi," said Bruce.

"Tammi's my sister," she said. "I'm filling in for her tonight. This is her uniform."

"What's your name?" asked Bruce.

"It's Rosie," she said.

Clarence smiled.

"Of course it is," said Bruce. "My favorite name."

"I'll get the drinks," said Rosie. She crossed to the counter.

"So, Hideki," said Bruce. "How come you didn't go back with the team?"

Hideki smiled.

"Okay," Hideki said.

"That's what I guessed," said Clarence.

"So did you finish your list?" Bruce said to Clarence.

"No, I've actually saved the one I'd like to hear the most for last," said Clarence.

"It's not 'Patches,' is it?"

"No."

"'Ode to Billie Joe?'"

"No."

"'Winchester Cathedral?'"

"No."

"Okay," said Bruce. "I give up. What is it?"

"'Two Triple Cheese, Side Order of Fries,'" said Clarence. "Recorded by Commander Cody and His Lost Planet Airmen."

Bruce laughed. Hideki laughed just after Bruce did.

"I don't know that one," said Bruce.

"It's great," said Clarence. "Old-time rock and roll. One of the lines sounds like it was written for you."

"I'm listening," said Bruce.

"It goes, 'Pickles, onions, special secret sauce / What goes in the patty's only known to the boss.'"

"Bullshit," said Bruce, laughing.

"I shit you not," said Clarence.

Bruce laughed. "What's it called?"

"'Two Triple Cheese, Side Order of Fries,'" said Clarence. Then he sang, "'If you like greasy eating and you wanna feel good / You got to cruise on down to my neighborhood / We got a funky little shack, just a hamburger stand / Right underneath the freeway down at Park and Grand.'"

"I've gotta hear this," said Bruce.

"I've got it in my bag in the car," said Clarence. "On my iPod."

"Good, good," said Bruce. He then turned to Hideki. "We're going to the Trump Hotel in the City. Where do you want us to drop you?"

Hideki nodded at the word *hotel*, took a card out of his pocket, and gave it to Bruce.

The card read "28 EAST SIXTY-THIRD STREET, N.Y., N.Y."

Later Rosie brought the pizza.

"My dad says you guys are famous," she said, as she put the pie down on the table. "Are you?"

"To some people of a certain age," said Bruce.

"And Yankee fans," said Clarence.

"You play for the Yankees?" she said.

"No," Clarence laughed. "But we think he does." He pointed at Hideki, who made a small bow and smiled.

"Wow," said Rosie.

After eating the pizza that Bruce said was second only to Federici's in Freehold, they posed for a bunch of pictures, and Bruce talked to Rosie's mother on the phone. She claimed Rosie was named after 'Rosalita,' even though her name was actually Rose. Bruce was gracious. Hideki posed for some pictures with Rosie's dad, Sal, and took pictures of the group. Clarence insisted on paying, but Sal wouldn't hear it. So Clarence left a tip on the table for Rosie. As they were leaving she caught up with them.

"You left too much money," she said.

"No I didn't," said Clarence.

"Oh, my God," said Rosie. "Thank you so much. This will go toward the car I need to get."

"That's great," said Clarence.

They said good-bye and hit the road.

Bruce and Clarence were singing "Mixed Up, Shook Up Girl" with Willy DeVille when they pulled up in front of 28 East Sixty-third Street in Manhattan.

They had actually spent the last hour of the ride singing songs from Clarence's iPod, including "Two Triple Cheese." They had sung "Ain't No Sunshine," "Baby Let's Stick Together," "Babylon Sisters," "Extremely Cool," "Travelin' Band," "Dock of the Bay," "I Wish I Never Saw the Sunshine," "I Put a Spell on You," "Keep Me in Your Heart," "Lake Marie," "River," "Real Real Gone," "Up on the Roof," "Walk on the Wild Side," and "Scotch and Soda," among others.

Clarence got out and stood on the sidewalk in front of a storefront French restaurant filled with beautiful people acting stupid. Hideki got out of the car and bowed to Clarence and to Bruce.

"Nice talking to you," said Clarence, shaking Hideki's hand.

"Good luck, man," said Bruce. "Win the World Series, okay?"

Hideki smiled and nodded. He then took out one of his cards, wrote something on the back, and handed it to Bruce. "Thank you," he said.

He bowed again to Clarence and crossed the street. He entered the building without turning back to wave.

Clarence got back into the car. Bruce was looking at Hideki's card and smiling.

"Son of a gun," Bruce said.

"What's it say?" asked Clarence.

"It says"—Bruce held it up so that Clarence could see the card for himself—"'Series of Dreams.'"

Two weeks later.

Rosie walked out of the restaurant to find the '69 Chevy parked at the curb with a big pink bow on the roof. Inside, taped to the steering wheel, was a card that said, "Our advice is to sell it on eBay and buy a Prius. All the best, Bruce and Clarence."

The Motorcade, Part I

Don

We were somewhere on the edge of London, doing about ninety miles an hour through the city streets around midnight. Our van was surrounded by motorcycle cops forming an escort. Police cars were leapfrogging ahead to block intersections so our breakneck speed wouldn't be impeded. We were in the second car of a ten-vehicle motorcade rushing through the night, all sirens, flashing lights, and tires in the rain. I was sitting in the backseat behind Clarence, who was riding shotgun. We had just done a "fast out" from the show at the Crystal Palace outside the city.

It was the night of May 27, 2003. Wayne Lebeaux, then the road manager for the band, had hustled me into the car while the last song "Dancing in the Dark" was still being performed. Then the band members, led by Bruce, came running through the night like some bizarre rock-and-roll *Braveheart* warriors and jumped into their assigned cars, and we were off and speeding through the suburbs before the crowd in the sold-out arena even left their seats.

The thing was there was no rush. The next show wasn't until the twenty-ninth in Manchester. We were just headed back to the bar at

Claridge's. And yet here we were flying around corners, frightening the children and the horses.

"Clarence," I said, "Why are we going so fast?"

He half-turned with a bemused look on his face. A man totally in his element; a man about to tell a secret. "Because we can," he said.

We continued our crazy ride through the night back into London. Having spent most of my life in the gridlock of LA, this was thrilling. I've spent more time in traffic than Steve Winwood.

"I wish that everybody I've ever met could see me," I said. "This is unbelievable."

"I know," said Clarence. "Believe it."

Earlier at the Crystal Palace fairgrounds, my wife, Judy, and I had sat backstage after the sound check and talked with tour manager George Travis about the complexities of mounting an undertaking like this. George was placid, and seemed genuinely puzzled and amused that anyone would think his job was difficult. We sat and discussed the intricacies of moving this many people and this much stuff around the world. We were and remain impressed.

We went into the catering tent and had dinner. It was both thrilling and bizarre to look around the tent and see Steve and Nils Lofgren and Garry standing in line with everybody else. They were eating just like normal people. (I have never seen Bruce or Clarence in any catering tent or E Street lounge anywhere in the world. It may have happened, but it's rare.) To say the feeling was surreal would be to understate the experience.

Things became even more dreamlike later when the band, led by Bruce, headed for the stage.

"It's time to rock and roll!" said Bruce, as they passed us.

"C'mon," said Clarence, gesturing to us.

We assumed he wanted us to follow him and then go to our seats. We were wrong.

"I've got some good seats for you," he said, as we walked up the ramp and onto the lower level of the darkened stage.

I lost track of the rest of the band in the darkness as I followed Clarence, Nils, and Danny to the stage-right area. We stopped just below the small riser that led to the performers' part of the stage. We stopped below Danny's organ, which was placed just behind and slightly above Clarence's horns, tambourines, and other percussive instruments. Clarence was in his Big Man mode, wearing his black fedora and smoking a cigar.

"One more time," he said.

This was the band's second show at this venue, but it was our first. We had arrived from Los Angeles the night before, and jet lag only added to the hazy quality of what was going on.

I became aware of a guitar playing and turned to look out over the audience. A huge cheer went up from the crowd. I looked to my left and there was Bruce, standing at center stage alone in a single white spotlight, playing the intro to the acoustic version of "Born in the U.S.A."

I was actually stunned. I really couldn't believe that I was standing there with Clarence watching Bruce from just a few feet away. Although we had been friends for years, I had never used that relationship to gain access to the shows at all. I actually took it as a point of pride that I never once asked Clarence for any special treatment, even though he would insist on it. Yes, I attended a lot of great shows over the years on all the tours, but I always bought a ticket. Most of our time together was spent away from touring. But in 2003 he invited me to come on the road with him and experience a tour through his eyes. He truly enjoyed sharing his world. For me, this show in London took things to another level.

"You guys can sit on my cases," said Clarence, pointing to the big, black rolling boxes a few feet to the right of his spot onstage.

We took the few steps and sat on the boxes. Just in front of us to the right was the stage soundboard. We became aware of all the people, the techs who were in constant motion on the stage, tuning and switching instruments, running them up to the musicians onstage, then scurrying off. All of them, everyone on and around the stage, were dressed in black.

Bruce finished BITUSA to thunderous applause. I was startled by it and by the energy coming from the crowd. There was a sea of people out there in the darkness. The rest of the band joined him on the stage and they played "The Rising." When the lights came up for "Lonesome Day" I saw the crowd for the first time. It took my breath away. It was a frightening sight. Thousands upon thousands of people, all staring at the stage. All of them into the music and the moment. This big, living thing that Bruce could control with the smallest movements. I noticed how aware he was of the cameras. He worked his performance in such a way that the people in the back had the same experience as those in front via the big screens. I guess it was then that I realized what a masterful performer he is. Of course he should be, considering how long he's been doing this. But the idea that a person could be comfortable doing *this* is unimaginable. Not only did he look comfortable, he looked more comfortable than he did offstage. He looked like he was home.

The whole band looked at home up there. This was their natural habitat. This was where they got to speak in music and style and attitude. Clarence was a different person. He moved differently when he was the Big Man. His face changed, and he appeared to get taller and younger. He walked into the spotlight with a swagger that said *Don't fuck with me,* and he leaned into the horn and spoke to every person in the audience about faith and love and passion. It was something to see.

Clarence

Once I arrive at a venue I never leave before the show. Sometimes we do a sound check at one o'clock in the afternoon for a show that doesn't start till after nine o'clock at night, but I won't leave. I stay in the Temple of Soul until showtime. I eat there and sleep there. I get whatever physical therapy I need there. I listen to music there. I play music there. But I don't leave there.

The reason I don't leave is because of what happened one night many years ago, when we were playing a gig at the Carlton Theatre in Red Bank. It later became the Count Basie Theatre, and we played there again in recent years.

But the night I'm talking about was back in the '70s. We did our sound check, and I decided to go home 'cause I lived across the bridge in the next town. "Across the bridge" is the most important part of the previous sentence. The bridge was between the towns of Sea Bright and Rumson.

I can't remember why it was so important for me to go to my house but I did, and on the way back I ran into trouble.

The bridge was closed.

Some clown had rammed into it with his boat, so I had to make this huge detour around through all these small towns filled with stoplights. It took me a long time to get back to the theater.

When I arrived I went back to the stage door and found that it was locked. Even worse, I could hear the band playing! I had never missed a gig in my life. I started pounding on the door, and eventually somebody inside heard me.

"Who is it?" said some guy from inside.

"It's Clarence," I said. "Open the door."

"Clarence who?" he said.

"Clarence Clemons," I said.

"Bullshit," said the guy. "Clarence is onstage."

"Listen to me," I said. "Go look onstage. If you don't see Clarence there, come back and open this motherfucking door!"

So the guy went all the way out front and looked at the band playing and saw I wasn't in it, then he came back to finally let me in.

It never happened again, and it never will.

Don

On the night of November 19, 2005, Clarence drove from his home to the Hard Rock Hotel in Hollywood, Florida, where Bruce was playing solo as part of the "Devils and Dust" tour. Steve Van Zandt was also in town and went to the show about the same time. About halfway through his set, Bruce brought them both onstage and, as they say, the crowd went wild. They played a song called "Drive All Night," a rarely heard ballad from *The River*. It was spectacular. Bruce sang the shit out of it and played piano. Steve was his usual fabulous self, and Clarence soared. His horn floats above everything with a soulful elegance, diving and dancing around the melody like a gull drifting on warm summer winds. The sound of his horn becomes a living thing made of beauty and breath and brass. It was a masterful performance; a perfect blend of music, friendship, and shared history. Go find it on YouTube. It's worth the effort.

People are surprised to hear that Clarence lives in Florida. He seems like such a city guy. But there are many things about the man that are surprising:

He plays golf. In fact, he puts on a celebrity golf tournament every year. Lots of friends from the world of music show up. Last January, in the jam session at the postgolf festivities, there were seven drummers present. But there was only one sax player.

He lives in a penthouse in West Palm Beach, with views out every window that will make you cry and curse the fact that you quit music lessons as a kid.

He drives a Rolls Royce convertible.

He's one hell of a fisherman.

He plays the bagpipes (well) before every show.

His favorite cigar is the Hoyo de Monterrey double corona. The same as Michael Jordan.

His nephew Jake, a fine sax player in his own right, was the star of an ABC Family television series.

He is both deeply religious and religiously phobic.

He can drink more Irish moonshine than most Irishmen and remain upright. The E Streeter he hangs out with most these days is Roy Bittan.

He doesn't hang out with Roy all that much.

He's always on a diet.

He's never on a diet.

He's always on time.

He's always in pain.

He has made a film of his spiritual journey to China in which he plays his saxophone on the Great Wall.

His likeness is on the wall at the Palm restaurant in LA.

He knows more about grappa than he should.

He has roast chicken and lobster after every show.

Except the nights he eats caviar.

He is a prolific writer of prose as well as music.

He once played pool with Fidel Castro and won.

Robert De Niro once told Clarence a secret that he swore to keep for twenty-five years.

He has a brother who is a college professor.

He's got a great singing voice.

He loves gospel music.

He's a great cook specializing in Italian dishes.

Especially meatballs. If you ever get the chance, try his meatballs. They are really good.

He is the first one to arrive before a show and the last to leave.

Bruce often calls him after shows with compliments. Those calls mean a lot to Clarence.

He knows more dirty jokes than you do.

If you're over thirty, the odds are good that he's slept with some woman you know.

He in fact likes women who are older rather than younger. Relative terms, to be sure, but it's a fact that women "of a certain age" still stand a chance of becoming his next ex-wife.

That last statement is no longer true.

He is now with a beautiful Russian girl named Victoria.

He has been married five times and has four children; Clarence Jr., who is known as Nick, is the offspring of Clarence and Jackie (hereafter known as "Black Jackie").

Nick is called Nick because Clarence's middle name is Anicholas.

His second child is Charles Oliver, whose mother is also Black Jackie.

His third son is Christopher, who lives in Sweden with his mother Christina.

And his youngest is Jarod, who lives near Tampa with his mother (White) Jackie.

Clarence loves all of them, and the feeling is mutual.

He has been known to use hydroponically grown herbs for medicinal purposes.

He wears size 17 shoes.

Yes.

His uncle is a preacher.

His grandfather farmed using a mule named Big Red for power.

He grew up in a house surrounded by white people.

He's still surrounded by white people.

He had to travel miles from home to get to the black school.

He used to run five miles a day.

He worked three jobs at the same time as a teenager.

He and Bruce used to dive off the stage into the crowds. One night Clarence badly sprained his ankle, got back onstage, and kept playing.

Sometimes when you ask him to tell you interesting facts about himself he lies.

The Legend of Key West, 1976

We've used a bar as a fictional setting for the next story. But there's a story within the story that's true. It's the story of a secret that Robert De Niro did in fact tell me many, many years ago that I'm now free to reveal. —C.C.

T wo more beers, please," said Robert De Niro.

"No worries," said the waiter, as he scurried off to get them.

"All this fuck says is 'no worries,'" De Niro said to Clarence. "He's starting to worry me."

Clarence laughed. "Me, too."

They were sitting on the upper deck of the Schooner Wharf Bar. It was five o'clock in the afternoon, and the town was fueling up for sunset.

"I was surprised to see you here," said Clarence.

A half hour ago he had walked onto the upper deck and heard a familiar voice say, "You, you, you…" He'd looked over to find De Niro sitting at the bar alone. He was wearing blue and white running shoes, black shorts, and an orange Schooner Wharf T-shirt that said WRECK RACE on the back.

On his head was a hat with a picture of a girl holding a surfboard and the words KEY WEST. The hat was black and matched his sunglasses. Clarence wouldn't have recognized him had it not been for the voice and the smile. De Niro stood, opened his arms, and said, "Big Man!"

Now, two beers later, they were talking like old friends. In truth, they had never met before.

"I was pretty shocked, too," said De Niro. "I can tell you that. I always expect to see Dennis Hopper, but I never expect to see you."

"Is Dennis Hopper here?" said Clarence.

"Not that I know of," said De Niro. "But I expect him anyway."

Clarence could see no point in pursuing this, so he moved on to something else. "What are you doing down here?" he asked.

"I'm scouting," said De Niro.

"For a movie?"

De Niro shrugged that famous shrug, turning down the corners of his mouth and nodding his head as his shoulders went up.

"For a location," he said. "Not just for movies but restaurants, too. I'm expanding my interests."

"I lost a bunch of money in the restaurant business," said Clarence. "You'd be better off taking your money and buying a boat."

"I hate boats," said De Niro. "They're nothing but floating prisons. When I'm on the beach and I see a boat go by I think, *I want to be on that boat*, but every time I actually get on a boat all I can think is, *I want to be on that beach*. Life is funny."

Clarence nodded his agreement, as the waiter returned with the beers.

"Thank you," said Clarence.

"No worries," said the waiter.

De Niro watched him go. "I find that guy annoying," he said.

"I hear you," said Clarence.

"You know how they have all this southernmost shit here? The southernmost hotel, the southernmost bar, the southernmost house?" said Bobby.

"Yeah?" said Clarence.

"I think our waiter is the southernmost dipwad."

Clarence laughed and Bobby joined in. The sky was beginning to turn a shade of pale orange.

"I'm a huge fan of yours, Bobby," said Clarence. At first he had called him "Mr. De Niro," but Mr. De Niro had insisted on "Bobby."

"And I you," said Bobby.

"I'm down here fishing," said Clarence.

"For what?" asked Bobby.

"Tarpon and pussy," said Clarence.

Now it was De Niro's turn to laugh. "Not necessarily in that order," he said to Clarence.

"Well, I'm pretty sure I'm not going to catch any tarpon in this place," said Clarence.

The truth was that he was only interested in new tarpon on this trip. His new girlfriend was the love of his life. She was back at the hotel getting ready for dinner. They were going to some Italian place on the other side of the island. He'd only talked about pussy 'cause the joke was just sitting there to be taken, and it was a guy thing to say, and Robert De Niro was certainly a guy.

"No," said Bobby, "but you might catch some crabs."

"Rim shot!" said Clarence.

After a while their laughter petered out and there was a momentary silence. They sipped their beers.

"I had the conch fritters before you got here," Bobby said.

"How were they?" Clarence asked.

"Pretty good, pretty good," said Bobby, once again nodding. The second time he said "pretty good" he hit the T sound hard, stretching it out to sound like *tee*.

Clarence couldn't wait to tell the guys about this. Robert fucking De Niro. Steve and Max would shit. They all did De Niro impressions. Steve's was the best.

"We ever meet before?" asked Bobby.

"No sir," said Clarence.

"You sure?"

"I would remember."

"You're positive?"

"Positive."

"Yeah," Bobby said. "That's right."

"Right," said Clarence.

"Those conch fritters are similar to the clam cakes they make up in Rhode Island. I'm thinking of serving them in a restaurant. Clam cakes and chowder. Red chowder. Call it the Shore Dinner Hall, like the one that used to be at Rocky Point," said Bobby.

"In Rhode Island?"

"Yeah," said Bobby. "It was an amusement park. I used to go there when I was a kid. In the summer. August. We used to take a house at a place called Bonnet Shores. Not a big house. Nothing fancy. A shack, really. No heat. A summerhouse, you know?"

"Yeah," said Clarence.

"Bonnet Shores is a good name for a restaurant, too," said Bobby.

"Names are important," Clarence agreed. "I was in a band once called Closed for Repairs, but when they put that on the marquee nobody came."

De Niro laughed hard. Rocking back and forth a little.

"That is funny," he said. "Is that true? If it's not true, lie to me, okay?"

"It's true," said Clarence. It wasn't.

"Funny," said Bobby. This time he made one word into two so it sounded like *fun knee*.

"It's true," Clarence lied again.

They drank and sighed. They both shifted in their chairs, getting comfortable.

"*Peter Gunn,*" said Bobby. "Remember that show?"

"Yeah," said Clarence. "Great theme song."

"Mancini," said Bobby. "I loved that show. Maybe I should do that as a movie."

"Good idea," said Clarence.

Downstairs a band was playing something that featured steel drums.

"You get sick of that sound fast down here," said Clarence.

"Yeah," said Bobby. "You know what else I noticed? People don't swim in the ocean here. Too shallow, or too much coral or jellyfish or something. They like to look at it and float on it, but they don't go in it much."

"I never noticed that," said Clarence. "But you're right."

"You ever done any acting?" said Bobby.

"No."

"You interested?"

"Sure, why not?" said Clarence. If Robert De Niro asks you if you're interested in acting, the answer has got to be yes.

"I'm doing this thing with Marty," he said. "I'm playing a saxophone player."

"No shit?" said Clarence.

"There's a part in it you'd be good for."

"Where do I sign?" said Clarence.

"You think I'm shitting you but I shit you not. It's called *New York, New York*."

"I'm interested," said Clarence. "Very interested."

"I'll get into it," said Bobby. "Maybe you could give me some lessons."

"I'd be happy to," said Clarence.

(Note: This did in fact come to pass. When Clarence went to LA to start the movie, Mr. De Niro came to his room overlooking the pool at the Beverly Wilshire Hotel. It was late when he got there, and his first efforts at playing a saxophone were bad. They were also loud and discordant. After a half hour of this an old woman came out of a room on the other side of the pool and screamed, "Shuuuuuuuuttttt uuuuuuuuppppp!" To this day, whenever Clarence sees Bobby he yells, "Shuuuuuuuuttttt uuuuuuuuuppppppp!")

On the wharf below them a man was dancing wildly by himself. He was wearing three-inch platform sandals, a pair of black spandex shorts, and a shiny white T-shirt that was very tight and left his flat stomach exposed. On his head sat a round, sharply pointed straw coolie hat equipped with a chinstrap. Nobody paid any attention to him at all.

"I gotta tell you something," said Bobby.

"What's that?" said Clarence.

"I say 'I gotta tell you' but I don't gotta tell you. I'm trying to stop using that word. *Gotta*. I want to tell you something. Want to," he said.

"Okay," said Clarence, thinking, *Where the fuck is this going?*

"But you gotta promise me not to—" He stopped. "I did it again. You fucking believe that? I just finished telling you how I gotta stop saying *gotta*, and the next fucking word outta my mouth is *gotta*! Jesus fuck!"

Clarence didn't know what to say, so he just smiled. Clarence was also wearing shorts and a T-shirt, and the Panama hat he'd gotten in Puerto Rico a long time ago.

"I'd like it if you didn't repeat what I'm about to tell you for a while," said Bobby.

"How long?" asked Clarence.

Bobby looked out at the boats in the harbor and thought about it.

"Twenty years," he said.

"I can't repeat it for twenty years?" asked Clarence.

"Make it twenty-five," said Bobby. "By then nobody will give a fuck."

"Twenty-five years," said Clarence.

"Yeah," said De Niro. "Or longer."

"Okay," said Clarence, uncertain if he could keep a secret for twenty-five seconds.

"Your word?" said Robert De Niro.

"My word," said Clarence.

They shook hands. Shit. Now he really couldn't say anything.

"Have you seen *Taxi Driver*?" said Bobby.

"Of course," said Clarence. "Everybody's seen it."

"Okay," said Bobby. "You know the thing I do in it?"

"Which thing?" asked Clarence.

"The thing," said Bobby. "'Are you talking to me?'"

"Oh, shit, yeah. Of course. 'Are you talkin' to me? I don't see anybody else here,'" said Clarence, wishing he hadn't just done a Robert De Niro impression to Robert De Niro.

"Yeah," said Bobby. "I stole that."

"You stole it?" said Clarence.

Bobby nodded his Robert De Niro nod again. "It's not original," he said. "I stole the whole thing."

"From who?" Clarence asked.

"Bruce," said Bobby.

"My Bruce?" said Clarence.

"The Boss," said Bobby. "Mr. Springsteen."

Clarence thought about it for a minute. Bobby watched him think. Then Clarence remembered.

"Oh, yeah...," he said.

"He did it in concert," said Bobby. "At some point he's got the whole fucking crowd in a frenzy. Everybody's on their feet screaming their lungs out and saying his name, and he stops in the spotlight and looks out into this howling mass of people, and as cool as a fucking cucumber he says, 'Are you talking to me?' Then he looks around to see, to make sure that there's nobody else they could be talking to and he repeats it. 'Are you talking to me? To me? Is that who you're talking to? Are you talking to me?' Fucking brilliant."

Clarence just stared at him for a while and smiled broadly. "Son of a bitch," he said.

"Are you talking to me?" said Bobby.

Don

Here's an absolutely true story that complements the previous piece. Believe it or not. —D.R.

I was walking down State Street in downtown Santa Barbara on a Saturday afternoon in March 2001 when a painting in a gallery window caught my eye. It was a night scene, a street in the rain lined with cars from the '50s. I went into the gallery and found out that the artist was a Canadian woman named Danielle Borbeau. Then I saw the rest of her work.

She had done a series of paintings called *Jazz,* and I loved them. They featured musicians and street scenes. Horn players, close looks at hands on valves, nightclubs, phone booths, etc. She really captured that smoky feeling of backstage at two a.m.

I bought a few of the paintings and put them in my office above stage 5 on the Disney lot.

On Monday mornings we always had our reading of that week's script on *My Wife and Kids,* the show I was writing and producing. All the players attended, including actors, writers, and executives. That week, our guest star was Clarence. After the reading there were very few notes from the network, so we had some time to catch up. He came up to my office, and we talked about what had been going on in our lives and made plans for dinner during the week. He was sitting on the couch under one of Danielle's paintings of musicians on a bandstand. From his point of view he could see two other paintings, which hung on the wall behind my desk. One was the street scene and the other was a guy on a pay phone.

"That guy looks like De Niro," said Clarence, looking at the guy on the phone.

He wasn't the first person to say that. Although Danielle did not paint distinct features, something about that guy said it was De Niro.

"Yeah," I said. "In that one, too." I pointed to the picture above his head.

In that one, there are two sax players on the bandstand. One black and one white. The white guy is leaning over and saying something to the black guy.

Clarence turned and looked at it. He stood and looked at it some more.

"I think that's me," he said.

"What the fuck are you talking about?" I said.

"I think that's me and Robert De Niro," he said. "It looks like a scene from a movie we did together."

"What movie?"

"*New York, New York*," said Clarence. "I played Cecil Powell."

"I'll be damned."

"Coincidence?" he said.

"If it is, this is the biggest coincidence I've ever heard of," I said, as I reached for the phone. "I mean come on, I randomly buy a painting of you without realizing it until you spot yourself in it?"

A minute later I was talking to Danielle.

"What did you base the *Jazz* series on?" I asked her.

"I saw this Robert De Niro movie on TV one night and the images just spoke to me," she said. "It was called *New York, New York*."

The Legend of the Big Man Meeting the Chairman, Miami Beach, Florida, 1979

This is one of my hospital dreams. Mr. Sinatra and I did cross paths a few times, and every one of them was thrilling. He was the original Boss, and he loved all kinds of music. I hope that comes across in the story. He is still one of my idols. —C.C.

Frank Sinatra walked into the room like a vision. He was impossible. He couldn't actually be there, could he? Moving like a mere mortal, a linen shirt, white pants and shoes, no socks, the silver antique Rolex...the entire package was difficult to accept. Frank Sinatra couldn't really exist on a mortal plane. He walked across the room with so much history, so many legends, and so much music. Clarence was impressed and reflexively stood up. They shook hands.

"Big Man," said Frank.

"Mr. Sinatra," said Clarence.

"Frank. Sit. Please. This is Jilly Rizzo," said Frank, indicating the balding hulk next to him with the gold-tinted glasses and the gold crucifix on a heavy gold chain. Clarence hadn't even noticed the guy. Sinatra took up that much space...that much oxygen.

"Honey loves you guys," said Jilly.

"Honey?" said Clarence.

"That's his wife," said Frank. "I call her the blue Jew."

"Where's Bruce?" said Jilly, his one crazy eye wandering off to Clarence's left.

"Jersey, I think," said Clarence.

"I thought maybe you guys lived together," said Jilly.

"You calling him a fag?" said Sinatra, half-turning.

"No, no. I'm just saying…not for nuthin', you know…that's all." Jilly signaled for the waitress.

The entire poolside bar had been cleared out for Mr. Sinatra so he could conduct this meeting in peace.

"Sweetheart," Jilly called.

She crossed to the table. Tall. Beautiful. Holding a tray.

"Whatcha want, kid?" said Frank to Clarence.

"A Coke," said Clarence. Jilly snorted.

"You don't want to drink with me?" said Frank with mock incredulity.

"It's a little early for me," said Clarence.

"Three Jacks. Put some Coke in his," said Frank. "And here." He handed her a C-note. "That's for being gorgeous." He smiled.

"Thank you," she said, and walked away. All three men followed her departure.

"If I could catch it I couldn't ride it," said Frank.

Clarence and Jilly laughed.

"I'd like some olives," said Jilly to himself.

"Let me get to the point," said Frank. "I know you're a busy guy."

"There's no place else I'd rather be," said Clarence. "No place in the world."

"That's very kind," said Frank. "The thing is, I've been listening to your records. I like to keep up with what's going on in music."

"Sure," said Clarence.

"When I heard you were here in the hotel I thought, what the hell, why not ask him, see what he thinks."

"Green olives," said Jilly.

"You can ask me anything, sir, and chances are the answer will be yes," said Clarence.

"I love this guy," said Frank to Jilly. Jilly nodded. "Okay, here's the deal," Frank continued. "I'm thinking of recording 'Born to Run.'"

Clarence didn't know Frank Sinatra, and he wasn't sure if Frank was serious or joking, so he didn't react at all. It seemed like the best response.

"What do you think?" said Frank.

"Uhh...I think you can do anything you want," said Clarence.

"It would require a different arrangement, of course," said Frank. "Less percussive. More keyboards, I think. Course I'd use my own guys. Bill Miller is my piano player."

"He's great," Clarence said. Clarence had never even heard of Bill Miller, but he assumed that if he played piano for Frank Sinatra he must be pretty good.

"I love olives," said Jilly.

"Charlie Greenface," said Frank.

"Who?" said Clarence.

"That's what Frank calls Bill," said Jilly. "On account of his skin tone."

"The guy's never seen the sun," said Frank, who was very tan.

"Oh," said Clarence.

"You know Sammy?" said Jilly.

"Davis?" said Clarence.

"No, Sammy Schmendrick. Of course Sammy Davis. 'Davis,' he says."

"No, I've never met him," said Clarence.

"I just thought maybe...you know, you guys..."

"Guitars, naturally," said Frank, who gave no indication of having heard Jilly speak. "I'm not looking to cut the balls off the song. It has to have guitars in there."

"Yeah," Clarence said. He wished the waitress would hurry up with the drinks.

"But acoustic."

"Acoustic guitars?" said Clarence.

"Yeah. It's more my style. You ever hear my stuff with Jobim?"

"Yeah, it's great," said Clarence, who had no clue.

"Maybe I'll get him. Jobim, Greenface, some strings, and you."

"Me?" said Clarence.

"You'd be the bridge between Bruce's world and my world," said Frank.

"The common domination," said Jilly.

"Well...Mr. Sinatra, it would be an honor and a privilege to record anything with you," said Clarence.

"Good," said Frank. The sun reflected the water from the pool onto the ceiling of the room, giving the whole place a dreamlike quality.

"What the fuck is a hemi-powered drone?" said Sinatra.

"Uhhh...I'm not sure," said Clarence. "Some kind of a car, I think. You know, with a hemi engine."

"But why a drone?" asked Frank, leaning forward slightly. Clarence moved back slightly. "That word is very specific. I looked it up. It can mean a driverless vehicle. Which would go with the hemi-powered thing, but it's also a male honeybee. So I asked myself, could this be about some kind of crazy souped-up insect? Or is the point that we don't know what the point is?"

"You'd have to ask Bruce," said Clarence.

"He's asking you," said Jilly.

"It's important to know what the composer had in mind," said Frank. "So the song has the proper interpretation. For instance, when he says, 'The boys try to look so hard,' does he mean they have hard-ons?"

"No," said Clarence. "I think it means they're trying to look tough. Badass."

"Is this Wendy a real chick?" asked Jilly. "Some hot little piece of ass you and Bruce are banging?"

"'I wanna die with you Wendy on the street tonight / In an everlasting kiss,'" Frank sang. To be accurate, he crooned the line, stretching out the word *kiss*. "Beautiful lyric," he said.

The waitress arrived with the drinks.

"Bring us some olives, would you, doll?" said Jilly.

"Three olives comin' up," she said.

"No. A bowl of olives," said Jilly. "Green olives."

"On the way," she said.

Again they watched her walk away.

"She couldn't be more lovely," said Frank.

"I'd like to stick my cock up her ass," said Jilly.

"'Someday girl, I don't know when, we're going to get to that place / Where we really want to go and we'll walk in the sun,'" sang Frank. Clarence noticed that he pronounced every vowel and every consonant. "'But till then, tramps like us, baby, baby, baby—'" he paused, letting the final *baby* hang in the air "'—we were born to run.'"

Jilly applauded.

Clarence, just about to kill his drink, instead put it down and joined the applause.

"Stop it," said Frank. "It's a marvelous song." He sipped his drink and snapped his fingers. Jilly instantly produced a gold cigarette case and flipped it open. Frank selected a single unfiltered Lucky and put it in his mouth. From nowhere Jilly pulled a Dunhill lighter and lit Frank's smoke.

"So, shall we do this thing?" said Frank.

"Sure," said Clarence. "When?"

"We'll be in touch," said Frank.

"How much you weigh?" said Jilly.

"Depends on the scale," said Clarence. "Sometimes, if it's a friendly scale, it could be—"

Frank Sinatra stood up. So did Jilly. Frank smiled. "Big Man," he said. Clarence stood and Frank hugged him, slapping his back three times. "Keep that horn ready, you hear me?"

"Yes, sir," said Clarence.

"You hear me?" Frank repeated.

"I hear you," said Clarence, wanting to make it absolutely clear that he heard him.

With that, Frank Sinatra turned and walked out of the room. Jilly Rizzo followed him out. Clarence sat down alone. In the distance he could hear splashing pool sounds. The room was spectacularly empty. After a minute or two the waitress returned, holding a bowl.

"Here're the olives," she said.

"You can just leave them," said Clarence. "And I'll have another drink."

"Jack and Coke?" she asked.

"Hold the Coke," he said.

Clarence

I sat under my caricature in a booth at the Palm Restaurant on Santa Monica Boulevard in West LA in Hollywood, 1985.

I loved it out here. As Ray Charles once sang, it has movie stars and cocktail bars and fancy cars — and it's on an ocean of some size.

The band was big there, too. It was a hotbed of rabid Bruce fans. Therefore the female talent pool here was large and deep. I used to really like swimming in that pool.

The truth was, by 1985 the band was big everywhere. We had blown up in a way that was hard to imagine.

Except I did imagine it. I saw it all that first night at the Student Prince. I saw the success and the stardom and the stadiums, and I knew without a doubt it was going to happen.

Bruce, however, was a very reluctant star. He never wanted to be Elvis. He saw himself more like Dylan. But the power of the songs made the pull of giant stardom irresistible, and he had to eventually find a way to deal with it.

I found a way to deal with it, too. I climbed aboard and swore to ride it until the wheels fell off and burned. To receive all this for something I would do for nothing was a blessing that fell on very few people in the world, and I tried to appreciate all of it every day. I'd been poor enough as a kid to know that I shouldn't take it for granted, either. This wouldn't, couldn't, last forever.

Could it?

Maybe.

I hadn't foreseen any failure or any diminishment in popularity. In my mind we would continue to enjoy nothing but good things until we just ran out of time.

I remember something I heard attributed to Colonel Tom Parker. The Colonel had said, "You don't have to be nice to people on the way up if you ain't coming back down."

Still, I planned to be nice to people. Why tempt fate by acting like an asshole?

But, yeah, California appealed to me in a major way.

I felt different out here, too. Younger, somehow. The weather suited me. It was a place where if you planned a picnic on Sunday you knew you'd be able to have it.

The girl I was with was talking and I was answering, but I was not really aware of what was being said. Something about her uncle's boat.

I was actually looking around the place. Everybody was beautiful or famous or both. Stallone had stopped by to say hello, as had Larry King and some TV actor whose name escaped me. Bob something.

LA was lousy with celebrities, and they all belonged to the celebrity club. Members who greeted other members with the secret handshake. They seemed compelled to sniff around each other like dogs.

I was just thinking about how much my life had changed since meeting Bruce. That was how I thought of my life now: before Bruce and after Bruce. I was thinking how I was in the club now and was congratulating myself on not really being overly impressed by anybody, when the front door opened and Muhammad Ali stepped into the room.

He was with his wife, Lonnie, and some other guy watching out for them. He was smiling at people. He was shaking, yes, but shit, he was still the greatest.

My heartbeat increased as Ali turned and looked around the room.

His eyes came to rest on me. Ali smiled and pointed. I returned the smile and bowed, my hands clasped in prayer mode.

Lonnie said something to the host and they turned and headed into the room. They were going to pass right by the table. Should I say something? If so, what? *I'm a big fan,* or one of those equally bland things people were always saying to me?

Was it possible that Ali knew who I was? Could he conceivably be a Bruce fan?

As he got closer, Ali looked at me and smiled again. I realized it was one of those moments where I was aware of everything. I knew the girl was talking to me. I was aware of every sound in the room. All the voices and all the restaurant sounds. I was aware of the music playing under all the other sounds. Improbably, it was War singing, "Cisco Kid was a friend of mine."

I was about to speak when Ali reached out and put his hand on my shoulder. He leaned down and whispered into my ear.

"We two bad niggers, ain't we?" he said.

My Grandma's house. That's me and my sister Geraldine.
Credit: Clemons Family

At my Mom's graduation. Me, Mom (Thelma), Geraldine, and my cousin Caroline Jenkins.
Credit: Clemons Family

My high school
yearbook photo.
Credit: Clemons Family

The young Boss. This
was taken in the early
'70s one weekend when
Bruce came to visit my
folks in Virginia.
Credit: Clemons Family

Geraldine, Bruce, Me, Tina Clemons, and Mom. This is from that same visit as the previous picture. *Credit: Clemons Family*

In Hawaii for my son Christopher's christening. Bruce, Dad, Quincy, and Bill Clemons. Bruce is Christopher's godfather. *Credit: Clemons Family*

Me and my horn in 1975. *Credit: Barbara Pyle*

Mr. Tambourine Man. *Credit: Barbara Pyle*

The band and a broken-down bus in Dallas. *Credit: Barbara Pyle*

The Big Man in the mir-
ror. Taken in my dressing
room in Wiedner, PA.
Credit: Barbara Pyle

Some things never change. This one is from Texas in the summer of '75.
Credit: Barbara Pyle

A dawn rehearsal at the Record Plant in New York City. *Credit: Barbara Pyle*

We'll meet 'neath that giant Exxon sign... Barbara Pyle, my friend who was at some of the *Born to Run* sessions, took this great picture of me and Roy.
Credit: Barbara Pyle

Some pretty sweet hats. Pauls Valley, Oklahoma. *Credit: Barbara Pyle*

An alternate cover for *Born to Run*. This one is a lot sexier. *Credit: Eric Meola*

Shea Stadium, 2003. This was taken before sound check at the end of *The Rising* tour. *Credit: JoLopezPhotography.com*

The Legend of Havana

I actually did play pool with Fidel in Cuba, and this is a reimagining of that night. It features a guest appearance by Dr. Gonzo himself. It is set on a piece of surreal estate. —C.C.

The dates here are difficult to pin down due to excessive consumption of drugs and alcohol by the participants, but we are somewhere between late 1979 into the first part of 1980. —D.R.

Hunter Thompson had been quietly refilling his glass for over an hour, and now Fidel Castro was drunk. Clarence knew this was an excellent time to challenge El Presidente to a game of nine ball.

Castro loved nine ball and was in fact an excellent player. He actually hustled many visitors over the years and had kept every penny he'd won. He especially liked bilking Americans. He'd always look over at his bodyguard, Fernando Dinardo, with a sly smile as he pocketed the cash. He had a box on his nightstand filled with thousands of U.S. dollars, which he would give to the whores he liked the best. The ones who made the most noise.

"Wanna shoot a little pool?" asked Clarence from the big leather chair by the window that opened onto the veranda. The veranda itself was deep and elegant, and it wrapped all the way around the beautiful wood-framed house Castro called his "real" home. The house could've been anywhere in America where people had money and taste, but it was actually located on a private street in a suburb of Havana.

"Yes, of course," said Castro in English. "Are you a betting man?"

"Oh, yes," said Clarence. "Yes indeed."

"Then by all means, let's play," said Castro. "But you'll have to spot me a ball or two as I'm not very good, but I am very drunk."

He stood, swaying and smiling.

"Let's play the first game straight up and then we'll adjust," said Clarence.

Fidel made a slight bow. "As you wish," he said.

"A hundred a game?" Clarence suggested.

Castro laughed. "You are a famous rock and roller. I was thinking more like a hundred a ball."

Clarence looked over at Hunter, who was puffing on the cigarette in his holder. He kept it between his teeth and it bounced up and down when he spoke.

"You can take him," said Hunter.

"Rack 'em up," said Clarence.

While this was going on, Fernando was having a problem.

He didn't realize that Hunter had slipped some very potent liquid LSD into the glass of water he had drunk earlier, and now the pool table was melting.

Hunter had considered dosing Castro, too, but he had only so much acid left, so he opted to debilitate the person most likely to be armed.

Fernando was staring at the pool table and beginning to drool.

Hunter sidled up to him. "Anybody ever tell you that you look like Handsome Dick Manitoba?" he asked.

"¿Que?" said Fernando.

"Do you speak English?"

"Si," said Fernando.

"Good answer," said Hunter. "We should go for a stroll and check out the local talent, as it were."

"What?" said Fernando, who seemed to be alarmed that he was being spoken to as if he were still human.

"Your skull is glowing," said Hunter.

"What?" said Fernando.

Castro beckoned Fernando, who crossed to him, and whispered to him.

"Go," said Castro in Spanish. "Take the tall one away while I steal the big Negro's money."

Clarence, who had heard the words *big Negro* in many different languages, some of them nonverbal, said nothing. But he did resolve to take this fuck's money. Nine ball was the one thing Clarence played as well as the saxophone.

It's impossible to say if Fernando understood anything being said to him, but he nodded and turned back to Hunter, who was drinking a mojito.

Hunter was very, very twisted at this point in time. He didn't care what happened to him. What set him apart was that he was actually used to feeling that way. This made him one of the most dangerous men in the world.

"He's hiding something from you," he said to the bodyguard. "There is something deadly going on here that he doesn't want anybody to know about. Do you know what it is?"

"No," said Fernando.

"Do you have family here?" asked Hunter. "Loved ones?"

"Yes, my mother and my sisters," said Fernando. "And Camilla."

"Yes, Camilla," said Hunter. "We may have to deal with her later."

"What do you mean?" asked Fernando in one of his final lucid moments.

"Have you ever heard of rat lungworm disease?" asked Hunter.

"*¿Que?*" said Fernando again.

"Let's go find a bar," said Hunter. "I have much to tell you."

After they left, Clarence and Castro began to play pool. There were still other people around, servants and some uniformed soldiers outside, but the dictator and the sax player were alone in the game room.

Castro won the lag and broke first.

Clarence noticed immediately that Fidel was no longer drunk. He was still acting drunk, slurring and swaying, but not when he was playing pool. He was stone-cold sober when he lined up a shot. He must've been dumping the drinks into a plant or something, because he had clearly clocked onto Hunter's game early and played along. You don't get to steal an entire country by being stupid, Clarence thought to himself. This was one clever motherfucker.

Castro ran the table.

Clarence had expected him to blow a shot on purpose to sucker him in, but the guy didn't do that. In fact, he made every shot look easy. The cue ball ended up in a perfect position every single time.

"Shall we continue?" said Castro.

"As long as we keep playing until I get a shot," said Clarence.

"I can't guarantee that," said Fidel. "Let's just play until you run out of either time or money."

"Works for me," said Clarence.

Clarence lit a Cohiba, sat back, and watched Fidel Castro play pool.

This trip had been in the offing for some time. Clarence had met Hunter when the writer was staying at Jimmy Buffett's place in Key West. Clarence liked the guy. They spent many nights drinking and talking sports and politics with Jimmy and Tom Corcoran, who was writing some movie with Hunter. What Hunter was writing was always unclear to Clarence, but somebody was paying him to do something even though all he seemed to do was party.

He was very good at that.

The idea for the Cuban trip had come up when Hunter was staying out on Sugarloaf Key. He had called Clarence and invited him down to have some fun. Having "fun" with Hunter could be exhausting, so Clarence put it off until Hunter called back with the promise of "cocaine, whiskey, and bitches." Plus everybody enjoyed trying to beat Clarence at pool in one of the local taverns. Nobody ever did.

They had a fine time. At least the parts of it Clarence could remember had been fine. Hunter had a thing where he would hit on every woman in proximity just to prove to you or himself that he was the top dog. Clarence was with a beautiful French model named Chloe, and Hunter followed her around as if he were in heat. Clarence was amused.

One night the whole group traveled north to the Moorings Village, where Clarence had taken a beautiful house on that perfect white sand beach. There was a full moon over the water. After a dinner of spaghetti and meatballs made by the Big Man, he took everybody out on the deck and he played the horn. He played soft, slow jazz and filled the night with soul. When he was done, Chloe turned to Hunter.

"Do you still think there's a chance I would leave him for you?" she asked.

"No," said Hunter.

It might have been the highest compliment he ever paid to anyone in his life.

"A friend of mine in the State Department has cleared the way for me to go interview Castro," said Hunter the next afternoon when they all awakened.

"Really?" said Clarence. "That would be interesting."

Hunter opened his third beer of the day and took a long drink.

"Wanna come with me?" asked Hunter. "We'd fly to Puerto Rico on Monday then take a boat to Havana. Some kind of a launch."

"Sure," said Clarence. He doubted that this would ever actually happen.

"Good," said Hunter. "I understand Castro plays pool."

Now Hunter and Fernando were in a bar on a side street near the National Hotel. The bar was actually called El Hole, and Hunter liked it. It was dark and filled with cheap-looking women.

There was a jukebox in the corner that kept playing "The Piña Colada Song," which was actually titled "Escape," although nobody called it that. It seemed to be the only song the jukebox played, and they were listening to it for the third time since they'd come in and sat on adjacent stools at the circular bar. Fernando was studying the steady stream of spiders that were crawling out from under his fingernails. Hunter had put on lipstick and was drinking rum.

"Do you have a weapon?" asked Hunter.

"Yes, of course," said Fernando.

He just wasn't sure why he was saying "Yes, of course," because he couldn't recall the question the tall American with the lipstick had asked him so long ago.

"I think you should shoot the bartender," said Hunter.

This was a very good idea because the bartender's face had split open, and a lizard had popped out and was flicking a forked tongue at Fernando as it approached him with something in its claw that was smoking.

"Yes," said Fernando, as he took out his gun and pointed it at the lizard.

The lizard stopped and its mouth opened and it started to scream. Fernando was just about to pull the trigger when he realized the lizard was holding a cocktail in its claw. A smoking cocktail called the Volcano, which Fernando had ordered. Well, he didn't actually order it, but he did point to a picture of it on the bar menu.

He lowered the gun; the lizard stopped screaming, put the drink down on the bar, and scuttled away.

"You showed him," said Hunter. He took the gun from Fernando, turned, and shot the jukebox.

The noise was deafening. There was a shattering of glass and plastic and then screaming as everybody ran out of the place.

"I hate that fucking song," said Hunter, who then yelled at the fleeing patrons, "This man is with the secret police. This is official business."

Just then the jukebox miraculously came back to life and "The Piña Colada Song" started up again.

Hunter shot the thing three more times. The music stopped for good.

"How are you feeling?" he asked Fernando.

"Not well," said the bodyguard.

"There's been an outbreak of this hideous disease and nobody knows about it. We've got to take care of you and then we've got to get the word out. This thing is vicious."

"What is it?"

"It's called rat lungworm disease," said Hunter, turning toward him. "It's a nematode that hatches in the lungs of rats. From there the larvae pass through rat feces to slugs and snails, who then crawl all over contaminated backyard vegetables. The effects are horrifying. Excruciating pain, uncontrollable itching…you see, it affects the nerve endings. In twenty-four hours you go into a coma. Meningitis is common. There are people who had it twenty years ago whose skin is still so sensitive that they can't wear long pants."

Fernando began to scratch his arm. "So what do I do?" he asked.

Hunter took out a small plastic bag filled with pills.

"Fortunately for you I'm a doctor," he said. "I'll give you some medicine."

"Why don't we stop this dance now?" said Castro. "Why not play for fifty thousand dollars, one game, winner take all?"

He smiled at Clarence. He had dropped all pretense of drunkenness.

They had been trading games for over an hour and were even.

"This is why you've come, no? There's no interview. Your friend is a world-famous drunk and drug addict. This is about nine ball, isn't it?"

"It is for me," said Clarence. "You're on."

They lagged again for the right to break, and this time Clarence won.

"I'm going to enjoy this," he said, as he chalked the cue he'd brought along. The cue had been made for him by a man named Nick Arnold in a trailer in Palmdale, California. Nick made the best cues in the world but was reluctant to make them. It had taken Clarence five years to convince him to build this one.

"That's a Nick Arnold cue, isn't it?" asked Fidel.

"It is," said Clarence.

"Would you consider selling it?"

"No," said Clarence, "but maybe I could get him to build you one in exchange for a few cases of this wonderful cigar."

"Anything is possible," said Castro.

"Yes," said Clarence, as he hit the cue ball mightily into the diamond. The balls flew around the table at warp speed. Not one of them dropped.

"Well," said Castro finally. "It looks like it's my shot."

He sunk the first seven balls in under a minute. But after pocketing the eight the cue ball just grazed the nine, which then rolled to within a Gwyneth of the side rail.

[According to Clarence a "Gwyneth" is the smallest unit of measurement, equal to the presumed width of one Gwyneth Paltrow pubic hair. —D.R.]

"You have an interesting dilemma," said Castro.

And he was right. There was no apparent shot. The correct move would be to play safe back and forth until somebody made a mistake or an incredible shot.

"True," said Clarence, as he picked up his cue and approached the table.

Then he smiled. He smiled because he could see the shot. It was the same thing as hearing the music in his head when he was writing. He could see and feel the shot and he would not miss.

"Something amusing?" said Castro, leaning on his cue.

Clarence took a puff on the cigar and rested it in the big stand-up ashtray a few feet from the table.

"I think so," said Clarence. "Nine ball, three cushions, side pocket."

Castro actually laughed.

Clarence made the shot as easy and true as any in his past. The nine bounced off the rail, then to the end cushion, back across the table under him, and straight into the side pocket.

"Game," said Clarence.

Castro had stopped laughing.

"I have become interested in the scansion of language," said Hunter, as he popped open another beer. They were on the flying bridge of the sport fishing boat they had chartered that morning in Havana.

It hadn't been difficult to find someone with a boat to take them to Key West. They were offering a thousand dollars for the trip, and there were many takers. The cash came from the box that had once sat on Castro's nightstand. They finally went with an old leather-skinned Cuban hand called Martin aboard his forty-two-foot Grand Banks named *Tempo*. The deal was that Martin would get them into the harbor and they would find another boat there to take them to shore, thereby avoiding the authorities.

"The what?" said Clarence.

"The rules of poetry, basically," said Hunter. "Stuff like spondees and dactyls, but mostly anapests. I'm fascinated by the anapest."

"What the fuck are you talking about?" said Clarence.

They could see a boat on the horizon. Most likely somebody fishing off the Florida coast.

"I'm talking about prosody and feet and meter," said Hunter. "About rhythm, stress, and intonation. An anapest is two unstressed syllables followed by one stressed one. Kind of like you and me and Fidel."

"Pass me a beer," said Clarence.

"Next year we should attend the *mahu* parade on Molokai," he said, handing Clarence the beer. "It's a hoot. Last year Kyu Sakamoto was there. He sang 'Sukiyaki,' of course, but also his follow-up song, which was called 'China Nights.'"

"The real name of that first song was 'Ue O Muite Aruko,'" said Clarence. "They only called it 'Sukiyaki' so Americans would buy it. Sukiyaki is actually a kind of steamboat dish. That would be like calling "Born to Run" "Cheese on Toast.""

"Sweet Jesus on a stick," said Hunter, as he stood. "Slow down, Martin. We have something unusual here."

Clarence looked at the boat they were approaching. It was a sloop that went maybe ninety feet. A beautiful craft made from mahogany and canvas. It appeared to be filled with naked lesbians.

"There are naked women going at it with each other on that vessel," said Hunter.

"Appears so," said Clarence.

"That must be some sort of violation of maritime laws," said Hunter with his cigarette holder clenched between his teeth.

"*Laissez les bon temps roulez*," said Clarence, smiling.

To be fair not all the women on the deck (there were about twenty of them) were naked or involved in lesbian activities, but enough were to give that impression.

"Pull alongside, Martin," said Hunter. "We need to talk to these people."

NOTE FROM DON:

I'm going to end this story here at the point where I stopped believing it when I first heard it. It goes on and on and includes a chapter about Fernando Dinardo, who never really recovered from the drug-induced psychotic episode he suffered while in Hunter's company. He later found religion, took a vow of silence, and spent the last thirty years of his life as a monk in a monastery above Big Sur, California.

Then there is a huge, wildly speculative section that hypothesizes that Oscar Acosta, Hunter's old friend from Fear and Loathing in Las Vegas *and presumed dead, was in fact alive in one of Castro's prisons and was released during the Mariel boat lift a few weeks after Clarence's game of pool with Castro. The story hints that Oscar's release was somehow tied to the game. It goes on to posit that Oscar became the man the character of Tony Montana (from* Scarface*) was based upon, and he spent the next decade dealing drugs and indulging in a bit of the old ultraviolence. Rubbish. It's all rubbish.*

There are, however, a few details that give my doubting nature pause. For instance, one of the women on board the sloop was named Cammi Ann Carter. Cammi's father, a legendary South Florida real estate developer named Lawrence "The Swamp Swami" Carter, owned the boat. She'd been raised on the water and was herself a first-class captain. She chartered the boat out to groups, and this one was in fact a bunch of part-time lesbian strippers down for the weekend from Boca, where they all worked in a club called Diamond.

There were several other notable things about Cammi. She had a deep and passionate interest in Eastern religions, and on that particular day she had the greatest set of tits in the world. The Big Man's involvement with her would lead him on a spiritual quest, which resulted in him finding a guru named Sri Chinmoy to guide his life and to changing his name from Clarence Clemons to Mokshagun.

Clarence

A girl I knew introduced me to Narada Michael Walden, the brilliant musician and record producer who changed my life in a major way. Narada is the most spiritual person I know, and at the time I met him I was disconnected from spirituality totally.

We hit it off and became friends, and he introduced me to meditation. I had always thought that meditation was a bunch of bullshit until he insisted that I give it an honest shot. The first time I tried it I fell into a trancelike state that seemed to last forever. When I opened my eyes Narada was there.

"Come over here," he said. "I want to show you something."

He led me over to a mirror and when I looked in it I did not recognize myself. I swear to God I didn't know who I was. My mind had drifted so far from my body that for a few minutes afterward they didn't connect. It was a weird feeling. But I felt a peace, which was a feeling I hardly recognized. I have practiced meditation every day since then.

Shortly after that Narada called me and asked me to play on a track with Aretha Franklin. This was a dream come true for several reasons. First, I would get to work with the undisputed Queen of Soul. I would have been thrilled to stand in the same room with Aretha, and now I would actually get to play with her. Second, I would get to stand where King Curtis stood. King was one of my sax heroes growing up. I loved him. He used to play for Aretha, and now I was going to get a chance to do the same thing. It was unbelievable.

The track, called "Freeway of Love," ended up on one of her best-selling albums.

We even made a video of it, although it didn't turn out the way it was planned. It was all shot in a nightclub, but it was supposed to be done at an auto plant. On the day of the shoot Aretha didn't feel like traveling out to the plant, so we had to improvise. There are certain privileges that come with being the Queen.

I moved out to Marin around that time to continue to study meditation with Narada. But the next big change in my life happened when he encouraged me to travel with him to New York to meet his guru, Sri Chinmoy. Narada said that Sri was a true holy man, and that he could help me to define myself and my life. At the time I was drifting and had no clear purpose.

When he saw me walk into the room in Queens, New York, that night, Sri Chinmoy smiled, crossed to me, and embraced me. That night he gave me my spiritual name, which was Mokshagun. Sometimes getting a name can take years, but he said that was who I was. The name is Sanskrit for "Lord's All-illuminating Liberation Fire."

I went by the name for many years, but I finally decided to use it only privately because it confused too many folks. But more important than a spiritual name was the purpose he gave to my life. He told me that I was on Earth to bring joy and light to the world and to destroy ignorance. I'm still on that quest.

On the night that I met him I called my mother.

"I've got a guru," I told her.

"Get a good night's sleep," she said. "And maybe it will be gone in the morning."

Don

Many memorable things occurred during the three-night stand that closed the "Rising" tour. On the second night the fast out was sabotaged when the police directed the motorcade into the public parking lot because they were angry with Bruce for playing the song "American Skin (41 Shots)" the night before. It wasn't all that bad. We spent about an hour in the parking lot and met a lot of nice people. Clarence rolled down the limo window and signed autographs, the smell of his cigar smoke wafting through the cool October night.

I watched those shows from the stage, sitting on Clarence's trap cases or standing by the soundboard. On the last night it took awhile to realize that the twitchy guy next to me in the leather jacket and watch cap was Bob Dylan, who later joined the band onstage and did "Highway 61 Revisited." I've spent my life around famous people but some, like Dylan, have that special light around them that sets them apart. When I asked Clarence who impressed him that way he said King Curtis, the sax player who inspired him to pick up a horn in the first place when he was just a kid in Virginia. He said the only other person who left him speechless was the late Marcel Marceau, but I'm pretty sure he was kidding. I'd call him to clarify but, as Marcel demonstrated in his lifetime, some things are better left unsaid.

Al Franken was there that night, too. This was after his time on *Saturday Night Live* but before his entry into politics. I had first met him in the '70s when he and his then partner, Tom Davis, were a young comedy team. In fact, I gave them their first shot on television as part of an ABC late-night show called *Comedy Concert*. Bruce had invited Al to the show because he was a fan of Al's books. We started chatting, and I reminded him that I was the one who first gave him a shot. I even remembered the routine they had done. It was a local newscast on the day the world ends.

"The stock market closed today...."

"It's two thousand degrees in Los Angeles, three thousand in the Valley, and up to thirty-five hundred in firestorms."

And a bunch of other very funny stuff. I even quoted some of the lines to Al as we stood there on the side of the stage.

"You cut us out," he said.

"I did?"

"Yeah, we had a big party with our friends and families to watch the show, but we weren't on it. You cut us out."

"I totally forgot that. I can't imagine why I did unless the show was really long or something," I said.

"Well, you did," said Al.

"Well, shit, I'm sorry about that," I said. "I sure hope it didn't hurt your career."

"It only hurt for a little while," he said. "I've totally forgiven you."

"Well, I'm glad," I said.

"But if you see Tom coming? Run."

"I will," I said.

"Is it just me or is Bruce starting to look like Tony Bennett?" he said.

A brief digression: all this time hanging around with the Big Man and Bruce and the band and famous people can get a little heady. After being on the road in Europe, I stopped in New York on my way home and was standing at the bar at the Post House talking to my friend Joe Funghini, the bartender. There were a few people at the bar, and I guess I might have raised my voice a little when telling stories of how "we" played a show here or "we" took the private jet there. What the hell, they were great stories. One guy at the bar got into it, asking me all kinds of questions about where "we" played, which venues, which hotels, etc. And I was happy to answer. I even talked about the unique perspective one gets from the stage, the almost voyeuristic view of the crowd. Finally after a lot of this even I got tired of the sound of my own voice and I asked him what business he was in.

"Oh, I'm in a band, too," he said.

"Really? What's it called?" I said.

"R.E.M.," he replied.

He was Mike Mills, the bass player. They would be working Madison Square Garden the next night.

"Okay," I said. "On a scale of one to ten, how big an asshole am I?"

Fortunately Mike was gracious and said he really was interested, as they were heading out on a European tour themselves. End of digression.

Back at Shea Stadium, the final night proved to be an emotional one for Clarence. It all hit him during the last song, which was a special version of "Blood Brothers," Bruce's tribute to his bandmates. At this point in their career it was in Clarence's mind that this could be it, the last time the E Street Band would ever perform together. He found it impossible to avoid tears. He remained in that fragile state in the car. As we were about to leave Bruce came over and tapped on the window.

"You okay?" he asked.

"Yeah," said Clarence. "It's just a lot of emotion, you know."

"Yeah," said Bruce. "But look, you're coming to the party, aren't you?"

"Absolutely," said Clarence.

"Good, good. I'll see you over there," said Bruce, as he turned to go.

"Hey, man," said Clarence. Bruce stopped. "Thanks," said the Big Man.

"For what?" Bruce asked.

Clarence grabbed his hand and held it.

"For everything," he said.

Clarence

Over the years the Temple of Soul has existed in many forms. It has been located in tiny dressing rooms and in lavish suites; in small tents and in huge RV's. But every place it is set up some things remain constant. There are always pictures of my family and my guru. There is always a picture of me, too, but that's just 'cause I'm so good looking I never get tired of seeing myself. You'd do the same thing if you were the sexiest man on the planet.

There is always a massage table and a massage chair. All of the Big Man's stage clothes are there including a collection of black fedoras made for me by Borsilino. There is always caviar and crackers and roast chicken and lots of sodas and beer and sports drinks. There is usually a bottle of something harder around, too; most often it's tequila.

The Temple of Soul is off limits to everybody except for members of my inner circle. In fact I often put a sign on the door that reads "Don't come in unless you are Jesus and you'd better have your Daddy with you!" That dissuades most people.

It is essential for me to have a refuge when I'm on the road and that's what the Temple of Soul is. It is my sanctuary.

One of my favorite incarnations was when the Temple lived inside a customized tour bus. That thing was like a beautiful house on wheels and I traveled in it for a while. But when the tour went international the bus couldn't make the trip and I missed it. To have a full kitchen and living room and, best of all, a private bedroom and bath was near the height of luxury. Near but not at the top.

The top for me was a private train car Don and I chartered in California. We took our families on a trip down the coast to San Diego in a gorgeous car that had a full galley, two bedrooms, and two sitting rooms. It was fabulous. I would love to have a car like that for my own.

I would keep it at a siding in a train yard and not tell anybody except for my family and close friends where it was. I'd trick it out with flatscreens and a killer sound system. I'd have a rear platform on it and I'd stand out there and wave at people as I went by. I actually got to do that on the trip we took and it made me feel like the president. Something about seeing a train go by makes people smile.

Now I've traveled a lot and much of it has been in luxury. In the band we fly on chartered jets and some of them are very beautiful. But nothing compares to the feeling of traveling in your own train car. It made me feel like a king. I didn't want the journey to end. If it weren't for the fact that we have to travel long distances in short periods of time I'd never fly. I would get myself that car and take it everywhere. And I would name the car Mrs. Silvers.

Mrs. Silvers is the name of a teacher I had in the seventh grade. She had a major impact on my life. She was unusual in a lot of ways. She was an African American woman teaching white kids, which was pretty rare back in the day. She and I were the only two people of color in the entire school. Maybe the entire neighborhood. I think that it was because of that fact that she was so hard on me.

"You're dumb," she'd say to me. "You're never going to amount to anything in this life, mark my words."

And I did mark her words. Or maybe they marked me. I was determined to prove her wrong, and that became one of my key motivators in life. Unfortunately she didn't live to see how things turned out for me, and that's a shame. I would've enjoyed taking her for a little train ride.

Don

D ublin is as good a place as any to talk about Clarence's rela-
tionships with women. We were in a restaurant one night, and
"Tenth Avenue Freeze-Out" came on the sound system. Bruce sang,
"'When the change was made uptown and the Big Man joined the band /
From the coastline to the city all the little pretties raise their hands.'"
Clarence smiled and said, "They did, too." The point being women love
Clarence and he returns the favor. Depending on who's counting, he's
been married five or six times (five, officially) and has had the numer-
ous relationships you'd think a man in his position might have. He also
seems to remain on friendly terms with all of them. One night I was in
the Temple of Soul after a show at Madison Square Garden. The room
was crowded. There were at least three women in the room I knew for
a fact had dated Clarence. They all seemed happy to see him and didn't
seem at all bothered by the presence of the others. And those are the
three I'm sure about. Katie Couric was in the room, too. I have no idea
if Katie has ever known Clarence in the biblical sense, but it wouldn't
surprise me.

So we get to Dublin as part of the "Rising" tour. At the time Clarence was dating a female basketball player from Yugoslavia who was

tall, beautiful, and funny. My wife and I spent three days with them in Dublin and, except for the few hours we slept, we were together almost nonstop. The only time we were not together was one afternoon when Clarence was having acupuncture to hopefully help his back, which had bothered him for years.

Two months later I was home in Los Angeles when the phone rang. It was Clarence.

"I'm at the airport in Atlanta," he said. "I've got the ring in my pocket and I'm flying to Dublin to ask her to marry me."

"Who?" I asked, thinking he must be talking about the basketball player.

"The acupuncturist," he said.

"You're marrying an Irish acupuncturist?" I said.

"No, she's Chinese," he replied.

That turned out to be Gina, from whom he is now divorced. But the story is illustrative of the romantic nature of the man. Now he's with Victoria, whom he met in Marin, near San Francisco. I wish them well.

The Legend of Fishing with Norman Mailer, Florida (Date Unknown)

The Naked and the Dead changed my life. The power of Norman Mailer's writing overwhelmed me. It still does. The stories about him in this book are a wish fulfillment. He was my companion on so many plane rides and in so many dressing rooms over the years that I began to believe I knew him. He is a hero of mine. —C.C.

Clarence and Norman Mailer were flatboat fishing in the Florida Keys. They were sitting on opposite ends of an almost new sixteen-footer. It was hot. Both wore sunglasses. Norman's glasses had a blue tint; Clarence's were black. Norman was shirtless. Clarence wore a white T-shirt with a picture of Willy DeVille on it. Clarence lit a cigar. Norman swatted and killed a mosquito on his forearm. It left a little spot of blood on his arm and another on his palm. He wiped his hand on his cargo shorts.

"Think I could take you in a fair fight?" asked Norman.

"No."

"I'm talking a street fight. Down and dirty."

"You said a fair fight."

"It'll be fair, but no holds barred."

"No."

"No what? No, you don't think I could take you?"

"That's right," said Clarence. "You couldn't take me."

"Why not?"

"You mean besides the fact that you're a hundred fucking years old?"

"Besides that," said Norman.

"I outweigh you by about a ton, I'm a foot taller...I'm quicker and blacker."

"What else?"

"That's enough."

"It's not the size of the dog in the fight, it's the size of the fight in the dog," said Norman.

"Sounds like something a small dog made up," said Clarence.

Norman noticed the blood on his forearm and licked it away. "Maybe I'll be the first person to catch AIDS from a mosquito," he said.

"Could happen," said Clarence.

They fished and smoked and sweated for a while. A heron flew by, its wings flapping in long, lazy strokes.

"I'll tell you who I could take," said Norman.

"Who's that?" Clarence asked.

"Cormac McCarthy."

"The 'Pretty Horses' guy?"

"Yeah," said Norman. "Pretentious bastard. Too good to use quotation marks. What the fuck is that? Is he some e. e. cummings lowercase cocksucker or what?"

"I don't know," said Clarence.

"I'd kick his skinny Texas ass from here to El fucking Paso. And don't sit there and tell me I couldn't."

"Would you wear those blue sunglasses when you did it?"

"What difference does that make?" asked Norman.

"Well, they're kinda faggy looking. Might add to the humiliation factor while you're kicking his ass. Have to tell his friends he got a beat-down from a hundred-year-old man with mosquito-blood AIDS wearing faggy blue sunglasses. That kind of thing could be a deal breaker down in Texas."

"I'll wear the glasses," said Norman.

Clarence opened the cooler and took out a Heineken. He offered it to Norman.

"I'll take a brown bottle, please," he said.

Clarence tossed him a bottle of Bud. Norman twisted off the cap and dropped it into the boat, where it lay with six others.

"You like white women?" asked Norman.

"Some of them," replied Clarence.

"You guys," began Norman, "and by 'you guys' I mean black guys, specifically famous black guys, seem to go nuts for white women."

"That's how you see it?"

"Yes it is."

"That's been your observation?"

"Yes."

"All the famous black guys you've seen were with white women?"

"Enough so I'd remark on it," said Norman.

"Forbidden fruit," said Clarence.

"No shit. I figured that part out on my own. But beyond the obvious, I don't get it. I mean I've been with a lot of white women, and most of them are incredible cunts."

"How many?" asked Clarence.

"What?"

"How many white women have you been with?"

Norman sipped his beer. "Eleven thousand," he said.

Clarence lowered his glasses and peered over them. "Even?" he asked.

"Last Tuesday at the Checca Lodge in Islamorada...remember the little cocktail waitress, Babbette?"

"No shit?"

"Who knew she was a reader?" Norman smiled. "I'd been stuck on ten thousand nine hundred ninety-nine for over four years."

"Is that a fact?" said Clarence. He started blowing smoke rings. It was still, so they hung in the air a long time before slowly losing their shape.

"Four years and a week, to be exact," said Norman.

It was quiet for a while. Clarence caught a fish. Norman worked the net. They brought it to the boat, removed the hook, and released it.

"Were you pissed when Springsteen went out with that other band?" asked Norman.

"I wasn't thrilled about it."

"I know my opinion doesn't count, I am a hundred years old after all, but without you guys it's just another band with some decent songs. There's no magic there. Plus he had that big black guy singing with him. That had to sting."

"Listen," said Clarence, "if it wasn't for Bruce there's no way I'm fishing in the Keys with Norman fucking Mailer, now is there?"

"No way in America," said Norman.

Both men laughed.

"Shit," said Clarence. "I can't worry about things I can't control. I'm on a spiritual path to enlightenment."

"Good luck with that," said Norman.

"You're not spiritual?" asked Clarence.

"Hey," said Norman, "I'm for whatever gets you through the 'four o'clock in the morning' of your soul."

"I hear you," said Clarence.

The sun was directly overhead. Clarence put on a straw hat he got in Puerto Rico many years ago. Norman poured beer over his own head.

"You working on anything?" asked Clarence.

"Yeah," said Norman. "I'm fooling around with a thing...a book."

"What's it about?" said Clarence.

"God," said Norman.

Clarence

My grandmother was blind. For a large part of my childhood she raised me when my parents were at work. She was tough on us kids. She used me as her eyes when she wanted to spank my brother Bill.

"Lead me to him," she'd say to me.

She'd put her hand on my shoulder and I'd have to take her to my brother, despite his silent pleadings not to.

"Don't run in the house," she'd always say. "You'll fall and cut your leg on something."

I think I heard that so many times that I unconsciously made it come true. I was running around the house and knocked a glass off the table. It broke, and I got a severe cut on my knee.

I went to the hospital and they stitched it up. When it healed I was left with a pretty horrifying scar. My knee felt and worked fine, but it looked like hell.

This turned out to be a life changer.

I got drafted. This was in the day when they told you to "bring your suitcase" when you reported to the draft board. I was headed for Korea until the doctor saw my knee. He took one look at it and told me to go home.

Thanks, Grandma.

The Legend of Big Sur, 1982

This next story is another work of fiction surrounding a truth. One night in Mr. Chow's, Nick Roeg did tell a version of the horrifying story contained within the piece to Harry Nilsson and me. The mitigating factor, and the reason we've fictionalized this one, is because Nick might have made up the whole thing. —D.R.

Do you know who he is?" Miki Dora asked Clarence, while pointing to the tall man wearing the huge cowboy hat. The man with the hat was sitting near the fireplace across the room.

"No," said Clarence. "I barely know who you are."

"His name is Richard Brautigan," said Miki. "I just finished reading this book he wrote called *The Hawkline Monster*, and it was fucking great."

"What's it about?" said Clarence.

"Hit men, twins, monsters..."

"Sounds good."

"Remind me to give it to you after dinner," said Miki. "We'll get him to sign it."

"I don't want to bother the guy," said Clarence.

"Bother him?" said Miki. "Look at the poor fuck sitting there by himself drinking alone. He's so freaky tall, and with that fucking hat he scares people. Nobody wants to make eye contact with him."

"He *is* odd looking," said Clarence. "Not that we're not strange ourselves."

They were in the dark dining room of the old Big Sur Inn. It was raining hammers and nails outside. The road to the south was closed because of the Devil's Slide moving again. If you didn't want to be in Big Sur you needed to head north now. Neither Clarence nor Miki had to be anywhere in the near future.

"How's the wine?" asked Miki.

"Good," said Clarence. "Real good."

Miki had ordered the wine, asking questions about it in French. He'd spent some time over there, he said afterward. It tasted expensive, and Clarence was already wondering how they were going to handle the check and they hadn't ordered their meals yet.

He'd run into Miki earlier that day. Clarence had been enjoying an ambrosia burger on the deck at Nepenthe.

"Big Man," Miki said, extending his hand. "I'm Miki Dora. I'm a surfer, among other things."

"How you doing, man?" asked Clarence. He always said that.

"Better now," said Miki, sitting down. "I don't know anybody in this place."

"Neither do I," said Clarence.

He had rented a car in San Francisco and was taking his time driving down the coast to Los Angeles. Bruce and Danny had told him how beautiful Big Sur was when they played a date for a bunch of naked hippies at the Esalen Institute down the road. He'd already checked in and gotten situated in a house on the grounds of the Ventana resort, and he was enjoying the place. Even though the rain killed the views he'd heard about, the place did have some kind of magical feel to it. It was good. It felt like a special place. The quiet here was almost a tangible thing. It seemed to have weight.

"That burger working?" asked Miki.

"It's delicious," said Clarence.

Miki had ordered one along with several beers, but when the check came his wallet was down in his car. Clarence paid, and Miki said he'd make it up by buying dinner. The guy was funny and charming, so Clarence went along with it. Miki was one of those people who rode giant waves in Hawaii when he was younger, working as a stand-in on films like *Ride the Wild Surf* back in the '60s. It was hard for Clarence to get a fix on what the guy had been doing since then.

Back at Ventana before dinner, Clarence called his friend Jefferson Wagner down in Malibu. Zuma Jay was the only surfer Clarence knew. After the usual catching-up bullshit he put it to him.

"Da Cat?" said Jay. "No shit? You're actually with him?"

"I was at lunch and I'm supposed to meet him for dinner," said Clarence.

"Watch your wallet," said Jay.

"I already got stuck for lunch," said Clarence.

"The guy you're with is a legend," said Jay. "His name has been on the wall at the 'Bu for twenty-five years. They sandblast it off and somebody puts it back up the next day. Nobody has seen Miki for years. I heard he was in jail, and then I heard he was in France, and then I heard he was in jail in France. Nobody has a fucking clue. The guy is part man part myth."

"I've got over a million dollars in certificates of deposit," said Richard Brautigan.

Miki Dora immediately ordered a bottle of cognac.

"Good for you," said Clarence.

"I'm going to need every penny of it," he said. "How do you want me to make this out?"

He was holding a pen poised over a beat-up copy of *The Hawkline Monster* that Miki had gotten from his car. It got wet in the rain, and the dust cover, featuring an old Victorian house, was bumpy with droplets.

"To Clarence," said Clarence.

"What do you need a million bucks for so bad?" asked Miki.

Brautigan signed the book and looked at his signature for a long time, then closed the cover and handed it to Clarence.

"I'm on the run," he said. He was pretty toasted, having killed a full bottle of wine while he had dinner alone.

"From what?" said Miki, who apparently had some experience at being on the run.

"I think I killed Nicolas Roeg last night," he said.

"Who?" asked Clarence, realizing that was not the first question he should've asked.

"Nick Roeg," said Brautigan. "He's a British film director. He did *Don't Look Now* and *The Man Who Fell to Earth*.

"Oh, yeah," said Clarence. "The one with David Bowie."

"Right," said Richard.

"That was a weird movie," said Clarence.

"Yes, strange and beautiful," said Richard.

"I didn't see it," said Miki.

Again it occurred to Clarence that they were burying the lead and ignoring the murder confession they just heard.

"You killed him?" Clarence asked.

Brautigan lowered his head and nodded. He had never taken the tall, flat-brimmed hat off, so the act of tilting his head forward took up a lot of space.

"Yes, I think so," he said.

"What do you mean you think so?" asked Miki, pouring the cognac into snifter glasses. He put more into Richard's glass than the others.

Richard sighed and picked up his snifter. He took a long drink then put the glass down. The flames in the fireplace were reflected on the lenses of his round glasses.

"We were in San Francisco last night," said Richard. "We'd met for a drink in the lobby bar of the St. Francis Hotel where Nick was staying. He's an incredible storyteller, so one drink led quickly to another and another, and pretty soon time doesn't mean anything anymore and we're barhopping in the Tenderloin and God knows where else. At some point I guess we had enough, 'cause we were back at the hotel in the living room of his suite. He actually had been reading *Trout Fishing in America*.

"I love fishing," said Clarence. "But I've never been trout fishing. Is that a book I should get?"

"Yes," said Richard. "But it's not really about trout fishing."

"Hold it," said Clarence. "It's called *Trout Fishing in America* but it's not about trout fishing in America?"

"Right," said Richard. "It's a novel. I wrote it."

"Fuck the book and the trout," said Miki. "What about the fucking murder?"

"It wouldn't be murder," said Richard. "Manslaughter maybe, but not murder. We were so drunk…"

"So what happened in the hotel room?" said Miki, refilling Richard's glass.

"At some point we began to argue," said Richard.

"I would've guessed that," said Clarence.

"Let the man tell the story," said Miki.

"And the argument became physical. I know we were punching and kicking each other and rolling around on the floor. It was bad. Then everything goes black. I can't remember what happened next."

"So why do you think you killed him?" said Clarence.

"'Cause when I woke up the room was covered with blood. There was blood everywhere. On the walls, the floor, the furniture. It was like a horror movie. I had blood on my hands and my clothes."

Nobody said anything for the next few moments. They all drank.

"Was he dead?" Miki finally asked.

"He wasn't there. There was no body. I must've taken it out and disposed of it."

"Maybe not," said Clarence. "Maybe you passed out, or he knocked you out, and he left."

"No," said Richard. "The bed was torn apart and the sheet was missing. I wrapped him in the sheet and probably threw him into a Dumpster."

"You're right," said Miki. "That's probably what happened. So now we've got to figure out how to get you out of the country."

Clarence noticed the use of the word *we* right away. "We?" he said to Miki.

"Not you, man," said Miki. "I'll deal with this."

"I'm a big fan of your music," said Richard.

"Oh, thanks," said Clarence.

"I've got all the albums," said Richard. "I think *Born to Run* is one of the greatest albums ever made."

"So do I," said Clarence.

"Well, ironically," said Miki, "you apparently were born to run 'cause that's what you've got to do now. How difficult will it be for you to access the million? We're going to need it and we're going to need it fast."

"I don't know, man, maybe I should just turn myself in," said Richard.

"Fine," said Miki. "And you'll spend the rest of your life getting butt-fucked every day by a guy who looks like Clarence. No offense to you, Clarence."

"None taken," said Clarence. "I wouldn't want that, either."

"Let me make a call," said Richard. "Where's the phone?"

"There's a booth out front," said Miki, pointing toward the front window.

"I'll be right back," said Richard.

He stood, swayed a little, then made his way to the front door, listing to the left all the way. He turned up his collar, opened the door, and stepped out into the rain.

"Jesus, what a story," said Clarence.

"Awful," said Miki. "A tragedy, really."

"Yeah," said Clarence.

"You must've made a fortune by now, huh?" said Miki.

"Nah," said Clarence.

"How's it work?" asked Miki. "Do you get a salary or a piece of the records or a piece of the gate or what?"

"I get a salary," said Clarence.

"Too bad," said Miki.

"I'm not complaining," said Clarence.

"You get the same money the drummer gets?" asked Miki.

"I don't know," said Clarence. "Everybody negotiates their own deal."

"I shoulda learned to play the fucking guitar," said Miki. "Got to be easier to pick up than a surfboard."

"What's that like?" said Clarence. "I mean riding those huge waves?"

"It's a rush," said Miki. "You got a credit card?"

"Yeah, why?" said Clarence.

"In case we can't get Brautigan to pick up the check, I'm broke. I think somebody stole my wallet."

"Is that right?"

"Yeah. I feel bad about it 'cause you got lunch, but what am I gonna do?" said Miki. "I've been riding a streak of bad luck. They busted me for kiting checks, but it was bullshit. Fucking judge just didn't want me to be so free."

"Right," said Clarence, wondering how much the cognac went for.

"Brautigan's a fucking millionaire. He's good for dinner."

"I hope so," said Clarence. "Assuming he's not shooting himself in the phone booth."

"He'll be fine," said Miki. "He's just a little shook."

"Yeah, well, if I just killed a guy I'd be a little shook, too," said Clarence.

The front door opened, and Brautigan entered and crossed back to the table.

"He's all right." He smiled. "He's not dead."

"Shit," said Miki Dora.

"Good," said Clarence.

"Apparently I broke his nose in the fight, and a nose bleeds like crazy. He did knock me out, then took the sheet to clean himself up. He threw it out the window. Perfect drunk logic, huh?"

"Wow," said Clarence.

"What a fucking relief," said Richard.

Miki stood. "You pick up the check," he said to Richard. Then he walked out of the place.

"Who is he again?" Richard said to Clarence.

"He's a big-time surfer," said Clarence.

"Seems like a nice guy," said Richard.

"Yeah," said Clarence. "Well, I'm going to hit the road, too. Thanks for dinner."

"Thanks for all the music," said Richard. "I hope you like the book."

*   *   *

Richard Brautigan died of a self-inflicted gunshot wound on or about September 14, 1984, at his remote home in Bolinas, California. His body was discovered by a private investigator on October 25, 1984.

Miki Dora died at his father's house in Montecito, California, on January 3, 2002. He was sixty-seven years old. The wall at Malibu still carries his name.

Nicolas Roeg was still directing at the age of eighty.

Jefferson Wagner, aka Zuma Jay, remains the coolest man in the world.

Clarence

To me music is like a river. I have lived my life beside the river. Every day I get up and I look at the river. I watch it and notice when it rises or falls. I see how the wind affects the surface and ruffles it, and how the lack of wind leaves it looking like a mirror. I follow the water as it flows over rocks and around obstacles. I have studied the river my whole life. I know it as well as I know myself.

Most days I swim in the river. Sometimes I float on it, looking up at the trees and the sky. Other times I dive beneath the surface and try to become the river. I feel it all around me and I feel like part of it. I find it difficult to distinguish between the water and myself, and I don't know where one begins and the other one ends. And then I am the river.

At night I sit beside it. I sit in the dark and listen to it and I feel like the Rain King and I listen to it and I close my eyes and I listen to the river. Some nights it's just noise. A nice noise, a peaceful noise, but just noise. But then something will happen. Something will move beneath the surface and the noise becomes something else. It's discordant like John Cage or Harry Partch, but then it sounds like music almost and it's Captain Beefheart and then Frank Zappa, and the noise turns beautiful and annoying all at the same time, and that's good and so unexpected that it makes me laugh out loud in the darkness.

But on other nights the river sings, and it can sing anything. It's a choir. It's the Edwin Hawkins Singers singing "Oh Happy Day," and it's all gospel all the time until it turns into opera and classical piano and violins and Wurlitzers and Hammonds and big church organs and Al Kooper on "Like a Rolling Stone" and Dave "Babyface" Cortez and whoever played organ on Del Shannon's "Runaway," and suddenly there are a million different voices and a million different instruments, and I can hear each and every one of them and they're all good. I can make out Speedo and Ivory Joe Hunter and some group singing about white port and lemon juice and Willie Dixon and Robert Johnson and Son House and Garnett Mims, and then the Darktown strutters dance by in the shadowy light, followed by the Viscounts playing "Harlem Nocturne" and "The Touch," and the Rockin' Rebels' "Wild Weekend," and then Hank Williams and Johnny Rodriguez and Mickey Newbury from a depot in Frisco, and the music just washes over me and makes me feel whole.

I can't be separated from the river. I cannot be away from it. It follows me; it changes its path to be with me and to stay with me and to define me. It is my purpose and it flows through my soul and it always will, and nothing in this world, including death, can stop that.

Burbank, California

Don

Clarence and I sat in the executive dining room atop the Team Disney Building, the building supported by the Seven Dwarves, having lunch with Steve McPherson, who was then the president of Touchstone Television. We were there to discuss an idea Clarence had for a TV show. It was called *Paradise Mississippi* and was the story of an aristocratic black couple in England who are broke but inherit what they think is a castle in the town of Paradise, Mississippi. It turns out to be a miniature-golf-themed amusement park with a castle motif, but they don't find that out till they get there. During lunch we pitched this notion to Steve, and he thought we might have a shot of selling it to Fox. He promised to set up a meeting over there, which in fact did take place a few days later.

After talking business for a while the conversation turned to E Street stuff. Clarence was his usual, charming self and we were having a good time. The chairman of ABC Entertainment was a guy named Lloyd Braun. He was in the room having lunch with Bob Iger, the future CEO of the Walt Disney Company. ABC and Touchstone Television had that week made a talent deal with an African American comedian named Earthquake. As Lloyd and Bob stood to leave, Lloyd spotted Clarence and made an assumption. He crossed to our table, with Bob a step behind him. When he got there he leaned across the table, extended his hand, smiled, and said, "Earthquake, I presume," as if he were meeting Dr. Livingstone in the jungle. Clarence is used to people approaching him and shaking hands and figured Lloyd for a fan. If the word *Earthquake* registered with him at all, I'd be very surprised. I caught Steve's eye but the damage, if there was any, had been done, so he just shrugged.

Bob Iger, however, didn't get to be a mogul by being slow. "Clarence Clemons," he said, extending his own hand, "of Bruce Springsteen and the E Street Band." If he had more time I think he would've started humming "Born to Run." Lloyd, to his credit, realized the faux pas he had made and chose to undo it by pretending it never happened. In the nanosecond after Bob spoke Lloyd said, "I love you guys. I've got all the albums. Are you playing in town?" It was a masterful correction, and it worked because Clarence hadn't really been listening and had no idea who these guys were.

Watching people react to Clarence is interesting. He commands almost any room he enters. He's big, yes, but he appears bigger in person. He looks like a building walking around. In recent years he's been wearing his hair in long dreadlocks that only add to the effect. When you couple that with his rock-star wardrobe, it renders those of us who travel with him invisible.

If I'm in a crowded restaurant with Clarence, I believe I could pick up my knife and stab our waiter in the neck and nobody, including the waiter, would be able to give an accurate description of me. I would appear in all the reports as "some guy with Clarence Clemons." But the upside is that when I go out anywhere with him, we're a star.

The Legend of Kaupo, 1983

This one takes place a few days after my club Big Man's West closed. It's a combination of many real conversations set in an exotic locale. Mahalo. —C.C.

Bruce and Clarence sat on the wooded steps of the Kaupo Store on the far side of Maui. The store was closed. The store was almost always closed. A sign on the door read, "This store is usually open Monday–Friday around 10:30–4:30. Don't be surprised if not open yet. Soon will be. Unless otherwise posted closed Saturday and Sunday and when necessary. Occasionally."

It was Monday, January 10, 1983.

Kaupo was more of a place on the map than a town. It was located on a four-wheel-drive-only road on the backside of the Haleakala Crater, far from the tourists in Kihei or Kaanapali.

They had been sitting on the steps for more than twenty minutes, and not a single vehicle had passed by on the rutted dirt road.

Both men wore shorts, flip-flops, and T-shirts. Clarence's shirt said, I SURVIVED THE ROAD TO HANA. Bruce's was plain white and said nothing. Clarence wore the Panama hat he had gotten in Puerto Rico years ago. Bruce's head was bare.

"Hot," said Bruce.

"I love it," said Clarence.

"Car rental company said you're not supposed to drive out here," said Bruce, nodding toward their rented red Ford Mustang convertible.

"I won't tell," said Clarence.

The wind was blowing hard out over the ocean, but the building and the mountain behind sheltered them.

"I like it here," said Bruce.

"Hawaii, Maui, or here?" asked Clarence.

"All of the above," said Bruce. "But especially here. No people."

"Somebody must live in these houses," said Clarence, referring to the few structures surrounding the store.

"Guess they're all at work. There's a ranch here. Cattle, looks like. Or maybe back in Hana at the hotel or something," Bruce said.

"Yeah," said Clarence. "I wonder if they ever open this place. I could use a Coke."

"I love the sign," said Bruce.

"Yeah," said Clarence.

They had flown to Maui the day before, after crossing the country in a private plane from Jersey earlier.

"Sorry about your club," said Bruce.

"That was fun Saturday night, though," said Clarence. "We went out with a bang. Thanks for showing up."

"Hey, what the fuck," said Bruce. "I love singing 'Lucille.' I'd go anywhere to sing it. Actually it had nothing to do with you or the club closing. I just felt like singing and I happened to be passing by your place at that exact moment."

Clarence laughed. "Sure," he said.

A man on a tractor drove by, followed by a slow cloud of dust. They watched him come and go. He never looked at them.

"How's *Nebraska* doing?" asked Clarence.

"Good, it's doing good," said Bruce. "You like it?"

"Yeah," said Clarence. "I thought 'Atlantic City' sounded good with the band."

"Better?" asked Bruce, turning to look at him.

"Different," said Clarence. "More heat."

Bruce looked out at the ocean. The wind line was a few hundred yards offshore. The water looked blue and flat, then suddenly turned white and stormy.

"You might be right," he said.

"I'm always right," said Clarence.

Bruce laughed. "I'm glad we're doing this," he said. "It's like the old days, before everything got so..."

"Big?" asked Clarence,

"That'll do," said Bruce. "I've missed hanging out, shootin' the shit, no place to be. You know what I'm saying?"

"I hear you, brother," said Clarence.

Bruce tilted his head back and felt the hot sun on his face.

"I've got some new songs," he said.

"More sad shit about losers?" Clarence smiled as he spoke.

Bruce laughed again. "No. Well...it's bigger stuff. Stuff for the band. It's got...I don't know, power. Yeah. Born in the U.S.A."

"That a song?" said Clarence.

"Not yet," said Bruce. "But it will be. I've got a lot of pieces." He sang the first line.

"Wow," said Clarence.

"I got the title from a screenplay somebody sent me. It comes out of the *Nebraska* thing but now it's happening fast," said Bruce. "All these songs. I can't write 'em down fast enough."

"I saw you on the plane," said Clarence. "You didn't even stop writing to eat."

"It gets like that. It was like that with *The River*, too. *Nebraska* was different. I was in a bad place."

"Yeah," said Clarence. "You write your way out of it."

"Right," said Bruce.

"So you think we might actually play again someday?" asked Clarence.

"Yeah," said Bruce, and he laughed the way he did when he was thinking ahead of what he was saying. "I think so. I hope so."

"Good," said Clarence. "I've gotta pay for some shit."

"Come to LA after this and I'll play you some stuff I've been doing in the garage," said Bruce.

"Okay," said Clarence. "But first I wanna get a good tan."

Bruce laughed.

"You ought to stand in front of a big American flag like in *Patton* for the cover. I mean if you call it 'Born in the U.S.A.'"

"That's an idea," said Bruce. "But I've got a song called 'Dancing in the Dark,' too. That's a good title."

"Like 'Dancing in the Dark'?" Clarence sang the old tune from the film, *The Band Wagon*.

"Same title, different song," said Bruce.

"Is there a sax part on it?" asked Clarence.

"I promise," said Bruce.

There was a noise behind them and the door opened. A tall, skinny, pale kid with long, stringy black hair set it in place, leaving the inner screen door exposed.

"We're open," he said.

"You got cold soda?" asked Clarence.

"Yup," said the kid. He looked about eighteen. He wore a HANA CANOE CLUB T-shirt and an old, faded gimme cap with some letters on it that were hard to read. "Been waiting long?" he asked.

"Nah," said Bruce. He and Clarence stood.

"You guys look familiar," said the kid. He had a wispy mustache and goatee. He, too, wore shorts and flip-flops. "You from the other side?"

"Of what?" said Clarence.

"Kahului," said the kid.

"No," said Clarence. "We're from the other side of the world."

The kid looked confused.

"The East Coast," said Bruce.

"Of what?" said the kid.

"America," said Bruce.

"Are you guys in a band or something?" the kid asked. "You look famous."

"Nah," said Bruce.

"Nah," said Clarence.

"Well, c'mon in," said the kid.

Inside the dark, cool store Bruce and Clarence took sodas from the old stand-up refrigerator and looked at the pictures of the store and the people who worked there in the old days.

"You going to Hana?" the kid asked.

"We were there earlier," said Bruce. "We're going to a place called Kula."

"Nice there," said the kid. "It stays cool up-country. Hardly any tourists unless they're on their way down the hill on bikes."

"More tourists than here, I'll bet," said Clarence, sipping his soda.

The kid laughed. "Yeah. More than here," he said.

"You live here?" asked Bruce.

"Yeah, my wife and I live in the back. Her dad works on the ranch," he said. "The Kaupo ranch."

"Quiet," said Bruce.

"Yeah," said the kid. "What do you do?"

Bruce looked quickly at Clarence then back to the kid. "We're dentists," he said.

"Really?" said the kid.

"Nah, we're musicians," said Bruce.

"I thought so," said the kid. "Have you guys accepted Jesus Christ as your personal savior?"

Bruce and Clarence just looked at the kid for a moment. Clarence realized that the air smelled like flowers. Orange blossoms or honeysuckle or something equally fabulous.

"I have," said Clarence, "but he's an atheist."

"Hey, thanks for the sodas," said Bruce. "We'd better get going."

"The road stays bad for another five miles," the kid said. "Then it gets to a kind of paved section down around Nu'u Bay, but that's pretty rough, too. It doesn't get real good again until you get to Ulupalakua."

"*Ulupalakua,*" Bruce repeated. "What does that mean?"

"I'm not sure," said the kid. "*Ulu* is breadfruit, so it's something about breadfruit. I'm from Florida."

"Me, too," said Clarence. "West Palm Beach."

"Tampa," said the kid. "I got in some trouble there. I used to be pretty wild before I found the Lord."

"Good for you," said Bruce. "Big Man? Shall we get going?"

"Yeah," said Clarence.

They turned toward the door. Another car pulled into the small, dusty parking lot outside with a young Japanese couple in it. They didn't have a "honeymooners" sign on the car, but they really didn't need one.

Bruce and Clarence took a step toward the door.

"God bless," said the kid.

Bruce stopped and turned back to him. "Your hat," he said.

The kid took his hat off and looked at it as if he were surprised to find it sitting on his head. "What about it?" he said.

"What do the letters stand for?" asked Bruce. It appeared to read REMBASS.

"I don't know," said the kid. "It's so old it's falling apart. Got it from my father-in-law. He's from New Jersey."

"He's from Jersey?" said Clarence, smiling.

"Yeah," said the kid, still looking at the hat.

"How much you want for it?" asked Bruce.

Clarence

The sound check for the first "Magic" show in Anaheim lasted over an hour and featured a blistering version of "The Ghost of Tom Joad," with guest Tom Morello sharing vocals with Bruce and performing a jaw-dropping guitar solo. Steve, Bruce, and Nils are all great guitar players, but of the three Nils is the best. Nils is an incredible guitar player. When Tom finished his solo, Nils turned to me and said, "Holy shit." That's the highest compliment Tom could ever get.

Sound checks are very private things on E Street. No one who is not a guest of the band is allowed into the room when the sound-check songs are being played. On this day three people were sitting in the audience of the otherwise empty Honda Center. One was Barbara Carr, from Bruce's management team, and the other two were friends of hers, a mother and her handicapped daughter. As the sound check ended, Bruce called to the guys as they began to exit the stage.

"One more," he said.

He then proceeded to perform "Girls in Their Summer Clothes" for the young lady in the stands. And he really performed it. The same way he did it in concert to an audience of twenty thousand people. Toward the end of the song he climbed down off the stage and danced across the pit doing two slow pirouettes, walked up into the stands, kissed the young girl's cheek, and finished the song sitting next to her.

It was a beautiful moment.

Don

I've seen Clarence do the same kind of thing.

After the show in Oakland a few days earlier, there were some fans lining the sidewalk outside the arena hoping to get a glimpse of their heroes as they drove past behind blacked-out windows.

One of the fans on the sidewalk was set apart from the others. A middle-aged woman in a wheelchair. She had just seen the show and was as thrilled as she had been at her first show thirty years ago. During that show she had danced in the aisle in front of the stage. Tonight she had been confined to the handicapped area behind the railing on the first level at the very back of the arena. But the giant video screens brought the stage to her, and she truly believed that she had the best seat in the house.

She had come to the show with her seventeen-year-old daughter tonight, who had been listening to the albums since she was little and was also a big fan. They both loved Clarence, and tonight when he'd stepped forward into the spotlight for his first solo they had both cheered at the top of their lungs. There was something so pure, so emotional, to the Big Man's music that the sight of him brought tears to her eyes. Her daughter was still in the arena. She wanted to try to get backstage and meet somebody. Of course that wasn't going to happen, but there was a thrill and a lesson in trying.

The people clustered off to her left began to cheer as headlights appeared at the mouth of the tunnel leading into the arena. The first vehicle was a black SUV that turned left and accelerated past them and off into the night. She waved and cheered with everyone else, even though none of them had any idea who was in the truck.

Two more SUVs followed, and she thought she saw Bruce waving from the passenger's seat in the second one, but she couldn't be certain.

Then the limo pulled out.

Surely one of them was in this car.

The other folks jumped up and down and waved at the car as it drove by them.

And then the car began to slow.

It cruised to a stop right in front of her. She sat in her chair on the sidewalk, speechless, as the back door of the car slowly opened.

Clarence Clemons slowly unfolded himself out of the car, stood tall, and smiled at her.

He was wearing a long black coat and some kind of hat that held his dreadlocks. He wore black sunglasses.

"Your daughter told me you could use a hug," he said, as he walked toward her.

This could not be happening. She knew for a fact that she had passed out and died and this was some kind of vision or maybe heaven itself.

But it was true. The Big Man was five feet in front of her and closing.

She began to tremble. Tears fell unbidden from her eyes.

"Oh, my God," she said. "Oh, my God."

Clarence bent down and embraced her. For a moment she thought he might lift her out of the chair and waltz her down the sidewalk, but he just held her.

"I love you, Clarence," she said.

"I love you, too," he answered.

He stood up. His sunglasses had slipped off and were on her lap. She handed them to him.

"Your glasses," she said.

"Thank you," he said. He took them and put them back on. Then he took her tiny hand into his giant hand. "I met your daughter. She's a lovely girl."

"She loves you, too," she said. "We're such fans. I saw you thirty years ago. Before my accident."

"I'm glad you made it back," he said.

The other fans had gathered around and were watching. The back door to the limo was open, and the driver was standing beside it waiting to help Clarence back into it. She could see a beautiful woman in the backseat smiling at her.

"Thank you," she said. She wanted to say much more, but that was what came out so that was what it would be.

"Thank you," said Clarence. "God bless you."

He leaned down again and kissed her forehead. Then he turned and waved to the others, who stood starstruck. He stepped off the curb and with what looked like a painful and practiced move got back into the big car. A moment later it pulled away, and he was gone.

She looked down the street in the other direction and saw her daughter running toward her, smiling, now laughing, as she got closer. The world felt like magic.

The Legend of Clarence Getting High with the Funniest Man in the World, Hollywood Hills, 1984

This story is based on actual conversations I had with Redd over a period of time. I've just rolled them into one story. It's as close as we can come to what it was really like to be with him. He is missed. —D.R.

Redd Foxx lit a cigarette, took a drag, and smiled. "My wife weighs four hundred and fifty pounds," he said. "She thinks I love her 'cause when I get in bed I roll toward her."

Clarence laughed.

"Not true," said Redd, "but funny."

They were standing in the living room of Redd's new house, located on the south side of Mulholland Drive near the top of Benedict Canyon.

"You just got this place, huh?" asked Clarence.

"Brand-new," said Redd. "Take a look at this." He crossed to the window and gestured. "How about that view?"

Clarence admired the view. It was daytime and very hazy, so you couldn't really see much besides the other houses that dotted the distant hillsides.

"On a clear day you can see Catalina," said Redd.

"Wow," said Clarence. He had only a vague notion of what Catalina was. An island, he thought. There was an old song about it. "Twenty-six miles," he said.

"Not that I give a fuck about Catalina," said Redd. "I've never been big on geography. I was parked up here with a girl one time and she said, 'Kiss me where it smells,' so I drove her to El Segundo."

Clarence laughed again.

"I like you, Big Man," said Redd. "You laugh at all my old jokes."

"They're not old to me," said Clarence.

"Then I like you even more," said Redd. He turned toward the hallway off the living room. "Hey, Honey," he called.

A moment later a beautiful, young Asian woman entered the room. She wore black pants and a white blouse with the top three buttons open. She wore heels that made a *click-clack*ing sound on the tile in the hallway. She smiled like a woman who didn't speak English but was acting like she did.

"This is Honey," said Redd, putting an arm around her waist and kissing her cheek. "My current wife."

"Hi, Honey," said Clarence. "Nice to meet you."

"Nice to meet you," said Honey, repeating it phonetically.

"Her real name's not Honey but I can't pronounce it. Her Japanese name," said Redd. He turned to her. "This is Clarence Clemons, the Big Man. He plays saxophone for Bruce Springsteen. You savvy Bruce Springsteen?"

"Nice to meet you," said Honey.

"Good. Get us a couple of drinks. Scotch." He looked at Clarence. "That okay with you?"

"Sure," said Clarence, who hated scotch. Once as a teenager he drank nineteen shots of scotch and was sick for three days. The smell of scotch still made him nauseous. "I'd love one."

"Two scotch," said Redd to Honey.

"Two scotch," said Honey, turning to go.

Redd patted her on the butt as she turned. She giggled. They watched her leave.

"Asian women are the best," said Redd. "They know the man is in charge. They like that. Part of their culture. White women think they own you. You ever see me with a white woman, I'm holding her for the police."

Clarence laughed. He'd been laughing at everything Redd said since he met him last night at the bar in Dan Tana's. The guy was funny when he said, "Hello." They'd hit it off, and Redd had invited him up to see the new house.

"And I'm done with black women," said Redd. "I'm too old to fight."

He stubbed his cigarette out in an ashtray with an elephant on it. There were lots of elephants in the house. Pictures, figurines, photos... Clarence knew people who got into shit like that. He had an aunt who collected turtles. When he finally asked her why she said it was because she liked turtles. He figured Redd must like elephants.

"Have a seat," said Redd.

They sat on different parts of the big red leather sectional couch that dominated the living room. Clarence sat on the long back section facing the view, Redd on the shorter section to the left.

"Nice couch," said Clarence.

"Had it made," said Redd. "Hard to find red cows. You wanna split a little reefer?"

"Sure," said Clarence. "I never turn down reefer."

Redd took a fat doobie out of his cigarette package. "This is Panama Red," he said. The joint was stuck in between the Salem package itself and the cellophane wrapper.

"Spark it up," said Clarence.

They smoked the joint. Honey returned, put down two glasses of scotch and a glass of ice, and left. She never stopped smiling. Redd and Clarence smiled back at her.

"So you okay in this white world you're in?" asked Redd.

"Yeah," said Clarence. "I love to play, and the music Bruce writes...I don't know, it speaks to me."

"He's a good guy?" asked Redd.

"He's my brother," said Clarence.

"Good," said Redd. "Just remember that he's white. I don't mean anything bad by that; it's just that he looks at the world as a white man. It's different."

"Yeah," Clarence agreed. It was difficult to argue with that logic. If it was logic. Shit, that dope was good. Clarence picked up the glass of scotch and sniffed it. It smelled good. He took a sip. It didn't taste anything like scotch as he knew it. "This is scotch?" he asked.

"Single malt," said Redd. "The best. It's from Scotland, where the Scotch people live."

"I gotta pay them a visit," said Clarence. Redd laughed and took a sip.

"See, black people are trying to get ahead," said Redd, as if he had been interrupted and was picking up some previous train of thought. "It's the niggers who are holding us back."

"That's deep," said Clarence, uncertain if it was in fact deep or just good-dope deep. "Heavy," he added. He had the feeling that someone else was talking, using his voice, and that he was outside himself, listening. Time began to fragment the way it did on strong shit. You had to float with it or you could get scared, and that would be so uncool. He floated.

"That's Agnes," said Redd, looking out the plate-glass doors to the lawn and the pool area.

"Agnes?" said Clarence about the same time a big St. Bernard lumbered into view. "Oh, Agnes," he said.

"My watchdog," said Redd. "A motherfucker comes in my yard, Agnes will tear his ass up. She will rip him long, deep, wide, and consecutively."

"Cool," said Clarence. He hadn't liked dogs since being bitten by Jimmy Lincoln's pit bull Fever when he was ten years old.

"I hate midgets," said Redd. "You want to cut a midget, you've got to stab him on top the head."

Clarence laughed. Longer and harder this time. The guy was hilarious. He really was.

"I'll tell you a secret," said Redd, lighting another Salem. "Agnes is trained to attack white people."

"No shit?" said Clarence.

Redd raised his right hand. "Swear to God and two other white men," he said. "I have to put her away when my agents and Jew lawyers come over."

"Huh," said Clarence. He was very high and felt like he could rise up and float out of the room, out over the yard and the lawn and the pool and Agnes, all the way to Catalina.

"I tell everybody she likes to eat crackers," said Redd.

Don

Clarence has drifted in and out of my life like smoke. As I wrote earlier, I had tried to book the band on my first producing job with Cher and I failed. Through the years I still looked for ways to incorporate the music into my work and, if possible, put Clarence on camera in something. If you don't believe that everything is connected to everything else, consider this: in the summer of 1989, I went to Florida to celebrate Dion DiMucci's fiftieth birthday. He's the same guy I met while doing the Cher show years before, when Phil Spector threatened to shoot me. While I was down there I noticed how Dion and his wife, Susan, interacted with their three daughters. Their behavior was normal. Normal except for the fact that the dad in this scenario was a member of the Rock and Roll Hall of Fame.

This gave me the beginnings of an idea for a show, a family sitcom, in which the father would be hipper than the ones who were then on TV. Those dads were like my dad and not like Dion or even me. Following a whole bunch of other stories, that notion became the NBC television series *Blossom*.

That show ran for more than five seasons and earned me acceptance into the ranks of television series creators and show runners.

Blossom led to *The John Larroquette Show,* another NBC series with its own book's worth of stories. I booked Dion to play a part on one episode. Another featured my old pal Kinky Friedman, the legendary Texas Jewboy and future president of the United States.

Down the road a ways I created a show called *My Wife and Kids* along with Damon Wayans. In the show's third season I cast Clarence Clemons as Damon's old friend. I finally got to put the Big Man on one of my shows, and he was great. It only took a little over thirty years to do it.

Clarence

R ingo and I were drinking tea in a Japanese hotel suite when the phone rang and the world changed.

We were in Japan as part of the "All-Starr Band" tour. Ringo had assembled a bunch of players who weren't busy at the time, each a "star" in his own right, and we went out on the road. It was a successful endeavor. There were some great guys along for the ride, including Rick Danko, Levon Helm, Joe Walsh, and Nils Lofgren.

I had been having a great time. I loved it there in Japan. I would've attracted attention on the streets here even if I weren't famous. Most of these people had never seen anything as big as me outside of Godzilla movies. They would stop and stare and giggle when they caught sight of me. I really didn't mind. As Dr. John, another member of the band, said, "Pussy is pussy." Some things were difficult to argue with.

Ringo and I had just been hanging out and shooting the shit about the old days and the Beatles and whatever else came up. Ringo's easygoing manner reminded me of Danny a little bit. Both of them stayed out of band politics, and that was not an easy thing to do. When Ringo talked about the first three years, it was amazing. Those four guys had taken a ride that very few people had ever been on. Sinatra and Elvis, maybe, but that was about it. It was one thing to have screaming fans and sold-out stadiums, but it was another thing entirely to change history. I was fascinated and wanted to understand how it had felt.

"It felt like we were traveling at a very high rate of speed." Ringo smiled. I had some sense of what he meant, although only the four of them would ever really know. What a remarkable thing to happen to a person—a drummer, yet—with no real expectations of any kind of fame much less overwhelming, impossible fame. It was astounding.

Ringo looked at the phone when it rang. Neither of us was in the habit of answering the phone. It was almost always somebody you didn't want to talk to. As luck would have it, at that moment all our assistants were off doing something else and the phone would have to be answered or ignored.

"What do you think?" said Ringo. He looked at the ringing phone then at me. I had just picked up a tiny cucumber sandwich from a tray of hors d'oeuvres.

"Maybe it's somebody trying to give you money," I said.

"More likely to be somebody with a problem," said Ringo.

"So let it ring," I said.

"On the other hand it could be one of the fucking loved ones," said Ringo.

"True," I said. I ate the tiny sandwich in one bite. When I looked at it before popping it into my mouth I was reminded of King Kong holding Fay Wray.

The phone kept ringing.

"Damn," said Ringo. "I wonder if they'd let it ring all day or would they give up after a while."

"Must be somebody important enough to get the switchboard to keep trying," I said.

"Damn," said Ringo, looking at the phone. It sat on a side table about eighteen inches away.

"Do me a favor," I said. "Either answer it or throw it out the fucking window."

"Damn," said Ringo. He looked around to see if anybody else was going to walk in who could solve this problem for him, but we were alone.

"Want me to answer it?" I asked.

"Damn," said Ringo. Then he picked up the phone and held the receiver to his ear. He didn't say hello. He just listened for a moment.

"Who is it?" I said, picking up another tiny sandwich. This one appeared to be either tuna or maybe crab. I smelled it. Crab.

"Who are you looking for?" asked Ringo, who then listened again and pointed to me.

"Me?" I said. "No, nobody knows I'm here. Nobody could find me here."

"Who is this?" said Ringo. Then he laughed and his body language changed. He uncrossed his legs and relaxed his shoulders. His face became more animated and his voice rose slightly. "Hey, cool breeze," he said.

Ringo was always saying cool shit like that, like calling somebody "cool breeze." I made a mental note to remember that and use it soon.

"Yeah, it's going great," he said. "You know how it is, I don't have to tell you, now do I?"

Ringo stood and began to pace around the room but moved steadily closer to me.

"I do, yes, and that would be fun. We'll be in your neck of the woods in three or four weeks, I think. I've lost all track of time out here. Exactly. Yes, we'll go eat something and lie to each other. It'll be fun. Yes, he is. In fact he's sitting here sipping tea and eating finger sandwiches. You've ruined him, I fear. Good talking to you, too. I'll put him on."

Ringo then proffered the phone and said, "It's Bruce."

I took the phone.

"Hey, Daddy-o," I said. "What's going on? How are you, man?"

Ringo watched as I smiled and looked toward the window, maybe picturing Bruce on a phone somewhere out there on the other side of the world.

This is what Ringo saw and heard me say:

"Oh, really? How so?"

I then listened for a long time. I didn't speak or even attempt to interject. I got very quiet and stopped smiling. In fact, it looked to Ringo like I was being told about somebody dying.

"No shit?" I said eventually. "I mean, I don't know what to say, Bruce. I don't know how to respond. You know I only want what's best for you. You know if that's what it's going to take to make you happy, then that's what it's going to take. No, no, I'm fine. I'll be fine."

Ringo watched as I stood and ran my free hand through my short hair. He started to leave the room, but something told him that I might want to talk when the call ended. He really wanted to support me if something bad had gone down.

"I understand," I said. "Yes, don't worry. No really, I'm good. I'm good. I love you, too, man. Bye."

I hung up the phone and took a deep breath. I let it out slowly and sat back down in the chair. I turned to Ringo.

"He's breaking up the band," I said.

"For real?" said Ringo.

"For real. Said he's been thinking about it for a long time and this is the road he's got to go down. He just told Nils," I said.

"Wow," said Ringo. "Wow."

"Yeah," I said. "Jesus, this changes everything. I mean . . . holy shit."

"Having been through this kind of breakup myself, you may have heard about it, I can tell you that life does go on. One door closes and another one opens and all that crap."

"I hear you, I know," I said. "I think I'm in shock or something, you know? It doesn't feel real yet."

"I know," said Ringo.

"Shit," I said. "This has been my whole life. I mean everything has been about Bruce for so long. Fuck. This is going to require a period of adjustment. And vodka, I suspect."

"It's tough to believe this right now," said Ringo. "But this might turn out to be the best thing that's ever happened to you. You don't know."

"I guess the not-knowing part is the scariest," I said.

"Yeah," said Ringo.

We sat for a while and said nothing. It did not feel awkward.

"I should go see Nils," I said.

"Yeah," said Ringo. "At least you've both got jobs."

"This is true," I said, smiling for the first time since hanging up.

I started to cross the room toward the door. Ringo stopped me and gave me a hug. It's difficult to hug someone as big as me. All the angles are wrong.

"It will be fine," said Ringo.

"Yes, I know," I said. "It's time for changes. I've been thinking that for a while, anyway. I'm not going to cut my hair."

"Your hair?" said Ringo.

"Yeah," I said. "I'm not going to ever cut my hair again."

"That's an interesting reaction," said Ringo. "I wouldn't have predicted that."

"I'm going to change my life, man," I said. "You're right. This is an opportunity to do new and different shit. To switch everything around."

"Starting with your hair," said Ringo, smiling slightly.

"As a symbol," I said. "As a sign of the new."

"That will be interesting," said Ringo.

The phone call from Bruce took place more than twenty years ago. Since then many things have happened.

But I have never cut my hair.

Don

"I have no idea what Clarence Clemons sounds like," said Chris Rock.

We were sitting in a restaurant on the Upper East Side. Clarence had just called to say he couldn't join us because his hip/knee/back was acting up.

"What are you talking about?" I asked. "You've heard him a thousand times."

"I've heard him *play* a thousand times," said Chris, "but I've never heard him speak."

"That seems so weird to me," I said.

"I would imagine he sounds like this," said Chris. He then proceeded to do the thing that makes him one of the funniest men in the world and a true genius. He created a version of Clarence who spoke like a saxophone. Obviously I can't describe it, you truly had to be there, but I can tell you that it was hysterical and in many ways accurate.

I've known Chris for a few years now and had the privilege to work with him on the television show he created with Ali LeRoi called *Everybody Hates Chris*. If you haven't seen the show you should. One of my functions on the series was to sit with Chris and punch up the scripts. In other words I got paid to sit and listen to Chris Rock. It was the best job in the history of the world. We ate lunch together often and talked about the events of the day. It was always interesting and always funny. In my entire career I've never encountered a mind like Chris Rock's. Not only is he amazingly insightful but he is quick. Quickness in the world of comedy writing is how pros judge each other. Nobody is quicker than Chris.

Once in a while I would write a joke that he liked enough to try in his act. One weekend I was at home watching CNN report on the movement to ban the N word. I always found that euphemism especially offensive. It sanitizes the actual word, which every listener plays inside his or her head. Anyway, the following joke occurred to me: "I hear they're trying to ban the N word. I see this as an opportunity. I immediately called my broker and told him to buy five million shares of *coon*."

Okay, that's the joke. And it's a fine joke. Unless, like me, you happen to be white. There were very few places I felt comfortable repeating the joke. Outside of the writer's room where anything goes, my choices were limited. So I called Chris.

"What's going on in your mansion?" he asked. "Not much happening here in mine."

"I just wrote a joke and I don't know what to do with it," I said.

"Let's hear it," he said.

I told him the joke.

"I know what to do with it," he said.

And he did know. He took the joke, added to it, and is currently using it in his act. When I say he "added" to it, I mean that in the way a musical genius could take a single note and turn it into a symphony.

At the restaurant that night, after he'd finished his impression of Clarence, I took out my cell phone and called the Big Man.

"Hello," said Clarence.

"It's me again," I said. "I've got somebody here who wants to talk to you."

With that I handed the phone to Chris.

"Big Man!" said Chris.

He listened for a few moments then covered the phone and spoke to me.

"I can't understand a fucking thing he's saying," said Chris. "He sounds like a saxophone."

Clarence

L evon Helm, Dr. John (also known as Mac Rebennack), and I
were in the back of a limo being driven to the arena, where we
were appearing with Ringo Starr in his first All-Starr Band.

"It feels like I've been up and down this road a million times," I said.

"Yeah," said Mac. "And you got a dollar on every ride."

"More like ten dollars," I said, laughing.

"Hey Mac," said Levon.

"What's up, Daddy?" said Mac. He was wearing a soft fedora hat and
sunglasses, even though it was a dark gray day.

"Did you play Woodstock?"

"Almost," said Mac.

"You almost played Woodstock?" I said. "How did that work?"

"Well, we were booked to play on the first day. In fact, we were
headed up there on this very road. Shit, it could've been this very spot.
We're listening to the radio and hearing about all the traffic problems up
there, and I got this premonition."

"What kind of premonition?" asked Levon.

"The money kind," said Mac. "I've been burned so many times I'm all
scarred up on my insides."

"I know that feeling," I said. "I did some TV show once and they asked me to play something. I think it was a kid's show. *Square One TV,* it was called. Anyway, I play the song and they all say, 'Thank you so much,' and I say, 'You're very welcome. That'll be a thousand dollars.'"

"Yeah," Levon laughed. "We got screwed all over Canada with Ronnie Hawkins. But that motherfucker was crazy. If some club owner tried to skip he'd chase him down and fuck him up. Or at least threaten to. Ronnie's a tough guy. I wouldn't want to fuck with him. So what happened after your premonition?"

He accented the *pre* syllable in *premonition.* It sounded like he added a few *e*'s to it. I love Levon. His voice is such a pure American thing. Levon is the most genuine person I've ever met.

"Well, we pulled off the road here at a rest stop to call the office. I get my assistant on the phone and I ask if we got the deposit from the Woodstock folks. She says, 'No, we didn't get any deposit.' So we got back in the car, turned around, and went home."

The Legend of Echo Hill Ranch, Texas, 1992

Kinky is a friend of mine and I have in fact visited him at the fabulous Echo Hill Ranch in the great state of Texas. He is a fine American and a brilliant individual. I have also spent time with Bob Dylan. This is what I imagine it would be like to hang out with both of them at the same time on a night that was, in all truth, significant for me. —C.C.

Kinky poured two fingers of Jameson's into each glass and handed Clarence the one shaped like Dr. Watson.

"Cheers," said Clarence, raising his drink.

"Seinfeld," said Kinky.

They killed the shots.

"I've never seen it rain this hard for this long," said Clarence.

"Spring in the hill country," said Kinky. He got up and tossed another log on the fire. The rain thundered down on the roof of the tiny cabin. They had just returned from checking on Kinky's cousin Nancy and her husband, Tony, who lived across the river in a far canyon on the ranch with all their animals.

"We got across the river just in time," said Kinky. "It's up now. Nobody's going to get through till tomorrow afternoon at the earliest."

"Well, you've got plenty of room," said Clarence.

"Yeah, just pick a cabin," said Kinky. Two dogs lay at his feet. A third, an older Lab, slept on the couch next to Clarence, who put his hand on her head. He was usually afraid of dogs, but the ones here at the ranch were so mellow his fear disappeared.

Echo Hill Ranch was a summer camp for kids Kinky had inherited from his father. The first campers were still over a month away.

"I haven't caught one fucking fish since I got here," said Clarence.

"Patience, son," said Kinky. "They're shy little buggers. They've never seen the Big Man before. Shit, they've never seen a Negro of any size outside of Big Nig the erstwhile Jewboy, and he don't fish."

"You stay in touch with all the Jewboys?" asked Clarence.

"Yeah, pretty much," said Kinky.

"You ever get back together and play?"

"Once in a while," said Kinky. "I'm a novelist now. I only play to promote the books."

"How many have you written?" asked Clarence.

"I'm in the middle of number six," said Kinky.

"What's it called?"

"I'm going to name it after the three things that make America great," said Kinky. "Elvis, Jesus and Coca-Cola."

Suddenly there was a knock at the door, startling both of them. The three dogs were up and barking.

"Who the fuck...?" said Kinky, standing.

"Nancy?" Clarence speculated, as Kinky crossed to the door.

"No way across the river," said Kinky. "Who is it?" he yelled. He had to yell to be heard over the rain and the barking dogs.

A muffled voice came from outside barely audible. "Bob," it said.

"Don't open it," said Clarence. "It could be some murderous lunatic here to kill us."

"Murderous lunatics don't normally tell you their names," said Kinky. "And they're rarely called Bob."

"Maybe this one is clever," said Clarence. A bolt of lightning hit nearby, followed by a huge boom of thunder. Kinky tried to quiet the dogs. "You got a gun?" Clarence asked.

"Of course I've got a gun," said Kinky. "But I don't know where it is."

"What good is having a gun if you don't know where it is?" said Clarence.

The knocking on the door came again, louder.

"I think it's under the bed. I'll go look," said Kinky, starting for the bedroom.

"Forget it," said Clarence. "We'll use mine." With that he took a pistol out of his jacket.

"You have a gun on you?" said Kinky, incredulous.

"I'm a black guy in rural Texas," said Clarence. "I should have six fucking guns on me."

"I see your point," said Kinky.

"Open the door," said Clarence, leveling the pistol.

"Okay, here we go," said Kinky.

He opened the door.

A figure in black stood there wearing a hooded slicker.

"KINKSTAH!" it said.

He threw back the hood and entered. Everything stopped. Even the dogs were still.

"Don't shoot," said Kinky. "It's Zimmy!"

Clarence lowered the gun and put it away as Bob Dylan, feigning boxing moves, stepped into the room.

Later.

The three men sat in the living room drinking. The rain continued to fall.

"How'd you get across the river?" asked Clarence.

"You can't get across the river," said Kinky.

Bob shrugged. "I got across," he said.

"You walked across?" asked Kinky.

"Drove," said Bob.

"What are you driving," said Clarence, "a fucking tank?"

"It's a seventy-one Bronco," said Bob. "Got a bored-out Hawaiian racing engine in it. Got a big winch. Didn't need it, though."

"Wait," said Kinky. "First of all, what are you doing out here in the Texas boondocks by yourself?"

"I was over in San Antone," said Bob. "Just looking around, you know."

"No, I don't know," said Kinky. "Bob Dylan's riding around San Antonio in some hot-rod seventy-one Bronco and nobody fucking notices?"

"Had it shipped down," said Bob, not quite responsively. "I like moving around. I drove out Highway Sixteen tonight, over to Flores Country Store. Joe Ely was playing."

"You went to see him," said Kinky, as if he were narrating a story he didn't really believe.

"Uh-huh," said Bob.

"Alone," said Kinky.

"Right," said Bob.

"At Flores Country Store."

"Yup."

"And nobody recognized you?" said Clarence.

"Not that I know of," said Bob. "The show was indoors on account of the rain, so I just kinda stood in the back over there by the pool table."

"Fuck all," said Kinky. "I mean it sounds almost normal the way you say it but...you're Bob Dylan!"

"Not all the time," said Bob.

"How do you guys know each other?" asked Clarence.

"I'm a big Kinky fan," said Bob.

"Bob was one of the Jewboys last year," said Kinky. "Backed me up on a song I did for the Chabad telethon out in LA."

"True," said Bob, petting the dog asleep on the floor next to his chair. "I believe the song was 'Sold American.'"

"That's right," said Kinky.

"Joe did a hell of a song tonight about a rooster," said Bob. "A Tom Russell song."

"Tom wrote a song about a rooster?" said Kinky.

"White people," said Clarence, shaking his head.

"No." Bob smiled. "It's good. It's about a fighting rooster. It's called 'Gallo del Cielo.'"

"And it was good, huh?" asked Clarence.

"Yeah," said Bob. "And I'm hard to impress."

It was quiet for a while. They sat and listened to the storm.

"I always meant to ask you, Bob, who's your favorite performer?" said Kinky.

"I've always liked Gary Unger from St. Louis," said Bob. He put his hand to his chin and thought awhile.

Clarence stole a glance at Kinky and mouthed the question *Gary Unger?* Kinky shrugged.

"Bobby Clarke," Bob continued. "Dan Maloney, Butch Goring..."

"I thought I knew every musician in the world," said Kinky. "But I've never heard of these guys."

"Me, neither," said Clarence.

"They're hockey players," said Bob. "When you said 'performers' I thought you were talking about hockey players."

"Why the fuck would you think I was talking about fucking hockey players?" said Kinky.

Bob shrugged. "I guess I was thinking about hockey," he said.

"He was thinking about hockey," said Clarence to Kinky.

"I'm hungry," said Kinky.

"I'm a hell of a cook," said Clarence. "You got any stuff out in that kitchen?"

"Be my guest," said Kinky. "Rattle them pots and pans."

"Let me take a look, see what you've got," said Clarence. He got up, stepped over the sleeping dogs, and went into the small kitchen.

"I like applesauce," said Bob.

"I know for a fact that I don't have any applesauce," said Kinky.

"I still like it," said Bob.

Later they sat at the tiny kitchen table eating. A TV set on the counter was tuned to the local news. Three more days of rain were predicted.

"What is this?" asked Bob, looking at his dish.

"It's fucking delicious is what it is," said Kinky.

"Yeah," said Bob. "But what is it?"

"It's an Italian peasant soup called pasta e fagioli, or pasta with beans, or pasta fazool," said Clarence.

"How'd you make it?" said Bob.

"Olive oil, garlic, onions, and pancetta diced up and sautéed," said Clarence. "Then I put in two cans of cannelini beans, drained and rinsed, and about four cups of chicken stock. I brought that to a boil, then put in the cavetelli pasta."

"I didn't know I had shit like pancetta and whatever that pasta was," said Kinky.

"Cavetelli," said Clarence. "I found it in a gift basket from Ester Newberg."

"My agent," said Kinky. "I'm going to send her ten percent of this soup."

"So the reason I came by," said Bob, "was 'cause this fella at the bar told me you had some stray dogs here."

"Well, cousin Nancy, she lives over that way with her husband, Tony. They rescue dogs," said Kinky. "I support that and . . . but it's not organized or anything, at least not yet. But I like doing it. Dogs don't bullshit."

"What do you call these three?" asked Bob, indicating the three dogs sitting patiently by the door waiting for leftovers or for something to fall.

"From right to left, which I think is fair since two of us are Heebs, that's Shadrach, Meshack, and Abednego," said Kinky. The dogs' ears perked up as their names were mentioned.

"Good names," said Clarence.

Saturday Night Live came on the TV.

"Guy said you had a heeler," said Bob. "An Australian heeler."

"Yeah," said Kinky. "Nancy found him wandering around Kerrville. Hadn't eaten for days. The dog, not Nancy. He's looking good now, though. She named him Willie, after Willie."

"I'd like to meet that dog," said Bob.

"Soon as we can get across the river," said Kinky.

"Oh, we'll get across," said Bob.

They ate quietly for a while.

"I had a dream about Elvis," said Kinky. "I guess 'cause I'm sort of writing about him, but in my dream he was president and Dick Nixon was visiting him and Nixon, as in 'take a Nixon,' was wearing the jumpsuit and the cape. Weird, huh?"

"What the hell happened to Elvis, anyway?" said Clarence. "How does it get like that?"

"Got in over his head," said Bob. "Thought he could stand up in the deep end."

They finished eating. Kinky gave what was left to the dogs. Bob was doing the dishes while Kinky and Clarence lit cigars. Tom Hanks was on the television, but the sound was off.

"What the fuck?" said Kinky, grabbing the clicker off the table and turning up the TV's volume. They all looked at the screen.

"That's Bruce," said Bob.

Bruce and his new band were doing "Living Proof," Bruce exchanging guitar licks with Shane Fontayne.

"Shit," said Clarence. "Don't make me watch this. It's too painful."

Kinky clicked the set off. Outside thunder rolled.

"That's a bitch," said Bob. "But shit, I know where he's coming from. I play with everybody. So does Neil."

"Yeah, but he always comes back to Crazy Horse," said Kinky. "Bruce'll come back to E Street. He's no fool."

"I hope so," said Clarence. "It's like seeing your girl with somebody else."

"I know what," said Bob. "Let's do something together. Get whatever E Street guys are around. I've got some songs. I could be the Boss for a while, right?"

Kinky and Clarence laughed.

"Sure thing," said Clarence. "Let's do it."

"Yeah," said Bob.

"In the meantime, where's the whiskey?" asked Clarence.

* * *

Later, in the first hour of Sunday morning, Kinky threw another log on the fire.

"I could use an Abba-Zaba," said Bob.

"Sorry," said Kinky. "I think I've got some frozen Snickers bars."

"I was thinking about Odudua, the Santeria mistress of darkness," said Bob.

"What's that got to do with candy?" Clarence asked.

"Odudua sounds like Abba-Zaba," said Bob.

Clarence looked at Kinky. "I give up trying to understand this man," he said.

"Santeria," said Bob, "is a blend of Bantu and Catholicism."

Kinky couldn't think of anything to say, so he took a drink of brandy. They all held snifters. A cloud of cigar smoke hung in the air. The dogs had retreated to the back bedroom. The rain sounded like applause.

"I ran into Mac Rebennack last week," said Clarence.

"How is Dr. John?" asked Kinky.

"He's good," said Clarence. "He told me this amazing story about a tour he was on in the late fifties. Mac was the piano player for some big star, he wouldn't say who, on the guy's first tour. The guy had a big hit record and was going on the road behind it. It was thirty dates starting in New York and working down the whole East Coast, ending in Miami. Well, Mac says that guy only played the New York and Miami dates. He hired some other dude who sounded like him to be him at all the other shows."

"Wow," said Kinky, laughing and shaking his head. "I'd love to know who that was."

"Next time you see Mac ask him," said Clarence.

"Well, it's possible that nobody is who they say they are," said Bob. "For example, everybody knows that I'm not really Bob Dylan, but what if I'm not Robert Zimmerman, either? It's an interesting question."

"Yeah, but if you're not you," said Clarence, "then who the fuck are you?"

"No telling," said Bob. "I could be Wink Martindale or Alan Alda."

"Those two are already taken," said Kinky.

"Are they?" asked Bob. "I know we all believe that, but what if it isn't true? What if nobody is who they say they are?"

"Could explain the collapse of the banking system," said Clarence.

"If I said I was Stephen King I'd sell a lot more books," said Kinky, drawing on his cigar.

"Why don't you try that with *Elvis, Jesus and Pepsi-Cola*?" said Clarence.

"Coca-Cola," said Kinky.

"Who gives a shit?" said Clarence. "Call it whatever you want, but then put Stephen King's name on it."

"You can't do that," said Kinky. "It's highly illegal."

"How about this," said Bob. "You call it *Elvis, Jesus and Coca-Cola by Stephen King*, written by Kinky Friedman. You could do that."

"Yeah," said Clarence. "And you make the Kinky Friedman part real small."

"I'll give it some thought," said Kinky, as he was forgetting it.

"Assuming," said Bob, "that you really are Kinky Friedman."

"Well," said Clarence, "whoever you motherfuckers are, good night. I'm going to bed."

With that he put his drink down, put his coat on and stepped out into the rain. Later, in his cabin, he thought about what Bob had said. Maybe people weren't who they said they were, maybe it was all an illusion.

He fell asleep and had crazy dreams. But the next morning when he woke up, he couldn't remember any of them.

Clarence

If Barbara Walters were to ask me what kind of animal I would be, I think I would say a Newfoundland with hip dysplasia. Big, black, friendly, lovable, and in constant pain. But despite that pain I try to continue on with a great attitude, and I always come when called.

I spoke to Don today before the show. I was calling to check in, like I like to do with all my friends when I'm on the road.

"There's a new addition to the stage," I said.

"What's that?" he asked.

"A throne," I said.

"A throne?"

"A big gold throne," I said. "It's great."

It was a funny idea and a good solution to my problem, and the idea to do it was Bruce's.

One night Bruce came into the Temple of Soul because I wanted to discuss the need for me to descend and then climb the stage stair for the encore. "No need to," said Bruce. "When the lights go down just go back to the chair. I want you to be comfortable. I'll put in an elevator if you want."

Recently I have been standing on two bad legs, with two bad knees, two replaced hips, and a very bad back.

My body suffers the results of age and a life on the road. For several years Bruce and I routinely jumped off the stage into the crowd at every show. One night I was surprised to find the drop was over ten feet. I landed hard and severely sprained my ankle. But of course I kept going. For the next two days I was on my back, the ankle packed in ice.

"You didn't miss a show?" Don asked.

"I've never missed a show," I said. "It's not an option."

Missing a show is not part of my work ethic.

"Now we can title the book *Big Man on the Throne*," Don laughed.

On the morning of March 3, 2008, the Montreal *Gazette* music critic T'cha Dunlevy wrote a review of the concert the previous night at the Bell Center. It was a glowing review of the show, calling it an enthusiastic celebration of a musical career that has spanned thirty-five years. But for me the best part of the review is found about halfway through. It may be the most memorable sentence in the history of E Street, except for Jon Landau's "future of rock and roll" line.

It reads as follows: "Next, Clarence Thomas stepped to centre stage for one of his trademark sax solos, with guitarist Nils Lofgren answering in kind."

I guess Mr. Thomas slipped away from his duties on the Supreme Court to play with the Boss for a few shows.

Now I love the Canadian people, but what the fuck? I've only been playing up there for thirty-five years. Can't you get my name right by now? On the other hand, maybe I could stop by the Supreme Court and make some small changes in the marijuana laws.

The Legend of Central Park, 2000

This story is based on truth. I did go to see Jacob play in the Park. What happens after I leave is made up, but it's a story that makes me laugh. I not only believe that it could happen, I'd be willing to bet that it has happened. Somewhere there are pictures to prove it. —C.C.

Clarence watched his nephew Jacob play the sax in the small bandshell on the east side of the Park. Clarence sat with Jacob's new wife, Jackie, and smiled as Jacob led the four-piece band through an elaborate Charlie Parker–inspired riff.

Jacob had always been a special kid. Always big like Clarence and always charismatic. Like his famous uncle, Jacob was born with an aura of warmth. And he could play. This group was put together through his church, and they were in New York to perform at a three-day quasi-religious festival, but informal events like this one were just about the music.

Jacob and Jackie met in church, too, and had fallen in love and gotten married within six months. They lived in Virginia and were using this trip to New York as a honeymoon. She sat next to Clarence and smiled as Jacob soloed sweetly, his eyes closed, his body arched backward. The music floated up over the trees in the park and off toward the surrounding city.

*   *   *

Annie Leibovitz slammed the door and headed down the stairs in front of her building. If you wanted something done right you had to do it yourself. Her assistant had just called from Barneys, unable to find the shirt Annie needed for Brad Pitt. She'd be photographing him at six o'clock tonight, and she wanted that blue shirt she'd seen in the window yesterday. Brad was blond at the moment, and the blue shirt would be stunning. Her plan was to have him wearing only the blue shirt so it had to look good, otherwise Brad wouldn't go for it. She wanted to do a take on the classic shot of the pretty girl wearing the guy's shirt in the morning, her hair tousled from a recent roll in the hay, standing in the doorway coyly holding a cup of coffee and smiling conspiratorially at the camera.

The trick of course was to somehow include his feet. To her knowledge Brad's feet had never been photographed. The rumor was that when he made *Troy,* they had to throw out the custom-made sandals and custom-make boots instead to hide his feet. Apparently he thought his feet were ugly, and when you're the most beautiful man in the world imperfection is intolerable. She knew he'd want to wear socks. White socks. She had to find a way to talk him out of that. The blue shirt would help.

She turned right and crossed the street. She had decided to walk, she could use the exercise, and so she headed into the Park. She walked with her head down but her eyes never stopped observing. She was a watcher, a framer of scenes, and the Park was full of them. She felt naked without a camera. She was almost never without one in easy reach. But in another, more subversive way it was kind of liberating. She felt momentarily unencumbered by the facts of her life. It was a beautiful day.

Clarence applauded along with the others in the small audience when the band finished.

"He's good, isn't he?" said Jackie, smiling.

"He's real good," said Clarence. "Better than I was at his age."

Jacob was twenty-two.

"You should tell him that," she said.

"You tell him," said Clarence.

Jacob put his horn in its case, shook hands with the other guys in the band, and crossed down from the stage to where Clarence and Jackie were standing. A few people stopped him on his way and complimented him on his playing.

"Thank you so much," he said, smiling that big smile. His hair was fashioned into a long and wild Afro that looked a lot like a halo when he was backlit.

"Come over here," said Clarence. He grabbed Jacob and hugged him. "You were great."

"Thank you, sir," said Jacob. "That really does mean a lot."

"He said you're better than he was at your age," said Jackie, standing on tiptoes to kiss his cheek.

"He's a liar," said Jacob.

"That's true," said Clarence. "But I'm not lying about this. You are the shit, my man."

"Maybe someday I'll be half as good as you," said Jacob.

"I'm not going to argue this point anymore," said Clarence. "You're right. I'm the best, but you're still okay. How's that?"

"Better," said Jacob.

Clarence looked at his watch.

"Oh, shit, I've got to bounce," he said. "I've got a fitting for my new stage clothes. I am going to be one fly motherfucker."

"You go ahead," said Jacob. "We're going to walk around the Park a little."

"It's so beautiful," said Jackie. "It's hard to believe it's actually here in the middle of this city."

"I think the Park *is* the city," said Clarence. "It gives New York its identity."

"I love it. I want to see the whole thing," she said.

"That'll take some time," laughed Jacob. "The place is huge."

"Enjoy," said Clarence. "I'll check in with you later about dinner tonight."

They hugged and kissed again and Clarence headed off toward the city's East Side.

*   *   *

Annie skirted the Great Lawn, crossed the road, and headed slightly north. Maybe the trick was to provide too much footwear. Socks, shoes, boots, footie pajamas, sneakers, and finally flip-flops. Maybe she could wear him down through attrition. She smiled to herself at the absurdity of the entire endeavor. Trying to get Brad Pitt's shoes off…ridiculous. For God's sake, she was in museums around the world. She was arguably the most successful photographer of her time, and here she was scheming to get a shot of some movie star's gnarly feet. She actually laughed out loud.

"Excuse me," said Jacob.

Annie looked to her right to see a young couple standing at the top of the mall, just below the small bandstand. They were a cute couple. He was a big guy with a great face and a big shock of hair. She was small and pretty and they had *newlyweds* written all over them. He was holding some kind of case. Maybe for a horn of some kind.

"Yes?" she said.

"Could you take our picture?" he said.

Jackie held out a small digital camera and smiled.

"We have no pictures together," she said.

Were they kidding? Was this some kind of elaborate trick to get her to take their picture?

"It'll just take a sec," he said.

No, they had no clue who she was.

"Sure," she said.

She crossed to them. The girl handed her the tiny camera.

"You just look through here and press this button," she said, pointing.

"I see," said Annie.

"There's a flash if you need it," he said. "But I think it's automatic."

"I don't think we'll need a flash," said Annie. "Okay, stand together and give us a smile."

They did, and she looked at the display. It was a nice shot. They were smiling and bright and young and attractive and framed beautifully by the trees on either side of the path. The light was perfect. But it wasn't special.

"What's in the case?" said Annie.

"My saxophone," said Jacob.

"Why don't you play it?" said Annie.

"Oh, that would be cool," said Jackie to Jacob. "Go ahead."

A few moments later the case was at Annie's feet, and the boy was playing something beautiful while the girl leaned against him and looked at him lovingly. There was pure joy in her face. Annie snapped the picture. Then another. Then another. She pulled the camera away and looked at the shots. They were good. Very good. The first one was the best, though. In it she captured the instant he connected with some soul note that spoke to him in music. It was a beautiful picture.

"Can I see?" said Jackie.

"Here you go," said Annie, handing them the camera.

"Hey, that's cool," said Jacob.

"Thank you," said Jackie.

"No problem," said Annie. "Enjoy."

She walked away, down toward the small tunnel on the way to the Delacorte Clock and the East Side beyond.

"Where do you want to go now?" said Jacob, putting the horn away.

"Let's go take a picture by the lake," said Jackie.

"Good idea," he said.

He looked at the photograph the woman had taken again, and he smiled.

"What?" said Jackie.

"This picture is good," he said.

Don

On the European leg of the "Magic" tour Clarence was a prisoner of pain.

His knees had become so bad that walking anywhere was very difficult, so he tried to confine his movements to the stage.

The rest of the time he stayed in his room. When he wasn't eating or sleeping or doing one of the many kinds of therapy he employs, he sat by the window and looked out at foreign cities and people he would never meet.

The highlight of his day was talking to Victoria via computer in the late evening. Without that and the joy that performing music still brings, he would've been a total recluse. Pain had forced the most outgoing of men to stay behind closed doors. Immigration issues had prevented Victoria from leaving the United States.

"I miss her so much," he said one night. "I cry real tears when I'm not with her. Yeah, I can talk to her ten times a day but I can't watch her walk."

In Sweden, Bruce coaxed Clarence out on an off day to go sailing. Other than that, the Big Man never left his room in any city until I arrived in San Sebastián on July 14.

I was traveling with my wife, Judy, a writer friend named Dean Lorey, and the famous comedian Damon Wayans. Damon and I had just finished a pilot for a new series, and he was looking to do some things out of his comfort zone. Spain and Springsteen were certainly that. Along with Clarence and his assistant, Lani, we had a fantastic meal in a hillside restaurant and went back to the hotel and closed the bar at about three a.m.

It would be great to see the show through Damon's eyes, as he had never seen Bruce perform before and was only vaguely familiar with his music.

"Major Payne!" said Bruce. "My kids are beside themselves. 'That's Major Payne,' they said."

"Yup," said Damon. "And Dean here wrote it."

"So what brings you to San Sebastián?" said Bruce. He was very tanned. He and his family had gone to the local beach that day like any other tourists and had gotten some sun. He had evidently left his sunglasses on and had white circles around his eyes like a skier.

"We just came to hang out with Don and Clarence," said Damon. "We just saw the Temple of Soul."

"It's unbelievable, isn't it?" said Bruce. "I've got concrete walls and an old couch, and he's got an entire fucking temple."

"It's very cool," said Damon.

"This is their first show of yours," I said. "They've never seen you before."

"Well, in that case we'll have to step it up a notch," said Bruce.

About an hour before showtime Judy, Dean, and I were sitting outside the E Street lounge when Damon came out dragging Little Steven with him.

"Look who I found," said Damon.

We all said hello and made small talk about his radio show, and Steven finally excused himself and left. After he left Damon shook his head and smiled.

"What are the odds we'd run into him here?" said Damon.

At first I thought he was kidding. Then I realized he wasn't.

"Actually the odds are pretty good," I said.

"Why?" said Damon.

"Well, he's in the band," I said.

"What band?" he asked.

"This band," I said. "Bruce's band."

"Bullshit," said Damon. "He's an actor. He was on *The Sopranos*."

"Yes, but he's also the guitar player in the E Street Band."

"No shit?" said Damon.

I raised my right hand.

"Swear to God," I said.

"I'll be damned," he said. "Bruce must be a huge *Sopranos* fan."

I don't think he really believed me until he actually saw Steven onstage.

He was equally amazed a few songs into the set when he recognized Conan O'Brien's bandleader on the drums.

Bruce held true to his promise to "kick it up a notch," and the show was amazing. Patti was onstage for the first time on this leg of the tour, and the whole evening had a house-party feel to it.

Damon took tons of pictures during that concert with a new camera he'd just bought, and he thoroughly enjoyed the show. We did one of those fast-out, police-escort things back to the hotel, and Damon waved to the crowds lining the street like he was in the band, too.

"I thought I knew what it was like to be famous," he said, as we drove through the crowded Spanish streets. "But there's nothing like rock-star fame. And Clarence is amazing. I think he's got to be one of the most interesting people I've ever met. There are so many facets to him. I mean he's black, but he lives in a white world and it hasn't seemed to affect him. He's still his own man."

Clarence had a particularly good night also. He knew he would. He had predicted as much in his suite the night before while sitting with Dean Lorey at three a.m. after a night of good food and friendship.

"You see how I am now? I'm this nice easygoing guy, we're laughing and having fun, right?" said Clarence.

"Right," said Dean.

"When you see me on that stage tomorrow night you'll be looking at a totally different human being. Another person entirely. You'll be looking at the Big Man."

He leaned forward and smiled that brilliant smile.

"And the Big Man," he said, "is a motherfucker."

After the show Clarence did something he does often, which is to hold court in the hotel bar. He sets himself up and basically receives people. They are always respectful and awestruck and want nothing more than a signature or a photograph of themselves with the Big Man.

I have never seen Clarence handle this situation with anything but patience and graciousness. He has a smile and a kind word for everyone and seems willing to sit with fans all night long. One night in Spain we sat in the lobby bar of the Maria Christina Hotel with Damon and Dean, and watched what seemed to be an endless stream of faces approach Clarence. It was an unusual situation for Damon, who went largely unrecognized in Spain. He spent the night photographing Clarence and the fans who stopped by. It was actually a lot of fun. It's easy to forget the impact that Clarence has had on people's lives. The emotion of the music touches people deeply, and they are anxious to communicate that to him.

After San Sebastián the band headed for Madrid. Our plans to join them were interrupted when I came down with a stomach virus that kept me in bed for three days. Judy and I set our sights on catching up with the circus in Barcelona, and Damon and Dean headed off to Paris by train. On Friday morning we made our way to the San Sebastián airport. We got there at 9:40 for the 11:00 flight to Barcelona. At the ticket counter the woman from the airline said in broken English, "The flight is delayed, maybe for two hours, or cancelled...forever." This did not sound good. I was still feeling weak having had little to eat for three days.

"There is a flight from Pamplona to Barcelona leaving in one hour, which is a one-hour taxi drive away," she said hopefully. She handed us boarding passes and luggage tags and pointed to the taxis lined up outside the small terminal building. "Of course there is no charge," she said.

This sounded reasonably optimistic. However "no charge" was not good news to the drivers of the beat-up old Toyotas, which served as taxicabs. *No charge* to them meant "no tip," so we ended up with a sullen mutant who decided if he had to take us to Pamplona he was going to make the ride as uncomfortable as possible.

A two-lane road runs through the beautiful mountains between San Sebastián and Pamplona. It rises and falls in elevation and is jammed with trucks and other slow-moving vehicles. We averaged 130 kilometers per hour. Our attempts to get this nail-biting fuckhead to slow down proved fruitless, and knocking him unconscious would have defeated the purpose. He dismissed us with a wave and sped up every time we spoke to him. Of all the people I met in my entire visit to this wonderful country, he was the only person I hated. I still hate him, and someday I will hunt him down and strangle him in an alley. He'll be stumbling out of some Tapas bar some night in winter, and a crazed ninety-year-old American holding a lamp cord will leap out of the darkness and squeeze the life out of his worthless shit-for-brains head.

Other than that the trip was good.

We arrived at the Gran Hotel Florida about the same time as the Springsteen family. We checked in and crashed for a few hours before venturing outside to take a look around and get the lay of the land.

The hotel is beautiful and sits near the top of the highest hill overlooking Barcelona. Next door is the Medieval Church of the Sacred Heart with its giant statue of Jesus, his arms outstretched in benediction over the city below. I say the church is next door but that's not entirely accurate. The two buildings are separated by what looks to be Coney Island.

A full-on amusement park is virtually on top of the church. It must be the world's closest juxtaposition between Jesus Christ and a Tilt-a-Whirl.

*   *   *

Later, we ran into Dennis Miller and Brian Williams at the Camp Nou concert, a high-energy affair with an audience of over eighty thousand singing all the lyrics to all the songs. Brian Williams turned out to be very quick and funny. When I knew I was about to be introduced to him I thought I would say, "Since you come into our home every night I feel like you're family," then I planned to pause to allow him to say "Thank you," or whatever, and then I would say, "So can I borrow twenty bucks?"

"It's a pleasure," I said, when we were introduced moments later. "Since you come into our home every night I feel like you're family."

"Yes," he said. "And as a family member I want to talk to you about the way you've been dressing lately."

The Big Man was on fire in Barcelona. Offstage he moved slowly and felt all the miles, but onstage he really was a different man. A stunning "Jungleland" capped his final night in Spain. It was time to head home and to his new love, Victoria, and a new tomorrow, perhaps once again as a married man. Time would tell.

Clarence

One day when we got back from Europe, Don, Victoria, and I were riding through the park in a horse-drawn carriage after having lunch at the Tavern on the Green. One kid was sent over to our table by his parents with a pen and a napkin.

"Are you Bruce Springsteen?" the kid said.

"Do I look like Bruce Springsteen?" I said.

"I don't know," said the kid.

"Then why did you ask?"

"My mother said you were . . . she said Bruce Springsteen."

"No, I'm not Bruce Springsteen. I'm Clarence Clemons."

"Do you know Bruce Springsteen?" asked the kid.

"We've met," I said.

"I mean are you in the band with him?" said the kid.

"Yes, I am," I said.

"Could I have your autograph?"

"Sure," I said. "I'll sign it 'Bruce Springsteen's friend, Clarence Clemons.' How's that?"

"That would be great," said the kid.

*   *   *

I sat back smoking a postprandial cigar while cruising through the park and riffing. Don loves it when I do this because my mind jumps around in space and time, and I'm likely to say anything. I started to tell stories that I knew neither Don nor Victoria had heard before.

"Big Red was my grandfather's mule," I said. "He was a stump-pulling mule. I used to watch him work. It was an incredible sight. He would pull and strain so hard, with such intensity I thought he would explode. Every muscle in his body was working and bulging out, and his eyes were like fire. I expected him to breathe smoke from his nose. And he would pull and pull and pull without stopping until he got that stump out of the ground. He was unbelievable! And I said to myself, 'I'm going to be like that. I'm going to have that kind of purpose and that kind of focus. And I'm going to work and work until my body looks like that.' And that's what I did. I modeled myself and my life and my work ethic after Big Red."

"Don't stop now," said Don. "Tell us some more weird shit."

"Okay," I said. "I'll tell you the story of Rolling Thunder."

"The Bob Dylan tour?" asked Don.

"No," I said. "Rolling Thunder was an Indian medicine man. Jerry Garcia called me one night when I was living in a small town in Nevada and said that I should visit Rolling Thunder, who was in a hospital there.

"So I went over there and walked into the room, and this old man is in bed. He radiated the most incredible energy I had ever felt come from another human being. He looked at me when I stepped into the room, and he waved me over to his bedside.

"'They cut off my leg,' said Rolling Thunder. 'Wanna see?'

"I didn't want to see, but he threw back the covers and showed me anyway. He'd lost his leg to gangrene. He'd gotten an infection somehow and was trying to treat it with herbs and sticks and clouds and shit, and it didn't work. Anyway, he says, 'I'd like you to sit with me tonight,' and I said, 'Sure,' and so that's what I did. I sat in a chair next to his bed and neither of us said another word all night, but I swear we were communicating the whole time. It was as if that whole room was vibrating with energy.

"We remained friends for the rest of his life, which was about ten more years. He'd always call me as his last resort to bail him out of trouble or help him in some way. I loved that guy. Rolling Thunder."

The carriage turned onto Fifty-ninth Street.

"Can you drop me off in front of my hotel?" I asked the driver. "I've got a handicapped sticker."

"Big Man!" yelled some guy passing by in the park.

"Guilty," I said, waving.

I handed the cigar to Victoria, who took a drag. We now shared cigars. The things we do for love.

"The first time I met Victoria's parents, I open the door, get out of the car, and fall flat on my face. They're standing there thinking, *Is he drunk? Is he dead?* It was a real ice breaker," I said.

Victoria laughed at the memory.

"Tell Victoria your story about that guy," I said to Don.

"Which guy?" he said.

"You know, the comedy writer guy. The one with what's his name…Dorf," I said.

"Tim Conway," he said.

"Right," I said.

"He's talking about a guy named Pat McCormick," Don said. "He was this brilliant comedy writer slash actor slash lunatic back in the seventies and eighties out in Hollywood. He did legendary crazy things."

"Like what?" said Victoria.

"Like one Thanksgiving at his house he brought out his newborn son, naked on a silver platter surrounded by fruits and vegetables, and served him to his guests, saying, 'They were out of turkey.'"

"Oh, my God," she laughed.

"That's hysterical," I said. Don Reo has some of the best show-business stories I've ever heard in my life.

"Anyway, one day over at ABC he and Tim Conway are leaving the lot and walking to lunch at some restaurant, when this carload of tourists pulls up. Husband, wife, two kids in the backseat, and clearly out-of-towners. The wife says to Pat, 'Excuse me, could you tell us how to get to the Chinese Theatre on Hollywood Boulevard?' and Pat says, 'Why of course, madam,' and he takes out his dick and points to the blue vein. 'This is Sunset Boulevard, that's where we are now,' he said. 'Just follow this three blocks and take a left here.' He indicated a tiny red vein extending off from the blue one. 'That's Sunset. You'll find the Chinese Theatre about a mile down on the right about here near this freckle.'"

We rode on through the park a bit more. It was hot and humid, and the forecast was calling for evening thundershowers.

Don

"That last show in Jersey was off the chart," said Clarence.

He was right. I got to watch that show from on the stage, and by the end of it I was amazed and exhausted. It started at nine-thirty and went virtually nonstop for three hours and twenty minutes. I saw a lot of the four-hour marathons in the '70s, but those included a thirty- to forty-five-minute intermission. The beast at Giants Stadium in the summer of 2008 exceeded those shows in terms of sheer performance and music played.

"During the encore," said Clarence. "I thought Bruce was trying to kill us. I didn't think he was ever going to stop." Then he smiled and drew on his cigar. He exhaled, lowered his sunglasses, looked at me, and smiled. "I loved every second of it," he said.

It had been quite a night.

This summertime show in 2008 was one of those that fall into the "best ever" category. That subjective list the true fans will argue about forever. The truth is that it is a pointless discussion. "One man's ceiling is another man's floor." But by any measure it was an epic show, stretching to three hours and twenty minutes of solid house-rocking, pants-dropping music.

Judy and I watched the show from on the stage sitting on Clarence's trap cases. I didn't think Bruce and this band could blow me away anymore, at least not like back in the day, but tonight I was proven wrong. I said "Wow" so many times even I got sick of hearing it.

We drove to the stadium with Clarence and Victoria from the city and arrived around five-thirty. A traffic accident delayed the start of the show and it didn't begin until nine-thirty. I sat to the side and behind the stage before the show and watched the crowd filter in. All the band members had lots of guests. Bruce and Patti had over sixty themselves. There were lots of folks wearing backstage passes and laminates. I sat and watched as people filtered out from behind the stage to find a seat or a place to stand. I saw Javier Bardem, who had been in Barcelona last week. Brian Williams, who seemed to be turning into a groupie, was there, along with Steven Spielberg and his wife. Steven was wearing a jaunty straw fedora that was almost as good as wearing a neon arrow on his head with a sign that read "Look at me!" Jimmy Burroughs and Tim Robbins and various Baldwins dotted the crowd. Mickey Rourke and Darren Aronofsky were up front. (After the show in his dressing room Bruce played Darren a song he'd written for a film Darren made with Mickey, called *The Wrestler*. So Darren got one more song than anyone else there.) Everybody was excited and seemed to anticipate that something special was about to happen.

I remember marveling at Nils Lofgren, in need of two new hips, actually doing a somersault during one of his solos. Music seems to possess him and free him from the pain of being human.

I remember Bruce throwing a bucket of water on the crowd in front and the way it was backlit in the air as he spun back toward the stage.

I remember the look and feel of the sold-out stadium when the lights came up at the first notes of "Born to Run." Yes, I've seen that many times before, but on this night it had that magic quality and an intensity that matched that of the audiences in Spain.

I remember seeing the elegant Barbara Carr, of Bruce's management team, standing on the side of the stage enjoying the show for the millionth time, as if it were the first.

I remember Bruce turning to Clarence onstage and talking to him about how they had both failed at marriage and Clarence's impending wedding and how he felt the Big Man had gotten it right this time. I remember the look of genuine affection on Bruce's face as he talked to his old friend in front of that huge crowd and then sang "Pretty Flamingo" for the first time in a long time. It was a beautiful moment.

I remember Candy Brown, an old friend of C's, coming to the Temple of Soul to feed us all.

I remember saying hello to Bruce as he arrived backstage, walking down the big hallway alone with his knit cap pulled over his head, looking like the world's hippest homeless person. I remember thinking that he looked somewhat tired. I was wrong. He wasn't tired. He was waiting.

I remember George Travis, still placid and smiling that small secret smile as he prowled the backstage area, quietly assuring himself that all was right in his world.

And I remember watching the assembly of the Big Man.

The process took well over two and a half hours, and it started with a nap.

Clarence came into the Temple and immediately laid down on the traveling bed, put on his CPAP mask and went to sleep. Assistants and friends came and went but he didn't notice. He was in the first stages of the transformation.

Judy and I left him alone and went up to catering for something to eat. A half hour later he called my cell.

"Where are you?" he asked.

"Upstairs," I said.

"Get down here," he said. "Candy Brown is here with the food."

What Candy brought was part of this list of things that went into the assembly process at that point in time. Here are a few of the others. This is not an all-inclusive list, but Clarence used, applied, ingested, or injected all of the following during the three-hour period before the show:

Two beers.

Glue and duct tape.

Several artificial joints and a myriad of other medical devices and equipment.

Two doctors.

A vitamin B12 shot.

Three pieces of Candy's incredible fried chicken.

A large serving of Candy's incredible greens.

A small serving of Candy's incredible mac and cheese.

A large bottle of Fiji water.

Two ginseng tablets.

A half hour of radiant heat from portable heat lamps.

Two ice bags.

Two knee braces.

Two elaborate back braces.

One deep tissue massage.

One Al Green album.

Two dressers (Lani and Freda).

Black boots, pants, and shirt. A long black military-style duster coat, a smooth black fedora, and black shades.

One fiancée (Victoria).

Lots of well-wishers.

Several prayers. Clarence prays every night before going onstage for God to let him bring joy to someone that night and to help him make it through the show.

A golf cart, which drove him right up onto the stage.

"The hardest part of all," Clarence told me, "is when I put my arm around Bruce and lean on him as we step onto the stage. I know I'm looking at three hours before I get to play my favorite song, which is the last one."

During the show another cigar was smoked and the rest of the Patrón bottle's contents was consumed.

After the show Clarence drank three beers in the dressing room while receiving guests.

In the limo on the way home he ate a small jar of caviar with crackers and drank most of a bottle of Dom Perignon.

By the time we got back to the hotel, which was well after two in the morning, Clarence was feeling as good as he can feel. He had done an amazing show. But, perhaps more amazing, he had survived another day as the Big Man.

Clearly nobody could do this every night and expect to function for long. Fortunately the shows are spaced luxuriously, and the Big Man has recovery time. And some nights the pain is not as bad as others, and certain ingredients of the formula can be eliminated. But Clarence is an old-school rock-and-roll animal and he's not going to change now. He's never even expressed a desire to change. He is a man in charge of his own life. Where most of us would be put on the floor if we consumed the way Clarence consumes, he remains steady and functions at a very high level.

I will remember that show at Giants Stadium for a long time. I'm getting out of the "best ever" business, but this show is connected in my mind to a show at the Santa Monica Civic Auditorium in 1974 and a private party at the Troubadour Club about the same time. It is linked to several shows at the Roxy Theatre and several more at the LA Sports Arena when the horns joined the band in the late '70s. There are others like the night in Arizona when the "video" of "Rosalita" was filmed, and several outstanding performances in New York in the '80s along with memorable performances in Italy and Spain, but again, all of this is in the eye of the beholder. We fans all have a desire, a strong desire, to say we just saw the greatest show we've ever seen. That may always be true. Sometimes it's just truer than others.

But the most enduring image I'll carry from that show is of what I saw when I was walking off the stage. It was dark in the cavernous area backstage, where the crew waits for the last note to fade so they can begin the job of tearing this thing down, loading it all onto trucks, and setting it back up in the next town. As I was leaving to walk down the ramp and back to the Temple of Soul I noticed a big metal trap case sitting by itself. It was dark green and there were two words stenciled on it in white. The larger one was FEDERICI and below it in smaller type was the word FRAGILE.

The Legend of Peahi (Dates Unknown)

Most of Clarence's stories are only partially bullshit. It's only fair to tell you that I think the next one is complete bullshit. —D.R.

The plane was extraordinarily luxurious. It was a festival of Connolly leather, cashmere, and crystal. It was a Gulfstream V. She had spent over three million dollars on the interior alone.

They were cruising at 550 miles an hour at an altitude of 42,000 feet. Their destination was the island of Maui, and they were both simultaneously confident and terrified. What waited for them was a defining moment, which would alter or end their lives.

The trip began when he appeared on her show. They challenged each other. Both fiercely independent and both very, very smart. It started as a joke. "What's the craziest thing you've ever done?" led quickly to "What's the craziest thing you'd ever do?" and then the one-upmanship began. Then it became serious. Then it became about life and death. Then it became about something beyond both of those things. Something more elusive.

They had been preparing for this trip both separately and together for more than a year. Both could swim a little at first, and both had a major fear of the ocean. They'd started doing laps both at his pool in Florida and hers in Montecito. They'd done most of their water work on the West Coast. Her estate there was set up for guests and trainers, so that was where they based their efforts at first. It was just a short hop to the beach when they graduated to ocean swimming.

But before any of that came the mental work. Preparing the mind for something the mind could not accept. They had spent a lot of time with Eckhart Tolle. Clarence was sure that this guy was full of shit, with his stupid accent and his stupid philosophy, but gradually he changed his mind. Tolle talked a lot about positivity and Clarence liked that. First of all he liked the word itself... *positivity*. It was a good word. It was rhythmic and percussive. It was a Chuck Berry word. Positivity. Accent on the *tiv*. Yes. It all started to make sense. If you could imagine it, you could become it.

The Hollister Ranch is a 15,000-acre enclave on the California coast north of Santa Barbara. Because beach access there is limited to ranch residents, it possesses some of the most undersurfed quality waves in the state. If you're not on the ranch, the only way to surf Razors or Big Drakes or Rights and Lefts is to boat in and out.

She had used her power to entice Laird to help them.

Laird had arranged ranch access for them through his old running buddy Dr. Brad Johnson, who had lived there for more than twenty-five years. Laird met the two of them, both in amazing shape, at the St. Augustine cabana, then drove them down onto the beach in an old restored Ford Bronco he bought from Bob Dylan. Dave Kalama followed in a Range Rover that carried all the gear.

They drove up to Johns Pond at the far western edge of the ranch and went to work.

Laird stressed hard physical training and breath control. On Maui they would be tested to their limits and beyond.

They had been running daily for over a year. They had been weight training for almost as long and deep diving for the last six months. A magician who had held his breath for more than seventeen minutes on her show had inspired her. He had worked with them on technique in the pool and then in the ocean off East Beach, where they had used one of Paul Allen's yachts as an extravagant base camp, far from prying eyes.

It is fair to say that when they began water work at Hollister, that is to say board work, they were both in the best physical shape of their lives.

They were the two most unlikely big-wave surfers in history.

They worked and worked and worked, and after months of falling their balance began to come around and they became competent. Then they became good. Then they became very good. They could more than hold their own in decent-sized surf. It was drop, turn, and set up for the glide stuff—no cutbacks or aerials, but those things wouldn't be needed where they were going.

After one super session on a double-overhead day they sat on the sand in front of the Bronco and stared out at the water. It was late afternoon, and except for a brief lunch break they'd been surfing since seven a.m. Laird was loading the boards and wet suits into the Range Rover with Dave.

"Nobody would believe this shit," said Clarence.

"I don't believe this shit," she said, laughing.

"I wish I'd starting doing this when I was young," he said.

"You are young, Clarence. It's all in your mind."

"Tell that to my knees."

"You're going to be fine," she said. "Just believe."

"I do," he said. "I didn't for a long time, but I do now."

She turned and looked at him. She was glowing with good health. The sun warmed her face. Her eyes were brilliant. Gulls danced behind her in the distance on the sands of the Laughing Cowboy Ranch, which used to be called the Western Gate, the place where Native Americans believed the Earth connected to Heaven.

"Are you happy?" she asked.

"Yes," he said. "I love what you said about the composition of happiness. The two ingredients of happiness."

"Gratitude and forgiveness," she said.

"Yes."

"That's all you need."

Laird closed up the tailgate on the Range Rover and started back toward the Bronco. The sun was sinking, and the sky was beginning to turn a soft pink.

"So tell me again why we're going over there to risk our lives," said Clarence.

"That I have not figured out," she said. Then she laughed that deep-throated laugh. He called it her dirty laugh. "It seemed like a good idea at the time."

They landed and went to the massive oceanfront estate she had leased in Paia. She owned property up-country and in Hana, but for this trip they needed to be closer to the action. She stayed in the big house while Clarence took the guesthouse, which was located right down on the sand. Clarence thought that if this were his property he'd live in this house and knock the big one down.

That night they met Laird and Gabrielle at Charlie's for dinner. Laird said the swell was big. Very big. He'd been studying weather charts and satellite photos for days. He'd alerted them a week ago and had put them on notice to jump on the plane the moment he said go.

Gabby was very supportive.

"You'll do great," she said to them. "With Laird and Dave out there with you nothing can go wrong."

"Something can always go wrong," said Laird with a small smile. "But it won't tomorrow."

Willie Nelson came by and sang a few songs. Clarence got up and sang "Moonlight in Vermont" with him. Willie introduced the song as the only classic standard that didn't contain a single rhyme.

Clarence had never thought of bringing his horn.

They turned in early and awakened early. Neither of them could remember dreaming.

Laird and Dave arrived well before dawn and drove them to the landing. It was too dark to see the waves, but they could hear them. They could feel them.

"Sounds big," said Clarence.

"It's big," said Laird.

"How big?" she asked.

"Sixty plus," he said. He searched their faces for any sign of hesitation. He saw fear, but he expected that. Hesitation out there was synonymous with death. He didn't see any.

"Let's ride," said Clarence.

"Go!" Laird shouted, then turned the Jet Ski hard to the right and disappeared from her vision.

She was aware of being alone. There was a clarity to this aloneness she had never experienced before. She could not have imagined this feeling. It was just her and the wave, and there was nothing else that mattered.

She leaned forward slightly and let gravity and God take over. She looked over the edge and dropped in, skipping down the face with a gathering speed that took her breath away. The enormous moving wall of water, which appeared to be smooth from the cliff onshore, was actually made up of jagged ledges, which seemed to be climbing upward toward the spitting lip, which was now some twenty-five feet above her.

For a moment she was sure she'd be pulled up by this lethal escalator and pitched screaming over the falls, followed by a million tons of falling water. But instead she shot off the edge of a huge shelf, sailed out into the air, reconnected with the surface a full ten feet below, and rocketed down into the pit.

She leaned hard on the inner rail and carved a deep and beautiful bottom turn, sending up a rooster tail of water.

As she began to climb, looking for her line, she became aware of the presence of the wave. It loomed above her and behind her. It was everything, filling all her senses with an absolute nowness. She was present.

She picked a line and set it. In front of her and far above, the wave began to pitch forward. She had no idea if she could make it, but in truth she didn't really care. If she died today so be it. *This moment,* she said to herself, *is perfect.*

Behind her time and space began to explode. As she raced across the face of the giant wave, chaos followed, closing fast.

*   *   *

Clarence dropped the towrope and glided slightly to his left, the wave lifting him up and propelling him forward. His speed was perfect, and when he found himself on the lip he looked down, seven stories down, smiled, leaned forward, and took the drop.

He extended his arms out and up for balance and looked like a great, black, winged bird flying down the face of a giant monster wave, both of them moving with majesty and grace and awesome, otherworldly power.

It seemed impossibly steep, and he felt like he was falling forever. He almost lost his position on the board and pitched forward, but the straps saved him and he leaned back, shifted ever so slightly, and hit the bottom of the wave angled a little to his right.

He could feel the g-force of the turn as he crouched down into it, using all the strength he'd built up in his massive legs to pull it off.

He continued turning now, traveling slightly upward toward the top.

He moved his back foot out toward the edge to set up for the glide.

His foot slipped.

He tried to pull it back but the laws of physics had been broken. The nose of his board turned violently to the right, pointing straight at the sky, while his body continued forward. He floated off the board and began skipping down the face like a pebble skipping across a stream.

Finally he was launched forward into the void.

He became airborne, and he twisted his body into a diving position. His goal now was to hit the bottom of the wave and knife backward under the beast. He knew that wasn't going to happen. The wave was way too thick. He would go down and then be sucked up over the falls of a seventy-foot *Jaws* giant and be buried, driven to the bottom.

His last thought before he entered the water was of his mother. He remembered the way she smiled.

She was flying through a green cathedral. The wave had broken and she was inside the tube. Although calling it a tube didn't do it justice. It was a moving, living cavern. The noise, the life of the thing, was beyond description. She didn't realize that she was screaming. She pointed the board at daylight, crouched down, and willed herself to go faster and then faster still.

When she shot out into the sunlight and saw Laird on the Jet Ski up on the shoulder, she felt weightless. She turned into an angel. She was transcendent. She raised her arms high over her head and yelled a kind of prayer to the sky. She felt like she had seen God, had touched God, and in some deeply human way she had become godlike.

Clarence was being torn apart. Immense forces pulled at his arms and legs, threatening to rip them off. The turbulence rendered him insignificant.

He tried to maintain a tuck position but it was impossible. He was being forced down and battered by tons of violently churning water.

He focused on his breath. He tried to remember everything he'd learned in training for this moment, but the panic was right there telling him it was hopeless and that he had no chance of survival. The panic told him to let go, to surrender and breathe in the sea.

But he found his center, the quiet place that both Eckhart and Laird had described, and he parked his mind. He took his being away from his body. His consciousness was calm and safe and still. What happened to his body would happen, but his soul would be unharmed no matter what.

Dave Kalama drove through the soupy foam close to panic himself.

Another megawave was building behind him and he knew that Clarence would not survive two hold-downs.

Then he spotted him.

Clarence had popped to the surface twenty yards closer to shore.

Dave raced toward him, expertly sliding the water sled into the Big Man's arms. Clarence grabbed it and Dave accelerated, charging out of the pit to the safety of the shoulder as the wave behind feathered and broke like doomsday on the reef.

She was sitting there astride her board next to Laird on his Jet Ski. Everything out here, the water, the sky, the air, had a unique quality. It all felt hyperreal.

"I'm fine," he said, answering the obvious unasked question.

"We did it," she said. For the first time that day he noticed that her bathing suit was red.

"No, *you* did it," he said. "I'm going back out."

On the plane again, headed east, they were quiet. He allowed himself a tumbler of whiskey and he enjoyed every sip.

She mostly smiled. There was little to say.

Finally he spoke. "As good as it gets," he said.

"You sure?" she asked, smiling crookedly with one eyebrow arched.

"Oh, no," he said. "I don't want to hear it."

"Okay, suit yourself," she said, sitting back.

He took another sip and felt the whiskey warm his throat. The horn didn't like it when he drank. The sugar in the alcohol made its valves sticky. The shoulders fell off the reeds.

"What is it?" he finally asked.

She turned in her seat and looked at him across the aisle. She looked like a little girl.

"Ski jumping," she said.

He said nothing for a long time. She kept watching him.

"Ridiculous," he said.

"Absurd, really," she said.

"Impossible," he said.

"I know that," she said. "The idea itself is stupid. Just like the notion that the two of us could surf big waves in Hawaii is stupid. It's a far-fetched fantasy. Couldn't happen. Not in a million years."

"That's right," said Clarence.

"Technically, what I have in mind is called ski flying," she said.

"Ski flying," he said.

"Right," she said.

"Sounds dangerous," he said.

"Oh, it is," she said. "The odds are very good that we'll get seriously hurt or killed trying to do it. But it looks so pretty."

"Yeah," he said. "Pretty."

They traveled through the sky in a metal tube going almost six hundred miles an hour for a few minutes before he spoke again.

"What the fuck," he said. "Let's do it."

She smiled at him. He looked at her and smiled back. Billion-watt smiles. World changers.

When she spoke it was soft, as if she hadn't intended it to be audible.

"Big Man," she said.

Don

I walked over to George Travis, who was standing backstage at one of the concerts looking like a guy who had nothing on his mind. George always looks like that. In fact he must have a lot on his mind, since he's in charge of everything connected to the business of touring. The phrase *Let's get this show on the road!* is where George begins. He does everything to make that happen. If you've ever taken a trip with your family, you know how complicated traveling with a group can become. Imagine traveling with a group like Bruce Springsteen and the E Street Band. Most people wouldn't last very long. George Travis is not most people.

Think about it for a minute or two, or just until your head explodes. You've got a crew of about two hundred people, lighting people, sound, video, security, hair, makeup, instrument techs, assistants, managers, friends of managers, haulers of heavy things, chefs, doctors, etc. First you have to hire most of them.

This alone would take a lifetime, because all of them have to be the best at what they do. You can't find these folks in the Yellow Pages. You get to know them through experience.

George started as a trucker, moving stage equipment and stages themselves from one venue to the next. Over the years he rose through the ranks and became the boss. Along the way he met and remembered key people. The real pros, the players who can get this done and get it done right the first time without asking stupid questions. He found people who anticipated. People who could suss out a situation and have a maximum amount of effect with a minimum amount of effort, which creates time to do other things. It is a huge job. George did the Pope's tour. He is the man.

Once you've assembled and hired all those people, and you've purchased or rented all the equipment you'll need, and you've got the trucks and the planes and the hotel rooms, you put this behemoth into motion. The entire circus moves every two to three days. It moves across the country and around the world. And it has to move smoothly and on time. Bruce and the band have to walk out onstage in Paris Tuesday night at eight o'clock and everything has to be in place and ready for them. Just like it was backstage and at the hotel and on the plane.

But George gets it done without sweating. He doesn't yell or scream; he inspires. Everybody wants to be at his or her very best for him. He moves all this stuff and all these people and all these egos, and he does it with grace and style. Like in the Pogues song, George Travis is so cool he could've put out Vietnam.

"How's it going, George?" I said.

"Fine," he said with that little smile of his that seems to say, *What've you got for me? Bring it on.*

"You busy?" I asked. The question was meant to be absurd. It was twenty minutes before showtime.

"Not really," he said.

"I need you to confirm a story for me," I said.

"Uh-oh," he said. "This could be trouble."

"No, it's nothing dangerous or illegal," I said. "Clarence told me a story about his right eyeball, and I want to know if it really happened or if he's just fucking with me."

"Houston," George said. "We were in another city, maybe Dallas, and Clarence started having trouble with the vision in his right eye. It was after the show. He described what he was seeing as a curtain coming down over his eye. It sounded serious, and I knew there was a hospital in Houston that specialized in eyes, so I put him in a car and drove him there."

Let's pause for a moment and think about what George said and how he said it. With very little information he went directly to the story with no wasted words. He recognized that Clarence's symptoms were serious. He didn't try to treat him. He knew there was a hospital in Houston that specialized in eyes, and he drove Clarence there himself. George is a very good person to travel with.

"So we're in the hospital, it's maybe two o'clock in the morning, and this guy in a suit walks by and recognizes Clarence. Turns out the guy is one of the leading eye surgeons in the world, and just happened to be there after giving a speech to a bunch of doctors. He stops and asks Clarence what was going on, and Clarence described his symptoms.

"'How's your tolerance for pain?' he asks Clarence.

"'Pretty good,' says Clarence.

"'Okay,' the doctor says, 'let's take a look.'

"And then," George says, "he puts what looks like a finger condom on his little finger and inserts it into the corner of Clarence's right eye and pops out his eyeball."

"That's what Clarence told me, but I thought he was bullshitting," I said.

"He wasn't," said George. "He looks in the back of the eye and says, 'Yeah, I can fix that. Check him into the hospital and I'll come back at nine and make this as good as new,' and then he pops the eye back into the socket and leaves. It was the damndest thing I've ever seen in my life. Sure enough, he's there at nine, fixes Clarence's eye, and he doesn't even miss a show. Amazing."

Everyone who works with George has a George story. Wayne Lebeaux has my favorite.

Wayne was the traveling secretary for the Boston Celtics for eighteen years, and he was looking to do the same thing in the world of traveling shows. George was an old friend, and Wayne decided to call him and basically ask for a job. George lives on a remote farm in Massachusetts, and when he's not running a traveling circus he does things like plow a field with an ox. This is true. His life at home is the opposite of his work life. His desire to simplify his home life extends to his telephone.

It doesn't ring.

It doesn't ring because George disabled the ringer.

If he wants to talk to somebody he calls them. Otherwise the phone doesn't ring. Ever.

Wayne didn't know this when he called.

George picked up the phone in his house to make a call and did not hear a dial tone.

He pressed a few buttons attempting to make his call and heard Wayne say, "George?"

Wayne got the job. He spent years as road manager for Bruce and the band, Bruce as a solo artist, Ringo Starr, and whoever else George agrees to bless with his expertise. When Terry Magovern passed away, Wayne did his best to fill in for him and is currently Bruce's right-hand man.

If you ever find yourself backstage at a Bruce concert a few minutes before showtime, when tensions are running the highest and the anxiety can actually be seen on people's faces and the crowd is growing in volume and anticipation and everybody's eyes are darting around and their movements get quicker and their responses a little louder and a lot more clipped, look around for the calmest person you can find. Look for the guy who seems to have nothing to do and looks like he doesn't have a care in the world. Cross over to him and say hello to George Travis. If you're backstage he'll already know who you are.

The Legend of Clarence
and Annie at Fenway,
Boston, 2004

This is another one of my hospital dreams. I had lots of them in the fall of 2008. To escape the pain I took these incredible flights of fancy. Still, almost everything I say in this one is true. —C.C.

He's going to steal," she said.

She and Clarence were in the first row of Monster Four. They had the two aisle seats but, like everyone else in the park, they were standing.

"You think?" asked Clarence.

"Oh, yeah. That's why he's here," she said.

Dave Roberts stood on the bag at first. He was Beantown's best and probably final hope. He needed to get into scoring position.

"It's not like Rivera to be walking guys," said Clarence.

Roberts stole second.

"If he scores and ties this thing, the building will fall down," she said.

The hot dog guy came by.

"Want a dog?" asked Clarence.

"I'm a vegan, Clarence. You know that."

"I think you should be allowed to eat anything that would eat you," said Clarence.

"Would a pig eat you?" she asked.

"Only a really hungry pig," said Clarence.

"Hey, you're Clarence Clemons," said the hot dog guy.

"How you doing, man?" said Clarence.

"I saw you guys in Hartford in seventy-eight," the guy said.

"You were the guy in the hat, right?" said Clarence.

The guy laughed.

"You recognize her?" Clarence asked.

"Should I?" the guy said.

"Yeah," said Clarence. "Ever hear of the Eurythmics?"

"No shit? Yeah, that's her. Cool," said the guy.

"C'mon, Mueller!" yelled Annie.

Mueller hit a single up the middle. Roberts scored from second. Fenway went batshit crazy.

Between innings, they sat.

"Was it better before there were chicks in the band?" she asked.

"Better? No," he replied. "It's different but everything evolves. Our new stuff is our best stuff. Always been that way."

"Tough having men and women together in a band. Killed me and Dave."

"Fleetwood Mac," said Clarence.

She laughed. "A bloodbath," she said.

"It's just that in the early days it was just the guys, you know?" he said. "All for one and that shit. Drinking, getting laid, playing…it was like the ultimate boys' club."

"Dave and I were drunk with each other at the outset," she said.

"Outset," he repeated. "That's like really English. The outset."

"Scottish," she said.

"Right," he said. "I don't think we've ever played up there. I don't know why, but I don't think we have."

"Oh, you've got to see the Highlands before you die, Clarence. They're so beautiful I'm hoping to see them after I die."

A scoreless tenth and eleventh passed. The crowd screaming or cringing with each pitch.

The hot dog guy came back and got autographs for his daughter. He asked them to make the autographs out to "Hector."

"Your daughter's name is Hector?" asked Clarence.

"Yeah," said the guy.

In the top of the twelfth Manny singled to left. Ortiz was at the plate, with Quantrill on the mound for New York.

"Can you imagine a future without Bruce?" she asked.

"I've had to from time to time," he said. "It's okay, but it's not as good."

"Do you think he feels the same way about you?"

"Yeah. I think he does," he said.

"I loved you guys on the *Born to Run* cover," she said. "Everybody did. This black guy and this white guy playing together...."

"I'm on the back," he said.

"What?"

"I'm not on the front of the cover. I'm on the back. I'm talking about the album as it came out. You've got to turn it over to see me. That's how they printed it."

"Really?"

"Really."

"Are you sure?"

"I'm sure."

"Huh," she said.

Then David Ortiz clocked a two-and-one pitch into the bullpen for a walk-off home run.

"Big Papi," he said.

"Red Sox," she said.

"Same thing," he said.

Don

Los Angeles is always a weird place for the band. There are so many celebrities who are fans and so many agents and managers all seeking special treatment or, at least, an acknowledgment of their specialness that it gets...well, strange. In other words, the place is filled with jerks like me. One unique thing that I've witnessed is a noncelebrity fan knocking over actual celebrity fans to get closer to Clarence. I saw a hefty young woman holding a *Born to Run* album and a magic marker knock Matthew McConaughey into another time zone because he was standing between her and the Big Man.

The show-biz crush can be overwhelming. At Dodger Stadium in 2003, there were two aftershow parties, one in the traveling E Street lounge, and another, smaller one in the band's tent compound. Tom Hanks was not in the E Street lounge.

Going backstage after the show is odd if you're not actually personal friends with whatever performer you've just seen. After "Great show," and/or "I saw you guys in Philly," there's not a whole lot to say. The only person I've ever seen backstage who looked like he belonged there, besides other musicians, was Chuck Zito of the Hells Angels. Chuck can go anywhere he wants to go and he's at home. Another guy who came to the Temple of Soul and fit right in was another Chuck—Chuck Plotkin, the famous producer/engineer of so many Springsteen classics as well as tons of Bob Dylan tracks, and many others. His was a name I recognized from years of reading album credits, but I couldn't remember ever seeing his face. He talked easily and almost instantly about mortality, one of Clarence's favorite subjects. Chuck said when he turned sixty he could hear the clock ticking, so he and his wife bought a boat and took off, sailing through Polynesia for two years. Chuck became my new hero.

Backstage at a Springsteen show is not like the wild crazy days of old, the "sex, drugs, and rock and roll" days. Yes, there are women around, but I've never witnessed any overt groupiness. Clarence has been known to have a shot of Patrón before going onstage (okay, maybe more than one), but, outside of legitimate prescription medicines, the most exotic drug I've seen is Lipitor. The thing runs like a clock. This is due to Bruce's personality and to the aforementioned George Travis, the man who produces everything but the music. He's the first person I've seen upon arriving at every venue, and his demeanor remains the same in all circumstances: placid.

In fact, everyone I've encountered operates at the highest level of professionalism. And some of the jobs that need to get done are unusual. For instance, consider that it takes at least five people to assemble the Clarence Clemons you see onstage. "Before they get to me I'm just a broken-down old man," he says. But the combined talents of his assistant, his personal trainer and physical therapist, various doctors, and the hair and makeup artists produce the transformation from old man into a rock-and-roll icon. He then gets the handwritten set list from the Boss, runs through the night's songs (although Bruce rarely sticks to the initial list), and stands in the hallway leading to the stage. He's always first. When Bruce exits his dressing room, Clarence says, "Boss man walking! Boss man walking!" Then the rest of the band arrives. They form a circle of solidarity and then head out to, in the words of the late Terry Magovern, "conquer yet another city."

Clarence

"Did you ever get to see Count Basie?" I asked Don.

"Oh, yeah," he said. "Several times in Vegas. He was playing at the Tropicana, and I was with Slappy White at the Flamingo."

"You worked with Slappy White?" I said.

"My first job in show business was playing straight man for him and writing jokes. We were on the road for almost three years in the sixties. Our first gig was opening for Jackie Wilson at the Apollo in 1967."

"You're an unusual white man," I said to my old friend. It's true, he is.

"Thank you," he said. "Anyway we were on the bill with Wayne Cochran and the C.C. Riders."

"Oh, shit," I said. "I remember him from Miami. Big, tall white guy with huge hair, right? Sang like Otis Redding?"

"That's him. He had ten horns. First trumpet player was also his hairdresser. Wayne was wild. He dressed like Elvis even offstage. Used to walk around the casino in a spangled jumpsuit with a cape. Had his wife on one arm and his girlfriend on the other. I hear he's a preacher now back in Georgia."

"I heard that, too."

"But I actually got to hang out with Count Basie. He used to like the old keno lodge at the Flamingo, and I met him and Sarah Vaughan there every night at six o'clock to play keno for a month," he said.

"Sarah Vaughan? No shit?"

"No shit," he said. "She was playing across the street at Caesars, and she and Bill were old friends, and we all had this keno jones, so we sat there every night playing five-dollar tickets. Nobody ever won much that I remember. They would just sit around telling stories and shooting the breeze. Basie wore this Greek fisherman's hat all the time."

"Do you remember any of the stories?" I asked.

We were in Campagnola on First Avenue on the Upper East Side. We had just ordered pastas and osso bucco with spinach in garlic and oil. We were drinking a bottle of Sassicaia.

"Not one," he said. "I was young and stupid and had no real sense of who these people were. We talked mostly about keno. I remember Redd Foxx came by a couple of times. I know we laughed a lot. But that's about all I've got. I did go across the street to see Sarah one night, and I was blown away. I mean the woman could actually bend a note in a way that would break your heart. She's the best singer I've ever heard in my life. We went up to see Basie twice. This was during the time that Sonny Payne was the drummer. Fantastic showman. Bill, not so much. He'd sit there at the piano and play a few notes and smile, but mostly he let the players play. That band had such incredible power. And they were playing in a small room. It was great."

"You were just a kid in Vegas when it was really Vegas," I said.

"Well, old-school Vegas," he said. "It's probably wilder now than it was then. It's just that it was so much smaller. Everybody knew everybody. We'd go to a club after work and it would be filled with people working other shows on the Strip. I learned to take my sunglasses with me when I left for work at night, because when you walked out of one of those clubs at six in the morning the sun was vicious."

"Yeah," I said. "When the sun comes up before you go to bed it feels like it's calling you an asshole."

"And it's right," he said.

"How many shows did you do a night?"

"Three in the lounge. It was a rotating schedule with Wayne, the Kim Sisters, and us. One night a week we went on last at two in the morning. That was a disaster because Wayne did this big show at one o'clock, and when he was done everybody left. One night we went out there and there was nobody in the room," said Don.

"Nobody?"

"Just the waitresses and the maitre d'," he said. "And the rule was you had to do at least forty-five minutes."

"What did you do?"

"Well, at first we just ordered drinks and played a few games of keno, because you could see the board across the casino from the stage. Then some guy stopped at the door. He was an older guy with a white beard. So Slappy says, 'Hey, Santa, come on in and sit down. I'll buy your drinks.' So the guy comes in, sits in front of the stage, and we start doing the act."

"For this one guy?"

"Yup. Plus we're buying him drinks. Anyway, about twenty minutes into the act he gets up and walks out on us."

"No!"

"Just walked right out. He hadn't laughed once anyway, so we didn't try to stop him. It was maybe the funniest thing that had happened in that room in years."

The pastas arrived. I had the special ravioli with ricotta, and Don had the penne with chicken sausage and a tomato sauce. We drank more wine and ordered a second bottle.

"There was a two-week period where we did five shows a night," he said. "The three in the lounge and two in the main room with Connie Stevens."

"How did that happen?" I asked.

"The comic who was booked with her had to drop out at the last second, I don't know why. Anyhow, we started out doing the dinner show at eight o'clock, which was about two hours after we woke up. I remember the smell of roast beef in the room filled with all these people who'd been up all day playing golf or sitting by the pool, and I hadn't had breakfast yet."

"It was like that for me and Bruce in the club days," I said. "We slept all day and stayed up all night every night. If I tried that now it would kill me."

"Me, too," said Don. "Connie Stevens was a lovely woman who had gotten famous on a TV show called *Hawaiian Eye*. She played a character called Cricket. In any event, she also sang and danced and put on a hell of a show. So she finds out that this is my first time in Vegas.

"'That means you're good luck,' she says, and asks me to come to the crap table with her between shows. So I go with her. I'm her good-luck charm, right?"

"Right," I said.

"In twenty minutes she lost a bunch of money."

"Oh, fuck," I said, laughing.

"I don't remember how much, but it seemed like a fortune to me," he said. "It's funny now, but at the time I was horrified. I felt guilty and frightened and I don't know what else."

"She liked to gamble, huh?"

"Well she did that night. Somebody in the hotel told me about all the entertainers who gambled there. Told me that Fats Domino was into them so deep that he'd be working there for free for the rest of his life. I don't know if that's true, but that was the story."

I had heard similar horror stories over the years about entertainers getting in debt to the company store. It was a scary thought, so I put it aside and concentrated on dinner.

"This ravioli is fantastic," I said.

A woman came over to the table from the bar. "You're Clarence Clemons," she said.

"Guilty," I said.

"I've seen you guys fifty times," she said.

"Really?" I replied.

"Well, at least ten," she said. "Can I get a picture with you?"

"Sure," I said. I always try to say yes.

She handed Don her cell phone, pulled out the empty chair next to me, and slid over. She put her left shoulder up against my right shoulder, looked at the camera, and smiled. Don had been through this before. He was there to snap the picture and hand the camera back to her. There was no need to speak to him unless she needed to give him instructions on how to operate the camera function on her phone. It's not the easiest thing to hang around with me. You have to put up with being ignored and interrupted all the time. I know how much this annoys Don, and that amuses me.

He took the picture and then another one just to be on the safe side, because everybody always says to do that.

She reached out and snatched the phone out of his hand, looked at the pictures, then, seemingly satisfied, stood up.

"Thank you so much," she said to me. "I love you guys."

"Love you, too," I said.

She went back to bar and showed the pictures to the people she was with.

"I hope she gets hit by lightning," said Don.

That made me laugh. "So did Connie talk to you after you'd cost her a big bunch of cash?" I said.

"It was as if it never happened. She was married to Eddie Fisher at the time. The next night he comes backstage with a huge bag of black chips. He was coming from the tables where he'd just won something like twice what she had lost."

"Jesus," I said. I never caught the gambling bug, thank God.

"Yes," he answered. "But years later Connie was one of the first people to use the Home Shopping Network successfully. She made a fortune selling cosmetics and got really, really rich."

"I love a happy ending," I said.

The Motorcade, Part II

Don

We got into the city of London itself and we didn't slow down. I felt like I was on Mr. Toad's Wild Ride.

"I'm going to call Kate," said Judy.

Kate Merrick-Wolf was an old friend of ours, an artist now living with her family outside of the city. Cell phones now made it possible to be in touch with everyone all the time, so a few minutes later Kate was on the phone.

Kate was a huge fan of the band and of Clarence, and she had been to many shows when she lived in California and also here in England. Other obligations had prevented her from attending the shows here this week.

"Hold on," said Judy. "I'll put him on."

I reached out for the phone but Judy handed it to Clarence.

"Say hello to my friend Kate," she said.

Clarence took the phone. Clarence always takes the phone.

"Hey, baby," he said. "What's happening? Yeah, it's really me. No shit." He laughed and listened. "The sirens? We're being chased by the police. Bruce stole some towels from the hotel and they called the cops." We could hear Kate's laugh from the backseat. The Big Man listened some more. "Well, next time you'll come to the show and I'll show you the Temple of Soul. You got it. All right, see you then. Bye." And he handed the phone back to Judy.

Kate was thrilled beyond beyond. And in December 2007 she did go to see the band when they came back through London and did in fact get to visit the Temple of Soul.

Kate died on September 23, 2008, after a four-year battle with cancer. There are circles within circles, and in the end we all share the same fate. As they say in the circus, "We're all Bozos on this bus." I miss her. I miss her big laugh and her fierce intelligence. I know how much pleasure music brought to her and how much she loved Bruce and the band. I know how special that meeting with Clarence was. I know how she escaped from her pain and fear for the hours she spent in the arena that night. I know that that is priceless. I know that it's a form of magic.

There is relief when someone's pain finally ends, but there will always be a void in the time and space they occupied. The balance of our lives is upset by death, and memories help us regain our footing. I remember the sound of Kate's voice when she called to talk about the show and meeting the Big Man, and that makes me feel a little better today.

September 23 is also Bruce Springsteen's birthday. I hope it's a happy one. He has brought so much happiness to others, he deserves some of his own.

Clarence

One night Victoria, Don, and I went to the Hard Rock to see Chris Rock perform. At dinner before the show I was in a lot of pain. My back problems seemed to be getting worse.

I try not to whine or complain, but Don says it hurts him to watch me walk. Stairs are my enemy.

I was okay through the show. Chris was his usual brilliant self, and afterward we made our way backstage. No matter who you are, there is always a stand-around time when waiting to see a performer. The stars, me included, need a few minutes alone to come down from the performance or to take a shower or whatever. This, combined with people—usually drunk people—who are trying to get backstage and overzealous security people often leads to uncomfortable situations. I just leaned against a wall and suffered through it. By the time we got to see Chris about ten minutes later I had reached tap city, and I just couldn't hang out.

The nice people at the hotel produced a golf cart to take Victoria and me to my car. I felt badly about not spending more time with Chris, but sometimes things just are what they are.

The tour would begin in Hartford in sixteen days.

"Are you going to be ready?" Don asked me.

"There's no choice," I said. "I'll be ready. I don't know if it'll take medication, magic, or miracles, but I'll be ready."

On his way back to his room on the fifth floor of the North Tower in the Hard Rock Hotel, Don was startled to find a display box by the elevator he had somehow failed to see earlier. For the uninitiated, the Hard Rock chain is decorated with rock-and-roll memorabilia ranging from gold records to guitars and articles of clothing. Combined with an aging baby-boomer clientele here in Florida, the whole thing is a little depressing. What startled him was a box behind Plexiglas containing a leather vest and a picture of Bruce and me onstage. In the photo I'm not wearing the vest. A sign proclaims that I wore this vest on the "River" tour.

Don called me.

He told me what he was looking at and asked if it was mine and if so how did it end up here next to the elevators on the fifth floor of a hotel. I said I had no clue.

Don took four pictures of the vest and the display and sent them to me. He stood in front of the vest and awaited my reply. It came less than a minute later in the form of a one-word e-mail.

It said, *Fake!*

Don

Somebody once said that there are only six hundred people in the world and the rest is done with mirrors. I have marked my life by a series of coincidences, which probably stem from what I do for a living. Show business is a world unto itself, and that world is relatively small. But still there are things that cross each other in ways that are a little eerie.

"There's someone else here who's in show business," said the host.

"Really?" I said. "Who?"

"Come with me," he said.

He led me through the crowd into another room of the massive apartment. There, in the center of the room wearing a black suit, stood Robert Altman.

I'm not good at parties. I was especially uncomfortable at this party because I knew no one and had very little in common with the other folks who were there. The party was attended by the society crowd and was held at 555 Park Avenue. There was no occasion for it, just the opportunity to get together and celebrate each other's fabulousness, which might be the best reason to ever do anything as a group. The doorman directed my wife and I to the elevator and said the apartment we were looking for was on the tenth floor. The entire tenth floor.

My wife had a friend who had lived for years with the woman who owned the place. He had become part of this Upper East Side society and loved hosting these get-togethers. We were on our way back to California, having just spent several weeks traveling with Clarence, Bruce, and the E Street Band. That group was a lot easier to hang with than this one.

I found a spot in a corner and was generally miserable when he noticed my plight and led me to Mr. Altman, whom I had never met.

"Bob," he said, "this is Don Reo. He's in show business, too."

Robert Altman turned and looked at me.

"I'll let you two talk shop," said the host as he left.

Mr. Altman extended his hand. "Nice to meet you," he said.

"Likewise," I said.

"You're in show business?"

"Yes, I write and produce TV shows," I said.

"Are you holding?"

"What?" I said.

"Do you have a joint?" he asked.

"No," I said.

He turned around and walked away.

It was one of my favorite moments in life. I had no dope and Robert Altman had no use for me. I stood there and laughed out loud. I went back into the living room to tell my wife what had happened and found her talking to another show business dude, the actor Peter Boyle. She introduced us, and this time I really did have a lot to say as we were both employed in the world of situation comedy. Peter was great and smart and friendly and made the rest of my time at the party a real pleasure.

But once again everything seems to be connected to everything else in surprising ways.

Four years later, after both Peter Boyle and Robert Altman had passed away, I found myself back in New York. I was walking around the upper reaches of Madison Square Garden during a show on the "Magic" tour. Bruce was onstage introducing the beautiful "Meeting Across the River."

"I'd like to dedicate this song to an old friend who passed away awhile back," he said. "He was one of the first people we met when we came to New York City and today would've been his birthday. This is for Peter Boyle."

Until that moment I had no idea that Bruce had even heard of Peter Boyle. It brought me back to that party and made me realize once again how tentative life is and how important it is to savor every day. It sounds trite, I know, but I also know that death doesn't fuck around and that it's waiting around some corner for all of us, and once you make that turn you're not coming back. Order the good wine.

Clarence

I was rocking a chocolate-colored Charlie Tweddle cowboy hat with a snakeskin band and a yellow feather, as I stood on the waterfall platform of the Glencalive Estate, on the River Carron in the Scottish Highlands, and cast my line into the root beer-colored water.

A soft, steady rain had been falling all morning. I wore a long oilskin coat from Australia and the waterproofed leather boots I had made in Spain. The rain was gentle enough to allow me to smoke a cigar. Today it was a fine Cuban Montecristo #2 I'd bought in London before heading up here on the overnight train to Inverness.

I was fishing for salmon.

In the distance I could see smoke tying the chimneys in the big house to the sky. I took meals there with the others, but I was staying at the remote stone lodge five miles away in the hills. *Remote* didn't quite describe the splendid isolation of the place. The estate was comprised of twenty-five thousand acres, which meant if you stood in the center of it you could walk about ten miles in any direction and still be on the property. The lodge overlooked a mountain loch.

I had come here to relax and unwind after the European leg of the tour.

I had another ten days before I climbed onstage again, and I was happy to spend that time here in this faraway corner of Scotland. A woman I knew had told me about this place and had set me up here through the owner, an English publisher whom she had known for years.

It was spring, and the stalking season hadn't begun. The herds of deer could be seen and felt thundering through the glen a mile below the lodge where I sat at night smoking and sipping whiskey in a beautiful wooden chair hand-built by the genius Petter Southall. It stayed light here until near midnight. I'd been told that the midges would eat me alive, but they didn't like my cigar or, I guess, dark meat.

I loved it here. It was high, wild country and it made me feel closer to God.

The fish weren't biting, so I sat in one of the dark green wooden chairs in the gazebo on the platform. I loved the sound of the rain on the metal roof. I took out a book I'd been reading. It was called *Someday This Pain Will Be Useful to You* by Peter Cameron. It was about a latter-day Holden Caulfield struggling to feel something. It brought to mind the Warren Zevon's lines "I'm going to hurl myself against the wall / 'Cause I'd rather feel bad than not feel anything at all." I read for a while then sat back and, like Zimmy, just watched the river flow. The sound of the waterfall had a hypnotic effect, and soon I was drifting, floating and flying on the wings of my imagination. It was as if my left lobe shut down and euphoria took me to the beaches and lovers from somewhere in my past. I was somewhere in honey-colored sunlight with honey-colored women and felt strong and fit and young.

These were the moments when things came to me. Today it was this image of a room on a sandy tropical shore somewhere that may or may not have been real. No matter. It was mine now and the languid, louche feeling of it would convert easily into music. The music I began to hear now. I started humming involuntarily, the sound flowing from me like maple syrup, all thick and slow and sweet and good.

The feeling of the room and the rain and the rushing water and the soft wind conspired and collaborated to produce this sound. "It sounds

like butterscotch," I said aloud. That's what I'd call it—"Sounds Like
Butterscotch," or maybe just "Butterscotch." Better. I ached to have the
horn right there so I could play it, but that would have to wait. Before
every performance I prayed the same prayers. One was "Let this horn
touch someone tonight." Tonight would be no different. I'd climb the
hill overlooking that green valley filled with mist and magic, and I'd
play it for no one and for everyone and the music would fall, tumbling
and rolling down to the water, and mix with the cold streams and the
heather, and for a little while I would be transported to a place of peace
both inside and out.

There was something about the Scottish Highlands that spoke to
me. There was a huge masculine beauty to the place. It was both hard
and soft at the same time. There was a great sense of peace tempered by
the faint scent of ancient blood on stone. Life felt a little more real to me
here. This was a place of basics. Wind and water and wood and rocks. I
could feel time passing here, a feeling I was unable to touch anywhere
else in the world.

And the people were smart and funny. They were as smart and as
funny as any group of people I'd ever met, including the community of
professional comedy writers. The Scots had that same sharp wit and the
dark streak in their souls that put them in touch with outrageousness. If
they didn't have a penchant for killing each other they would've ruled
the world. But while the clans fought over the small things, the English
moved north and stole the country.

Now here in the far North Country full dark had arrived, and I went
back into the stone lodge and built a fire. I sat in front of it on the leather
couch and felt where I was. Alone in a small house in a remote corner of
a foreign country in the blackest of nights, with the cold wind now carrying more rain, which began tapping on the windows. The logs hissed
and crackled. I took off my boots and put my feet up on the wooden table.
The heat from the fire felt good. I did not want the moment to end.

Boat ride in Scandinavia, 2008. This looks so peaceful, but we were surrounded by boatloads of paparazzi. *Credit: Lani Richmond*

Monday Night Football band. This was the second best band I ever played with. *Credit: JoLopezPhotography.com*

The authors at work. This is me and Don at the Trump Hotel in NYC making up a whole new bunch of lies. *Credit: Judith D. Allison*

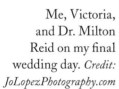

Me, Victoria, and Dr. Milton Reid on my final wedding day. *Credit: JoLopezPhotography.com*

The shrine onstage—Terry Magovern with Sri Chinmoy; Danny; me and Dick Moroso. I look at these pictures everytime I'm on the stage and celebrate my departed friends. They're all still with me. *Credit: JoLopezPhotography.com*

Scooter and the Big Man still having fun after all these years.
Credit: JoLopezPhotography.com

On stage with my son Christopher, 2007. What a night this was. I loved playing "Dancing in the Dark" with my son. *Credit: JoLopezPhotography.com*

After surgery, 2008. Me and Lani Richmond. The room had a great view but I didn't see it. By the time I came to, I was in another room.
Credit: Victoria Clemons

Danny. I will miss him every day that I'm alive. *Credit: JoLopezPhotography.com*

This is a unique perspective of the band at the end of a show.
Credit: JoLopezPhotography.com

Smoking in Spain. This was taken at a great place in the hills outside of San Sebastián. George Travis, Jon Landau, and Bruce were all there at other tables. We can't get away from each other even if we try. *Credit: Damon Wayans*

Damon Wayans and sunburned Bruce in Spain. Damon kept everybody laughing all night. *Credit: Don Reo*

Victoria and I going home in New York City just before dawn. Don took this picture from the limo when we got back from "The Ride Home" show. One of the best I can remember.
Credit: Don Reo

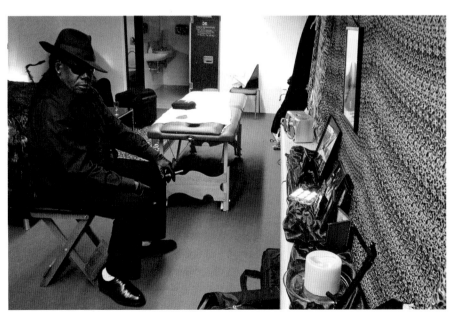

That's me in the Temple of Soul—Boston version. I'm locked and loaded.
Credit: JoLopezPhotography.com

Super Bowl. This is a great photo taken by my friend Jo Lopez during the half-time show. Even I have to admit that this is pretty cool.
Credit: JoLopezPhotography.com

Me and Bruce. What can I say? It feels like the *Born to Run* cover but it also stands on its own. I think this is a beautiful image that captures the relationship we have and the humor, the camaraderie, and the mystery of our friendship. I especially like the fact that it's black and white. *Credit: N.F.L. Photo*

Clarence

By six o'clock in the evening Islamorada is legally drunk. The sun sets early this time of year, and no one wants to face the darkness without fortification. We entered this broken-down dive bar on the gulf side of the road at six-thirty and found the place jammed with seriously monstered rednecks, hooting and hollering and stumble-dancing to a Jimmy Buffett cover band led by our fishing guide, Chris Miller. Some of these people, maybe most, were drunk from two days ago.

"In the Keys," Don said, "every night is Saturday night."

I had agreed to sit in, and apparently the word had spread because the place was packed. There was a rumor going around that Billy Joel was also stopping by because he and I had met that morning while having breakfast at Lor-E-Lei's, but I was there and Billy Joel wasn't. Besides, there was no piano in the joint even if he did show up. We pushed our way through the crowd, who broke into cheers when they saw me, and made our way to the stage. Don was carrying the horn in its case, while my assistant had the bag of things I always have with me. It contains medicines, reeds, pads, and some form of adult beverage and all kinds of other stuff. My paramour, Victoria, was also there, looking as out of place as a swan in the desert. Victoria is tall, elegant, twenty-nine, and

Russian. She in fact resembles the tennis star Maria Sharapova but is more beautiful. I swear she could charm a hungry dog off a meat wagon. I got set up while Victoria and Don squeezed into the two seats saved for them at a front table, which included some very drunk women and at least two kids. Seeing children in a bar is unusual, but then again this is the Keys. The kids were both blond and obviously brothers, about ten and twelve years old. I found out later that the older boy, AJ, was celebrating his birthday. It turned out to be one I'm sure he'll never forget.

Don had gotten to the hotel here in the Florida Keys a few hours ahead of us the day before. I called him when we got to the hotel to talk about dinner plans and fishing plans, and something else.

"I think there's going to be a wedding soon," I said.

I had been thinking about marrying Victoria for weeks. Last night we had discussed various locations where such a wedding could take place. I rejected the obvious suggestions of Vegas and Hawaii because I've already gotten married in those places. So we put the where of it aside.

"How soon?" he asked.

"Maybe soon," I replied.

"That's great," said Don. "As long as it doesn't fuck up the fishing."

That first night the four of us went out for dinner, and conversation turned from marriage to tequila, then (as it always does following tequila), life itself. Don tried to imagine what my life might have been like had I never met Bruce.

"I'd still be playing," I said. "Just in smaller rooms."

We were in a restaurant owned by a friend of mine. (At this point in time I have friends everywhere who own just about anything you can imagine.) The owner in this case was named Frank and was one of many men in the Keys who wears ponytails. I believe there are four hundred men in this country who still wear ponytails. Six of them live in Big Sur, four of them live on Maui, and the rest are in the Florida Keys.

Having dinner in any public place with me can sometimes be like attending a party. Everyone is in a good mood. They generally seem to feel fortunate, even blessed, that they chose the same place to eat that someone famous chose. They don't realize that I sometimes have really bad taste. People also like to buy me drinks. In fact it's difficult to pay for anything. This is one of the perks of fame that nobody talks about much. It's really, really nice.

I love it down here in the Keys. It is one of those end of the road places like Hana or Provincetown, where all that was once loose finally stops rolling. Many people here are outsiders and larger than life. Some are rich; the rest work for the rich. Two of them died in the days before our arrival. I read their obituaries in the morning paper.

A photograph that caught my eye accompanied the first. It was a headshot of a razor-thin guy with a tanned face wearing dark sunglasses and an old gimme cap. His black hair was pulled back into, you guessed it, a ponytail. He looked like he had spent his entire life on a bar stool drinking beer and smoking Marlboros. His name was John "Cockroach" Hart. He was from New Jersey but had been in the Keys for thirty years. He worked in the "fishing industry."

He had died of a heart attack. He was fifty-eight years old. A celebration of his life was to be held on Thursday afternoon at the Dog Pound bar in Marathon Key.

The second was Carl "Cappy" Carlson, also fifty-eight. Cappy was the owner of the "DUI cab company." A one cab operation that specialized in driving convicted DUI offenders to and from their DUI classes. After dropping off his charges the previous Saturday, Cappy had been stopped by the police and arrested for driving under the influence. He couldn't make bail and died in his sleep in his cell that night.

Rest in peace.

The next morning we made our way to Lor-E-Lei's, the funky waterfront open air restaurant in Islamorada. We ate fried egg sandwiches, drank coffee, and didn't see Billy Joel. (As it turned out later we may have passed Billy as he was walking in and we were walking out.) Chris Miller, our fishing guide and boat captain, arrived on a twenty-four-foot flat bottom Triton at about eight thirty, and we were loaded up and on the water by nine.

It was chilly at first, and Don was huddled behind the captain's chair, freezing. Victoria and I sat forward, looking like oddly matched figure-heads on the prow of the *Proud Mary*.

It turned out to be a beautiful day on the water. I caught four mangrove snappers, which we had for dinner that night. Chris caught a catfish that stabbed him with its poisonous barb while he was removing the hook. He swore and bled profusely, concerned mostly about being able to play his guitar that night. Fortunately I had a small taste of whiskey in my bag, which Chris poured on the wound. He said it also made sucking out the poison easier. It must have worked, because his hand didn't swell, and he was fine by the time we got back to the dock at three thirty.

But after our first day on the Triton we went back to the hotel, took naps, and left for the club at sunset. We stopped briefly so I could do a local radio show being broadcast from, of course, a bar. It was ostensibly a show about fishing but was actually a forum for the local gossip that fuels all small towns. We heard there that the club where I had agreed to sit in was jammed and had been for hours.

Most people hear something like a place being jammed and start to imagine difficulty parking or getting in. I never worry about stuff like that.

"My face is my pass," I said to Don once, and it's true.

It's easy for me to forget that I've been very famous for a very long time. Since the band still attracts young people, the size and scope of its fan base is vast.

"Do you realize what a magical life you're living?" Don asked me in the car on the way to the club.

"I do," I said.

"Most people don't get this kind of life. Most people can't even imagine it," he said.

I just smiled and pointed at the sky.

*   *   *

"My old boyfriend knew lots of famous people," said the drunk girl. "He knew Simon and Garfunkel."

"No kidding," said Don. "Both of them?"

"Yup." She nodded as she spoke. "And..."

She trailed off, trying hard to focus. It was after the show and the place was still electric, everyone ripping high and buzzed about what they had seen. Even I was stoked about what had happened earlier with the kid in the front row.

The drunk girl had simply plunked herself down next to us and started talking. She was skinny and slack-haired and on the dark side of forty, but we called her the drunk girl to distinguish her from the drunk woman, a fat, plastered sixty-year-old with a bleached blond Sandra Dee bouffant, wearing a muumuu and holding up the keys to her van.

"I can't find my passengers," she slurred.

"They're probably hiding," I said.

"From you," Don added.

"I'm the designated driver," she announced. "I've only had two beers."

"Jonathan Winters's brother," the drunk girl finally finished.

"People say I'm drunk but I'm not," said the drunk woman. "That's bullshit."

"Chilly?" I said to the drunk girl.

"No, I'm warm," she said.

"No, Jonathan Winters's brother...is his name Chilly Winters?" I smiled. "Or Long Dark Winters?"

She considered that. "No," she concluded.

"Juss bullshit," said the drunk woman, as she wandered away. "I can drive."

"I know Jonathan Winters," Don said to the drunk girl, "and I don't think he has a brother. If he does, I can't remember him mentioning it."

"My ex-boyfriend knew his brother," she said.

"The Simon and Garfunkel ex-boyfriend?" I asked politely, trying to keep up.

"Yup. He knew lots of famous people," she said, then turned to Don. "You know Jonathan Winters?"

"Well," he said. "I've met him a few times."

He had in fact met Mr. Winters a few times over the years. Most notably on the street in Montecito or at the drugstore coffee shop, where he often holds court for hours.

"He's a great guitar player," said the drunk girl.

"Jonathan Winters is a great guitar player?" I said.

"So's his brother," she answered.

"Wait a minute," I said. "Is his brother's name Edgar?"

"Yes!" She smiled and actually applauded. "That's it."

"Johnny and Edgar Winter," Don said to me.

"You might have mentioned the fact that he's a fucking albino," I said. "That would've been a good clue."

Earlier the thing with the kid happened. The band had just begun the third song, a bluesy version of a '60's tune called "Rhythm of the Rain," when the kid at the front table started acting weirdly.

I thought it was strange enough to see kids in a place like this, but everything in the Keys is strange.

He was sitting to Don's left in a chair turned to face the stage. He'd been watching me intently, ignoring his little brother who kept coming up to him from somewhere in the crowd behind us and hitting him before running away. A woman I assumed was his mother appeared a few times to tousle his bushy blond hair and give him another Happy Birthday kiss on the cheek. Each time she did it he'd wipe his face. He was a husky kid who seemed to be very serious and very focused, which put him at odds with this chaotic environment. Along the way I'd gleaned that his name was AJ.

About ten seconds into the song he seemed to make some inner decision, to reach some conclusion to a problem he'd worked on for a long time, and he took action.

He leaned forward and pulled something out from under his chair. I could not see what it was. He was bent over fiddling with something on the floor. His movements were fast and practiced.

Finally he finished and sat up, lifting the object in front of him.

It was a saxophone.

The people around the kid saw the horn and began to cheer. They all knew him and began to chant, "AJ! AJ! AJ!"

I smiled at him and with one finger beckoned him up onto the stage. The kid never hesitated.

He stepped onto the stage, turned sideways to the crowd, pointed his horn at mine, and began to play.

"I've had a lot of magical moments," I told Don and Victoria later. "But that was one of the best. When that kid started playing...I don't know...it was...everything."

Don showed me a picture he'd taken of us with his cell phone. I looked at it a long time.

"You know what this reminds me of?" I asked.

"What?"

"It sort of reminds me of me and Bruce," I said.

"Was the kid any good?" Victoria asked.

"He will be," I said. "But what he lacks in experience he makes up for in balls."

I looked at the picture again and smiled.

Don

I was walking across the tarmac toward the stairs leading to the door of the big rock-star jet that was going to take us to Ireland.

I was traveling with the band and the inner circle of assistants and managers who get to travel this way. Bruce was first up the stairs. Patti would follow in her own plane, as she and Bruce didn't fly together unless their kids were with them, the theory being that if one plane went down the kids wouldn't be orphans. Patti's plane was a Challenger 600; she was accompanied by her assistants and friends. On some days Soozie would fly with Patti but not today.

At the bottom of the stairs Jon Landau stopped next to me, extended his hand, and said, "Hi, I'm Jon Landau." Thereby inviting me to identify myself. The words he had used were "Hi, I'm Jon Landau," but everything else—body language, tone, and volume—all said, *And who the fuck are you?* (In my opinion Jon and Bruce have the best manager/artist relationship since Peter and Jesus.)

Things were fine after I identified myself as a guest of Clarence's, but it led me to ask Clarence if Bruce knew about me traveling with them on this flight.

"Bruce knows everything all the time," said Clarence.

It's hard to believe that this life of police escorts and private jets can become routine, but it does to those involved. It's another drive, another flight, another show. On these trips Bruce has a routine that dates back to the early days. He walks through the plane (or bus or whatever) and greets everybody on board before departure.

When he shook my hand that night I said, "Great show," referring to the performance earlier at Old Trafford. "Hey," he said. "That's my job." As he walked on toward the back of the plane Clarence turned to me.

"That's why he's the Boss," he said.

Clarence

It was December 10, and the band, now without Danny on the organ, was playing the Globe Arena in Stockholm as part of the "Magic" tour's European leg.

The Swedish crowd loved me and let me know. A chant of "We're not worthy!" began during my solo on "She's the One" and continued every time I stepped into the spotlight.

Eventually Bruce and the band started to chant along with the crowd. It was quite a scene.

This love was probably connected to the fact that I have ties to the country. Bruce calls me "the godfather of Swedish soul" during his introductions. My second wife, Christina, is Swedish, and I have always felt a deep connection to the place.

My son from that union, Christopher, now twenty-two years old, was at the show that night. He is a fine guitar player and, unbeknownst to me, was invited up onto the stage by Bruce to join us on "Dancing in the Dark."

For me, it was an astonishing moment. It's difficult to describe how it felt to be on that stage with my son. Especially on that song.

Why is that song so special? Because the day my wife told me that she was pregnant with Christopher was the exact same day we shot the video for "Dancing in the Dark." And here we were, twenty-two years later...It was very cool. In fact I think it might have been the best night of my life.

Don

The question I'm asked most is if Clarence and Bruce are really friends. Are they actually as tight as they appear to be onstage? The answer is yes. They are as close to being brothers as they can be. They have spent more time together in the E Street family than with their real relatives. At times their family has been dysfunctional, but all families are at one time or another. I have never seen or heard about any serious rift between Clarence and Bruce. I have seen many displays of love and respect and concern for each other. Except for Bruce's highly publicized decision to go out with a different band, I've heard of no problems between the two men. In fact, I think it's fair to say that Clarence is the biggest Bruce Springsteen fan I've ever met.

I was riding with Clarence to the Honda Center in Anaheim for the second of two shows. He was wearing earphones and rocking to music I couldn't hear. He had his eyes closed and he was smiling broadly.

At one point he laughed out loud and said, "God damn, this is good!"

He saw my look of curiosity and took off the earphones.

"'Light of Day' live," he said. "God, this guy is amazing!"

It took a second for me to realize that he was talking about Bruce.

Clarence could marvel at the Boss like every other fan, even though he's been standing next to him onstage for over thirty-five years.

Later in the Temple of Soul it was all Bruce all the time. Clarence played "Sad Eyes" over and over, followed by the beautiful falsetto performance on "Lift Me Up." When that song finished, Clarence shook his head in admiration.

"Sweet Jesus, he writes great songs," he said.

I guess it's obvious that I, too, have tremendous respect and admiration for Bruce Springsteen. And so does everyone I've met on the tour. I'm talking about roadies and personal assistants and bodyguards and other members of the band. Look to the sides of the stage at the next concert. You'll see friends and employees and occasionally celebrities singing along or watching the show with the same rapt attention as the rest of the audience.

There are a lot of celebrities who appear or are mentioned in this book. Elvis Presley once called me a namedropper.

I've seen the show a lot. I've seen the band perform live a lot. I saw them as an opening act, and I saw them do a four hour plus set in a tiny club. I have seen them in arenas and stadiums all over the world. I know these men and women personally. I have watched them grow and mature and survive for almost forty years now, and they keep getting better. When they take the stage now they take it with the weight of history and experience. They encompass all the others in rock who have gone before and include all who continue to play it now. They are, without question, the greatest rock and roll band in the world.

And there is a reason for that which lies beyond the brilliance of the songwriting and the arrangements, past the consummate showmanship and the dazzle and the lights and the screens and the energy of those audiences, something beyond the collective talent on and around the stage, and it's this: Bruce and Clarence.

Bruce and Clarence personify the dreams of the '60s, when we were all going to live together in peace and harmony. We may not have achieved those goals as a nation, but up there on that stage they do. Just like they did in Erik Meola's iconic photographs from so many years ago.

Black and white photographs. A black man and a white man who are brothers. That's what I see in these two men.

And some nights, once in a while, "the thing" happens.

It happened on the stage of the Student Prince the first time, but it might happen again tonight.

When the thing happens Bruce is more than Bruce. He carries the hopes and dreams and troubles and dark places of all who went before. When the thing happens Bruce is Sal Paradise and James Dean and Elvis and Otis and John Galt and Marlon Brando and Gene Vincent and Chet Baker and all the winners and losers and midnight gamblers and fringe players who ever had American dust on their boots; and Clarence is Jimmy Walker and Red Prysock and Stan Getz and Malcolm X and Gerry Mulligan and Iceberg Slim and all the Counts and Dukes and Kings and every black jazz musician who had to go in through the kitchen and every cool rockin' daddy who stood at the bar at the Metropole and watched Gene Krupa take drums into another dimension.

They stand on the stage and play like all the other nights and then, by some silent, ancient means of communication, they look at each other.

There are defining moments in the lives of men and women and nations.

I mentioned some of this to Clarence while we were sitting in the Temple of Soul, and he started talking about the first night at the Student Prince.

"At some point I turn and look over at him and he does the same thing at the same second, and there was this connection, and we both felt it and we both knew it was powerful and that our lives would be intertwined forever. I know it sounds like bullshit and it sounds faggy and all that shit, but it's as true as anything that I know in life. This thing just happened."

Bruce and Clarence are more than the sum of their parts. They are the whole package filled with dreams and aspirations and soul and talent and rhythm and *sha-la-las* and *bop-shu-bop*s and ass kicking guitar solos that make the girls act the way you want them to act, and they're

Leonard Cohen and Bob Dylan and Lord Buckley and Screaming Lord Sutch and all the Ronettes and Vandellas and Cadillacs and Infernos who ever put on sharkskin and stood on a stage and looked out into the darkness and opened their hearts and brought forth light. They are the complete contradiction and the complete explanation all in one moment, and the moment itself floats away, breaks away from time like an iceberg and floats into our collective memories of yesterday and our plans for tomorrow, and suddenly we're all in a car with no top on a summer night in a beach town with a hot, slow wind blowing, and our skin is sun kissed and soft and we're young and we're strong and the night is endless and we're headed for a better place.

Clarence

It was the last time Don and I went deep sea fishing. We spent the day aboard a sixty-foot sport fishing boat in the Atlantic Ocean. I had committed to this trip as part of a charity fund-raiser, a "Spend the day fishing with the Big Man!" silent auction item. The winners were three guys, Shelly, Chris, and Carl. Shelly and Carl had never seen me play and had barely heard of Bruce. Chris, a roofer who spent most of the day on his cell phone doing business, was a fan of sorts. He called me Mr. Clarence. After one of his calls — "I'm telling you those tiles better be on the dock in the morning!" — he snapped the phone shut, looked around at the turquoise ocean, and actually said, "This is great. I get to take a day off to recharge my batteries, and then tomorrow I'm back at work." Then he got another call. But they were charitable and generally pleasant people.

The seas today were what boat people call choppy. Nonboat people would call it hell. I like boats, but sometimes I have problems on the open ocean. Being on a boat at sea is like being on a floating prison. A prison from which there is no escape. It was worse for my assistant, Lani, who found out today that she gets seasick. She spent the endless eight hours curled into a fetal position in the cabin and wishing she'd never left Australia.

To make matters worse, the fish weren't biting, so the day was spent watching the kite from which the lines were strung. The first guy to do this (Rube Goldberg?) was a genuine genius. Eventually we collectively caught a few barracuda and a couple of dolphin. That day, I felt that catching fish was somewhat depressing. I often forget that the fish I eat was once a living thing that did not want to die.

I got bored after a few hours of kite watching, and we went inside. My fiancée, Victoria, stayed home today, because her last time out on the ocean she found out that she, too, was prone to seasickness.

"August sixteenth," I said to Don. "Save the date."

"For what?"

"On that day in Tiburon, California, I'm getting married for the last time," I said.

He congratulated me and called his wife to block out that weekend. Don has been around me enough to have lived through this before. A few times. But this has a different feel to it. I believe that Victoria, who was born in Siberia twenty-nine years ago, is in fact the perfect woman for me. I have never been this happy.

We talked about the road and the upcoming European leg of the "Magic" tour that was moving on to stadiums. We discussed my various ailments, including my bad hips, knees, and back. I've noticed that since the deaths of Terry and Danny, Bruce had become worried about me and had in fact asked the tour medical advisor to keep an eye on me.

"I've already got a ton of doctors," I said. "I don't need somebody else checking up on me like a babysitter. I'm a grown man."

In fact I had to write Bruce a letter and tell him that I appreciated his concern but I didn't need another person looking over my shoulder on the road to make sure I was eating my carrots. I'm there to do a job, and as long as I'm doing it well I'd prefer to be left alone. I said that I knew he was coming from a good place and I told him, "I know it's hard to believe but I actually love me as much as you love me. Maybe more."

"Did he answer?" Don asked.

"Yeah," I said. "He's great. He said he didn't mean to cause me any aggravation, and that he wants to keep doing this for a long time and that he wants me to be around. Hard to argue with that."

When we were returning to the dock the crew got excited when Alan Jackson, the country singer, passed going in the opposite direction aboard his boat *Hullbilly*. They seemed to think that I knew Alan and maybe they should turn our boat around and catch up with his and somehow lash the two together so that Alan and I could jam on one of the decks. I guess I put that notion to rest when I said, "Alan who?"

I told Don that I had played the rain forest concert last week at Carnegie Hall, and that I had run into Billy Joel and asked him if he had in fact been in Islamorada when we were there last February. He was. He said that he has a vacation home in Miami, and when he feels the urge to take a vacation from his vacation home he and a buddy put their motorcycles on a boat, take the boat somewhere, then take the motorcycles off the boat and drive around. One of those places was Islamorada. There are lifestyles and then there are lifestyles.

Our plans for the evening were still evolving. Either a chef was cooking at my place or we were going out for Chinese food. There was talk of going to a cigar bar to watch the sunset. This is often the way it is when you're hanging with me. You must remain flexible.

An hour later I sent Don the following text message: *You would not believe the shit I've been going through since I got home because I did not take her [Victoria] fishing. I'll call you in a few.*

I called him an hour later.

"It's unbelievable," I said. "She didn't want to go 'cause she got sick the last time, but apparently she wanted me to ask her to go even though I knew she didn't want to."

"Women are complicated," Don offered. "Relationships are complicated."

"I know. I've been in enough relationships and enough women to be aware of that, but I just don't understand this," I said.

"She didn't want to go, but she wanted you to ask her to go so that she would know that you wanted her to go, and then she would've said she didn't want to go," he said.

"That's just crazy."

"That's just women."

"I can't deal with this," I sighed.

"You keep talking like that and I'm going to have to rewrite this chapter," he said.

"Or write a new one," I replied.

Of course by the next morning this was all forgotten and life went on. Bruce had decided to add more shows, so the wedding date was moved up a week to August 8. We all went out to dinner that night and wound up in a cigar bar in a marina in West Palm Beach. Victoria shares my love of cigars, which, considering how much I like to smoke them, is a good thing. It's tough to hang with me if you're not cigar tolerant. (At least it was at that point in time. Now my cigar-smoking days are over.)

When I go anywhere down here I know that we're in for special treatment. It would be disingenuous to say I don't enjoy the attention that comes with fame. Don gets a big kick out of it. He says that it's fun to inhabit this glamorous world on a temporary basis. But that's bullshit 'cause Don's had a pretty glamorous life, too. I like to set Don up to tell some of his show-business stories and momentarily deflect the attention from me. That happened when an old guy with white hair that was way too long started talking about the first condo he bought in 1974 in a place called Inverrary.

"That's where Jackie Gleason lived," the guy said. "Everybody hated him."

I turned to Don and said, "Tell him some of your Gleason stories."

"You knew him?" the guy said.

"Actually I worked for him once in 1974 in Inverrary," Don said.

"Everybody hated him," the guy said.

"Yes," said Don. "He was not a nice guy. Brilliant but not nice."

"Everybody hated him," the guy said.

"I came down here for six weeks to help write a *Honeymooners* special," said Don.

"We met Gleason the first day outside of the tennis club they had there. It was about a hundred and sixty degrees. He sat with his back to the sun and ran down the show. He had most of it mapped out, and, in fact, we wrote the bulk of it that first week. The other writers were Allan Katz, Frank Peppiat and his partner John Aylesworth, and Gleason's guy, Walter Stone. Gleason would only look at and talk to Walter. If I asked him a question he would answer Walter. Walter, who was nearly bald, would break out in sweat along his former hairline whenever Jackie came into the room. We went to work on his opening monologue. I'll bet we wrote a hundred jokes a day. He asked for them to be put on separate pieces of paper, and he'd sit behind his desk while we watched him read them one at a time. Using one finger he'd slide a sheet of paper off the pile, look at it, then slide it to the other side of the desk and off it into a wastepaper basket.

"Walter said that after we left Gleason would go through the basket and pick out the jokes he liked."

"Everybody hated him," the guy said. "But his wife was an angel."

"I never met her," said Don. "He used to sneak around the condo where we were in the afternoon and peek in the windows to make sure we were working. It was six weeks of daily humiliation."

"Why did you do it and why did you take it?" I asked.

"To say we had done it. We had worked for the Great One. We had written lines for Ralph and Alice and Norton and Trixie. And that part of it was great. It's like you always say, 'I play the music for free, I get paid for all the bullshit,' right?"

"Right," I said.

"Anyway, at the end of all of this we finally move down to the Miami Beach Auditorium where the shows were shot. Gleason insisted it be fifty-five degrees inside the building. 'They don't laugh if they're warm,' he said. Frank and John and Allan and I moved to a hotel nearby at our own expense to avoid the hellish commute from Inverrary. Now you have to realize that Frank and John were rich. They had created and owned a show called *Hee Haw*, and after taking a considerable risk had cashed in big time by essentially syndicating the show themselves. So they didn't need Gleason's money; they just wanted to wear that T-shirt. I tell you this because of what happened the night of the show.

"We had one rental car they provided for us, so we drove over to the auditorium together. It was raining very hard that night. The kind of impossible tropical downpour that's actually hard to see through. As Tom Waits said, '*it was raining hammers, it was raining nails.*' Frank, always in control and elegant, was behind the wheel. He was one of the funniest human beings I ever met. John, his quiet and brilliant partner, was riding shotgun, and Allan and I were in the backseat. When we got to the stage entrance the guard, who was wearing a heavy slicker with a hood over his hat, looked at some papers he had on a clipboard and said, 'You're not on the list.'

"'We're not on the list?' said Frank.

"'No,' said the guard.

"Frank turned around and looked at me and Allan, wearing a gleeful smile. 'We're not on the list,' he said.

"'You need to turn around, go back out to the street, and go to the parking garage two blocks down,' said the guard.

"'I think not,'" said Frank.

"He put the car, a big Ford, in reverse and half-turned again to watch behind us. He put the gas pedal to the floor, and we went fishtailing backward across the driveway, over the curb, across the grassy lawn area in front of the building, and smashed into the flagpole. The trunk of the car was wrapped around the pole and wrecked. Frank opened the door and got out. He stood in rain falling so hard that it looked like a shower, and turned back to us. I remember the joy on his face. His smile was pure and full of life. He raised his right hand to his forehead and saluted us.

"'See ya!' he said, and he walked away, disappearing into the darkness and the rain.

"I never saw him again. Truthfully, that moment was so perfect I never want to see him again. Nothing could top that exit.

"John decided to go off after him and skip the show, so Allan and I made our way into the building to see Mr. Gleason perform.

"Gleason seemed to thrive on belittling people. A week earlier, everyone involved with the show got together for a cast reading and a production meeting. They were all there, from the fabulous Art Carney to the beautiful June Taylor. Gleason ran the meeting from the head of the table. He gave each department head his notes and finally came to Sammy Spear, his musical director for decades. 'Sammy,' he said. 'Work on the music, will you? It's never been any good.'

"For the writing staff he had one final fuck you. He had a monitor set up for us to watch the show. It was set up in the men's room. Allan and I sat on a couch along with Gleason's agent, the late Sam Cohen, and watched a TV screen across the tiled room, the row of urinals ten feet to our left."

"He was a bastard," the guy said.

"Yes, he was a bastard," Don agreed. "When he died nobody said 'What a great guy'; they all said 'What a great talent.' And that is true. After everything he did for those six weeks, we sat in that men's room and when Gleason went to work we laughed. The bastard made us laugh.

"About a month later Allan and I were standing backstage at a televised roast for Milton Berle. We were talking to Frank Sinatra. All the stars appearing on the dais that night had gathered in this green-room area to have cocktails. It was a different time."

"What have you guys been doing?" asked Sinatra.

"We were just in Florida for six weeks doing a show for Gleason," I said.

"Oh, really?" said Frank. "And you lived to talk about it."

Allan and I laughed.

"I take it you know him," said Allan.

"He's a bastard," said Frank. "A real bastard."

Clarence

I surf.
At least I used to surf.

That is not fiction. That is the truth. And in 1973 I surfed often and I surfed pretty well. So did Bruce and all the other guys in that famous David Gahr photograph on the back cover of *The Wild, the Innocent & the E Street Shuffle.*

In fact we had been out surfing that day.

We knew we had this photo shoot so we wanted to go inside and change. But Dave said, "No, you look great like this," so we ended up taking those pictures and then we went back out surfing.

You can feel summer when you look at that picture. You can feel the Jersey Shore. Everybody looks young and fit and sun-kissed. We all have that relaxed summertime attitude.

During the afternoon go out, I took off on a wave that closed out in front of me. I shot the board forward and fell back into the water like I'd done a thousand times before.

That time was a little different.

That time my board went up into the air, got stopped by my leash, and came straight back down and hit me in the mouth.

It broke my front tooth.

We had a show that night at this club. There was no fucking way I was going onstage with my front tooth missing, so we went on this mad search for a dentist. Anyway, I think Bruce's mother or aunt or somebody got in touch with a guy who agreed to see me right away. I went over there and he put on this temporary cap. It wasn't perfect, but at least I didn't look like an idiot.

Problem solved.

The next problem didn't occur until my first sax solo in the first song.

It might have been "Spirit in the Night," I'm not sure. In any event, I went to blow into the horn and my front tooth came flying out of my mouth and into the audience.

"Hold it! Stop the music!" said Bruce. "We're not playing another note until we find the Big Man's front tooth!"

Somebody did find it. I think it landed in some girl's drink. I fished it out and jammed it back in, and we finished the show.

Don

I sat alone at the very back of Madison Square Garden and watched Bruce and the band do "Jungleland." When I say I sat alone I mean that literally. I was the only person there who wasn't working for the tour. It was the sound check for that night's show. A few hours later I stood near the same spot and watched and listened with twenty thousand other people as Clarence played those magnificent solos again. (In Spain, one night, the entire crowd hummed those solos note for note. An amazing echo from the night so many years ago at the Record Plant when Bruce hummed his version to Clarence in the final hours of the *Born to Run* sessions.) After the show that night, Bruce brought a couple of young kids into the Temple of Soul to meet the Big Man.

"This is their first rock and roll show," Bruce said. "And they got to have the quintessential Big Man experience; 'Jungleland' in New York City."

Yes, Bruce is the kind of guy who'll use the word *quintessential* in front of innocent children.

"What does that mean?" one of the kids asked sensibly.

"It means it's a New York song played here in New York and it's the Big Man's signature song," said Bruce.

On the way home that night in the limo, I asked Clarence what it felt like to play that song again after so many years. "I didn't play it," he said. "God did."

After a respectful pause I said, "I thought God played the trumpet."

"He used to," said Clarence. "He kept working with horns till he got it right."

But perhaps the most interesting thing I ever heard Clarence say about "Jungleland" was this: the first time he heard it was on the record.

"What?" I said. I was sure he was fucking with me.

Now the story of the *Born to Run* sessions has been told many times. It always ends with Bruce and Clarence spending sixteen straight hours working on the "Jungleland" solos. Legend has it they finished at eight thirty in the morning, then jumped into waiting cars and drove to Providence to begin a tour. Clarence recently confirmed this. I always assumed that in those final hours they finally found the right notes and finished the track. Wrong. Bruce assembled it later in the editing process, but before it was finished the band performed the song in concert and the solo changed with every performance. You can hear those old versions on various bootlegs, which are now being played on E Street Radio.

But the version we've all come to know is the best of all for a number of reasons.

"The first time I heard the way Bruce had built it I couldn't talk," Clarence told me. "It spoke to my soul. It was the perfect combination of our talents and our abilities and our deep mystical connection. He took what I had played, all those little pieces, and married them to what he heard in his heart, and then put it together in a way that's timeless. Every time I play it I feel that it represents our musical partnership in a way that's beyond words. To me that solo sounds like love."

Clarence

Danny Federici died on the afternoon of April 17, 2008, in New York City. This changed the world of E Street forever. The band would never again have the lineup we've all come to know and love.

Danny was the quiet one. Bruce called him the Phantom. In truth he was a quiet, unassuming guy who didn't crave the spotlight but was genuinely happy to remain in the shadows playing those fabulous fills, like the ones that run through "Sandy."

His funeral, which took place in the same church where we all had recently said good-bye to Terry Magovern, was devastatingly sad. It seemed like he was there for my whole life. From the beginning there was always Danny, and now...

And now we go on, strengthened by his memory and weakened by his loss. Nothing will ever be quite the same. It makes me appreciate every single day that I'm above ground. I have a love of life now that's more powerful, and that's a gift from Danny. He's with me every day, and he'll continue to be with me till the day I'm with him.

At the end of May I made a personal appearance in a friend's dojo near my home in Florida. I had agreed to play a few songs and sign autographs to help him open this new business. It was an oddly sweet affair. With no advertising, somehow over a hundred people showed up carrying copies of *Born to Run* and wearing concert T-shirts. They took off their shoes and sat on the dojo's matted floors and patiently watched a martial arts demonstration. I was dressed in white and wore my straw hat and glasses, and I sat at the far end of the room with my horn. Don drove me over to the place. Jo Lopez was there and had set up an excellent sound system. I played live to tracks from my new solo album, answered questions, and posed for pictures for more than two hours. The people who came were true fans who knew which songs had been played on a certain night in 1978 and hadn't been played since, and asked if I'd be able to play those tunes if Bruce called for them. "Yes," I said. "Because I don't memorize the songs—I feel the songs." One guy had been to 131 shows and claimed to have listened to over 700.

It felt like a family reunion of sorts. Then near the end somebody asked a question about Danny. I spoke of my love for Danny and how much he would be missed. Bruce will never have a better organ player. Danny played Bruce Springsteen organ the way I play Bruce Springsteen saxophone. Then I was moved to pick up the horn one more time.

"This is an unrecorded song called 'Garden of Memories,' I said. "I'm going to try to play it for Danny. Forgive me if I can't get all the way through it."

Don

He did get through it and it was beautiful. Those deep, honey-coated notes floated out of the man and out of the horn and into the air. We were all transported from a small dojo in a strip mall in Florida to a place of bittersweet loveliness apart from or maybe adjacent to this world.

If music is the bridge between Heaven and Earth, we were all on that bridge. It was an eloquent and heartfelt good-bye to a friend expressed in the language that Clarence spoke most fluently.

The Night Skies over Europe

Don

The darkened interior of the E Street jet looked like a hospital plane. Everyone on board wore a surgical mask. All the musicians, the managers, the assistants, the physical therapists, the visitors, and the trainers wore surgical masks. It looked like a planeload of sleeping Michael Jackson impersonators.

Bruce had a cold. It wasn't bad enough to cancel a show, not yet anyway, but if it spread it could affect the entire tour—and the tour was big, big business.

This band, which has shown remarkable lasting powers, is starting to feel its age. You can't tell from listening to the shows, nor can you see any major differences onstage except for Clarence's throne, but these men are hurting in the ways that men this age hurt. Parts are worn down and need replacing. Nils rides a bike around backstage because it's too painful to walk on hips that need to be traded in. But watch him spin and twist onstage an hour later in one of those astounding solos and you believe in miracles.

Max is almost always trussed up to support his bad back.

Danny is gone.

Clarence is held together with bolts and wires and electrodes and is filled with plastic and metal in places where bone used to be. He needs new knees.

"You're the six-million-dollar man," I said to him one night.

"Shit," he laughed. "I passed six million ten years ago."

Bruce remains a remarkable athlete as he closes in on sixty years old. He works at it every day and he works hard. And that doesn't count the three hours of unbelievable aerobics he goes through every time he performs.

Someday soon, if it hasn't happened already, someone will write, "I saw Rock and Roll's past tonight and its name was Bruce Springsteen." In some ways that would be a fair statement. There is no other band like this and there never will be. This is the last and best rock aggregation with ties to the birth of rock in the '50s and '60s. And it is not a dinosaur act like the Stones have become. Bruce and the band remain vital and relevant like no one else of their ilk. U2 came along later and doesn't have the history of E Street to draw from. Bruce and this band are representatives of America at a time when the music moved a generation (or two) forward toward that elusive Promised Land.

So yes, they are rock and roll's past. The world of music, like the world itself, has become more fractured and secular. To have one supergroup or artist who could capture the attention of the majority like Elvis or the Beatles did is no longer possible. It won't happen again. And rock and roll itself has been eclipsed by other kinds of music. But Bruce and the Band are also rock and roll's present and its future. They continue to make new music, and Bruce may not as yet have hit the height of his powers. They may not leap off the stage anymore, but the music is as strong and powerful as ever. But now it resonates across decades and touches millions of lives.

Who knows how long they can continue? They have never been better than they are right now. I believe that Bruce will continue to make music until he is simply incapable of doing it anymore. I believe that the E Street Band will continue so long as Bruce and Clarence are able to stand on a stage together.

The Legend of Clarence and Thomas
(A Screaming Comes Across the Bar), 2008

I love Gravity's Rainbow *more than mac and cheese. It's lasted longer and has more nutritional value.* —C.C.

Having lived in China, Clarence was somewhat of an expert on Chinatowns. Having been a saxophone player all his life made him somewhat of an expert on bars. These two things led him to the Li Po bar on Grant Street in the heart of San Francisco's Chinatown.

He was sitting in front of the Buddha shrine drinking martinis with Thomas ("nobody calls me Tom") Pynchon. Clarence and Thomas had been friends for a long, long time. Pynchon had been to over 150 shows in person and also possessed a huge collection of bootleg CDs, which he listened to while writing in his study in Manhattan.

Thomas was on a sentimental journey here to his old stomping grounds from the '60s. Clarence was here to plan his next wedding. The wedding would be across the Golden Gate in Tiburon, but when he heard Thomas was in town he came into the city to hang out and have some dinner. Pat Buchanan, the conservative former presidential candidate, was across the room alone in the corner pounding shots of tequila. Neither Clarence nor Thomas paid any attention to him.

"Congratulations on your impending nuptials," said Thomas.

"Thank you," said Clarence.

"Remind me again why you're doing this."

"I'm in love."

"Weren't you in love the last five or six times?"

"Yes," said Clarence.

"So how is this time different?"

"It just is," said Clarence. "I truly love this woman."

"It seems to me that you're very good at getting married and very bad at staying married," said Thomas. "Or am I stating the obvious?"

"You're good at that," said Clarence.

"Stating the obvious?"

"Obviously."

"You're avoiding the question," said Thomas.

"What question?"

"The implied question of why you're getting married when history tells us you're a failure at remaining married."

"My lawyer tells me that with my prenup it's just like dating," said Clarence.

Thomas laughed and reflexively stroked his beard. He'd shaved it a few years ago, but nobody recognized him without it so he grew it back. He found no irony in that.

"Here's to you," said Thomas, raising his glass.

"Cheers," said Clarence.

"Antiques Roadshow," said Thomas.

They drank. Somebody put some money in the jukebox and "Oh Babe, What Would You Say?" by the late Hurricane Smith began to play. Clarence loved the sound of the organ on this song. It reminded him of summer at the shore and all those waterfront bars and, of course, of Danny. So many people he'd known had died. He didn't understand death. It felt like life was a movie with a bad ending. Hopefully the next life would make it worthwhile. Still, there was too much death that went with growing older. Too many fallen comrades.

"I know more dead people than living people," said Clarence.

"I hate death," said Thomas. "What was it Jackson Browne said about it in that song? 'It's like a song I can hear playing right in my ear / That I can't sing / I can't help listening.'"

"Yes," said Clarence.

"How's the tour going?"

"Great. This band is better than it's ever been at any time in history. It's unbelievable. We did a show in Dublin at the end of May that was as good as any show in fucking history."

"That's great," said Thomas. "I'll get a bootleg."

"That's what rock and roll says," said Clarence. "Fuck death."

"Yes," said Thomas. "Fuck death."

They left the bar and walked off the drinks. They went up Columbus and headed down to the wharf.

"Roky Erickson and the 13th Floor Elevators," said Thomas. "They were my favorites back in the day. Roky's made a comeback in recent years."

"Where was he?" asked Clarence.

"He was insane in Texas. Too many drugs. Lots of misdiagnoses," said Thomas.

They walked over to pier 39, drawn by the cries of the sea lions. There were hundreds of them on the barges and docks. Clarence and Thomas watched them for a while. Sometimes when they were together they didn't speak for hours. This wasn't one of those times.

"They started coming here after the last big earthquake," said Clarence. "Weird, huh?"

"Makes you wonder," said Thomas. "Maybe they just wanted to come in close and watch whatever was going down go down. Or maybe it's coincidence. Or maybe it's a sign of the end of days. Or maybe it's the herring. I'm going with the herring."

"Which reminds me of dinner," said Clarence. "Where do you want to go?"

"That's a tough choice in this city," said Thomas. "We could go to Capps Corner in North Beach, or Quince, or back to Chinatown."

"Where in Chinatown?" said Clarence.

"There's only one place in Chinatown," said Thomas. "There used to be two. One of those private booths at the Far East Café...but the food's not what it used to be. So that leaves only one."

"Let's go there," said Clarence.

An hour later they were at a table on the second floor in Sam Wo's restaurant on Washington Street, eating dumplings and drinking Chinese beer.

"So you still doing your mystery man reclusive shit?" asked Clarence.

"Not so much," said Thomas. "I don't know. In fact the only thing I know for sure is that I don't know anything for sure. And I'm not really sure of that."

"How'd you start that no talking stuff?"

"By not talking."

"Yeah, but why? I mean why at the beginning?"

"I never liked the attention. I didn't have much choice in the writing thing. I mean I had to write. I didn't feel like I had to talk about what I wrote. The writing did the talking," said Thomas.

"But you chose to publish," said Clarence.

"Yeah, to feed my family and my writing habit," said Thomas. "Then it turned into a thing. Then I became Professor Irwin Corey for a while."

"What?"

"I hired him to pick up an award for me," said Thomas, laughing. "I actually went with him but everybody thought I was his agent or something. It was very cool."

"Bob Dylan told me he could be somebody else," said Clarence.

"Somebody other than who he is?"

"He says he could be anybody," said Clarence. "He said identity is just an illusion and that maybe he's actually somebody else."

"Sounds like Bob," said Thomas.

"Course, you could be doing the same thing," said Clarence.

"How's that?"

"Well, how do I know you're you? I've never seen you write a book. Maybe Professor Corey wrote all that shit. It's possible that he's actually who you claim to be and you're somebody else entirely. See what I'm saying?"

"I do," said Thomas, as he ate a dumpling.

"It's confusing," said Clarence.

"I'd say it's vexing," said Thomas.

"You're the writer," said Clarence. "I think."

Clarence shrugged and sipped his beer. The place was jammed, as usual. Most of the customers were speaking Chinese.

"Tomorrow morning," said Thomas, "if you stay in the city..."

"Yeah, we're staying at the Ritz Carlton," said Clarence.

"Okay," said Thomas. "There's this place called the Liguria Bakery up on Washington Square Park that makes this incredible pizza focaccia in the morning. But they're sold out by nine o'clock so you've got to get there early."

"Pizza in the morning?"

"Yes. They sell it in slabs, but they'll cut one or two up for you. It's unbelievable. One of the best things to eat on the entire planet. And don't be fooled by the way the place looks. It looks empty, like it's closed, but it's not. Trust me on this. I lived on that shit for about a year when I lived in North Beach."

"I always thought it would be cool to live in that neighborhood," said Clarence.

"It used to be," said Thomas. "It's yuppified now, but back in the day it was the center of the universe. I used to eat at the Golden Spike three nights a week. City Lights, the Condor, Café Tosca, shit..."

He looked off into the middle distance, unstuck in time like Billy Pilgrim.

"I lived in Marin," said Clarence. "I loved it. Now the Keys are calling me."

"I hear you," said Thomas. "We go down there maybe once a year. Key West, mostly. Ride bikes. Sit in bars. You know, gathering material."

"This friend of mine, Paulie, says Key West is full of faggots, drunks, punks, and chickens."

"He's obviously been there," said Thomas.

"Where do you stay down there?"

"This place called Hidden Beach," said Thomas.

"Do you stay under your own name?"

"Nah, sometimes I'm Dr. Warren Kruger, but most of the time I'm Henry Porter," said Thomas.

"I'm C. O. Jones," said Clarence. "As in cojones."

Thomas laughed again. Then they ate for a while. "You knew Mailer, right?" asked Thomas.

"Yeah," said Clarence. "I have a tendency to hang out with writers. I don't really know why, but that's how it's worked out. Norman and I hit it off. We could just talk shit forever. I miss him. I miss him a whole lot. Last time we spent any time together was down in the Bahamas. We had a good time. He loved it down there. We sat around and smoked cigars and drank beer and worked on our tans. Solved all the problems in the world."

"Funny how we know so many of the same people," said Thomas. "Then again, maybe there's nothing unusual about it at all."

"I met Quentin Crisp once," said Clarence. "He was wearing makeup and a big hat and a fucking cape. He pulled it off though. All attitude."

"You and Quentin Crisp are a very odd couple," said Thomas.

"Like we're not?" said Clarence.

Thomas laughed. That was his response, he laughed. Then they ate for a while.

"You writing?" asked Clarence.

"Yeah," said Thomas. "I'm fucking with a kind of detective thing. Not really a detective detective..."

"Of course not," said Clarence.

"We'll see," said Thomas.

"Any talking dogs in it?" said Clarence, smiling.

"Not yet," said Thomas. "But I'm thinking there might be some seals."

"Assuming once again that you actually are who you say you are, which may or may not be the truth," said Clarence.

Thomas smiled.

"True," he said.

Then he said it again.

Clarence

I walked into DeAngelo's restaurant in Mill Valley, saw her, and said, 'I'm going to marry that woman,'" I said. "I kept going back and telling her she was going to be my wife."

"It's true," said Victoria. "It was incredible. I didn't know what to do. I called my sister and said, 'This guy named Clarence Clemons keeps sending me roses and asking me to go out with him,' and she said, 'Clarence Clemons? Go!' So eventually I did."

"I started out sending her one white rose a day," I said to Don. "Then it was two white roses, and eventually a dozen white roses."

"I started giving them to everybody in the restaurant," said Victoria. "There were so many of them."

We were at the wedding party rehearsal dinner at a magnificent house overlooking the San Francisco Bay the night before our marriage. Michael Indelicato, the owner of the legendary Record Plant recording studio, owned the house where the ceremony would take place. My family, in the persons of my three aunts and my uncle, who would perform the ceremony, had flown in from Virginia for the occasion.

"We never thought Clarence would amount to anything," Aunt Sara told Don. "He was in school and he still didn't know how to spell his own name. So in our minds we said, well, Clarence isn't the one who's going to make it, so we'd better focus on one of these other kids. Course, it turned out that we were all wrong. Took a while, though."

My family is a wonderful group of churchgoing people from Virginia, and it's easy to see where I got my deep spirit of love for all. They are genuinely nice folks who are filled with life and laughter. Lots of laughter.

"I've met Clarence's family and his friends," Don said to them. "I've even met his ex-wives. Well, not all his ex-wives. Nobody has that kind of time. I suppose I could do it, but I'd have to quit my job." They took his cheeky remarks with gales of laughter.

"I'm not certain that Clarence has met all of them," said Sara.

"I also think it's a good idea to marry a woman with a twin sister," Don said. "This way, if anything ever goes wrong with Victoria she can use her sister for parts."

It was a fun evening. The fifty or so people there were divided between my family and friends and Victoria's, including her mother and father from Siberia, who didn't speak a word of English. I wondered what they made of all this.

Earlier that day we had walked through the ceremony and were about as ready as we were going to be. This was still rock and roll. As I said earlier, the wedding itself would take place at the oceanfront home of Michael Indelicato. It is a spectacular modern house directly on the water in Tiburon. However, it sits at the bottom of a very narrow and winding driveway with little space to turn a car around at the bottom. It would be difficult to get over a hundred guests down there on time, and dinner on the deck could prove to be a chilly and damp affair, but I was certain it would be memorable.

"Is there an extension cable we can get for the speakers, or is there no such thing?" asked the Reverend Lawrence Rubin, who was the piano player who'd be working the wedding but not performing the ceremony.

"There's no such thing as no such thing," I said.

And I was right.

On the day of the wedding, disaster was avoided when my uncle Milton Reid, the preacher from Virginia, announced he had to be in Washington, D.C., at noon the next day. We had made flight plans for him to leave in two days. Since he had already signed the license, replacing him was impossible. For a while everyone was in a state of high anxiety, but the problem was solved when a red-eye was booked for a few extra bucks.

I spent the day relaxing. My doctor flew in last night and gave me the injections that enabled me to move pain free for a few days. Don came over and hung out with me for a while. I got a manicure and a pedicure, and I asked for sparkling blue toenail polish, but the girl was out of it. I settled for clear.

Bruce called and wished me well and apologized for not being able to make it to the ceremony. He reiterated what he told me onstage the week before at Giants Stadium, which was that he believed that I had finally found the right girl. He said that he, too, had made mistakes, but the real thing was worth waiting for. I sat in a chair by the window and looked out at the San Francisco Bay. I sipped white wine. I smiled a lot but, as always, I worried about the details.

I do believe in marriage. I believe in it despite all the evidence to the contrary. Much of that evidence was provided by me. We're talking about a man who's married different women in Philadelphia, Hawaii, Little Palm Island (also an all-white clothing affair), China, and now, finally, Tiburon. I am, among other things, an optimist.

An old friend called me this morning and said, "It's not too late. I can send a helicopter for you and get you out of there now."

But I'm staying.

"This time," I said to Don, "it's for good."

"I'm glad to hear it," he said. "I'll let you have a little peace and quiet."

He started to leave the suite and head back to his hotel to get ready for the wedding.

"But if you hear a helicopter go over," I said, "wave."

Don

The wedding was beautiful.

Clarence wore a white East Indian type of suit accented with silver and a white turban. Not a lot of guys can make a turban work, but he is definitely one of them. The overall effect left him looking like a raja.

Victoria wore a soft pink gown that Clarence had designed. She looked lovely.

The ceremony was a combination of music and prayer. Sometimes both at once.

Victoria's twin sister, Julia, was the maid of honor; Clarence's nephew, Jacob, was the best man. Narada Michael Walden and I served as groomsmen. Victoria's high school girlfriends, Marianna Darmina and Ekaterina Timokhina, were bridesmaids. Julia's daughter Natasha was the flower girl. Uncle Brother, more properly known as Dr. Milton Reid, performed the wedding ceremony in front of a hundred guests, all clad in shades of white.

Everything went smoothly. (With one notable exception.) Nothing unusual happened. (With one notable exception.) Nobody fell into the pool or off the deck into the ocean. The food was delicious and the wine flowed until late in the evening. A good time was had by all. (With one notable exception.)

I sat next to Clarence in the moments before things got under way. I have never seen him so nervous about anything. I have seen him get amped before countless shows but never to this degree. He kept repeating details of how the wedding was supposed to go, reminding Lani and Jacob of things they already knew. It seemed that he was almost in a state of shock until we stood and the song "Oceans" began to play, signaling the entrance of the bridal party.

The evening was sweet and reflected the heart and soul and love that Clarence professes for Victoria.

Bruce called earlier in the day to offer his congratulations and best wishes. Because of where the wedding fell in the touring schedule and in the country, none of the band members were there. All of them wanted to be, but it simply proved to be a logistical nightmare for them. But then these guys don't hang out together the way people imagine they do. They see each other at the halls and stadiums where they play but don't socialize beyond that, except on rare occasions.

Clarence and Roy have dinner once in a while, and Bruce and the Big Man do find time to spend together away from work, but that's about it. So no disrespect was intended or taken by their absence at the wedding. Plus, to be fair, Clarence has done this a lot, so they might have figured they'll just catch the next one.

All of this has been exhausting for Clarence. It's been exhausting for me, and all I do is ride along attached to the Big Man like a pilot fish on a whale. All the flights, hotels, time zones, stress, and shows take a very real toll both physically and mentally. In five days Clarence will be in Florida to pick up the tour, with eight more dates scattered around America. After that he'll be going to Atlanta to add his horn to the new music Bruce has been working on for the last six months. When that is done, Clarence faces double knee-replacement surgery and the difficult rehabilitation program that follows. After the first of the year another tour is in the offing. The question that comes up in my mind is: how long can he keep doing this? How long before that big body finally tells him enough is enough? Nobody knows, of course, but every time I see a show, especially the last show of a tour, I think I might be seeing Bruce Springsteen and the E Street Band for the last time. After one of those shows that will be true.

I hope that the knee surgery gives Clarence a new lease on life physically the way that his relationship with Victoria has given him a new lease on life spiritually. I hope there are many tours to come. But logic tells me that even if all the stars align, the next tour will be the last one. Clarence and Victoria have just purchased a new home in Florida, and I know he's looking forward to sitting back and spending most of his days fishing on the Gulf. On the other hand I could be wrong. This band could keep going and making relevant music until they're all in their seventies. They could, but I don't think so. Bruce will always be involved in making music until he is forced to stop, but the band, with Clarence at its heart, cannot. I will see as many shows as I can and cherish every one of them as if it is the last.

After the wedding while I was on my way back to the hotel I received a text from the groom. It read, *Today is the day "I" becomes "we."*

When they got back to their room they found that Jennifer Jacobs had worked her magic. The floor and the bed were covered with rose petals. The tub was filled with water and covered with rose petals. There was a beautiful floral bouquet with a card that read, "To Clarenze and Viktortya, Much, Much love and happiness. We love you. Bruce, Patti and Family." Bruce had spelled the Big Man's name the way Victoria pronounced it, and he used the original Russian spelling of Victoria's name. There was also a bottle of champagne on ice with two glasses. The room was filled with burning candles. Soft music was playing. Victoria fell back on the bed. It had been a truly magical evening.

"And then I smelled something burning," she said the next day. "I said to Clarence, 'Do you smell something burning?' and he did."

"It was her hair," said Clarence. "She fell back and her hair landed near one of the candles. Fortunately we put it out and no harm was done."

Which brings us to that notable exception.

Dr. Roberta Shapiro is Clarence's personal physician. She is very, very good at what she does. In addition, she is a lovely, warm, and intelligent person. She is dedicated to her patients and takes wonderful care of Clarence, who requires a lot of attention. Roberta, who specializes in the treatment and management of chronic pain, travels wherever the Big Man needs her, and she wouldn't have missed his wedding for the world. She flew in during the day on Friday and would fly back to New York on Saturday morning. That was the plan. And the plan was a good one.

Until she swallowed the cinnamon lozenge.

It happened back at the hotel lobby after the wedding. Roberta swallowed a mint that became lodged in her throat and she began to choke. She gave the choking signal to the people around her, and fortunately one of them was Jacob. He knew what to do and immediately gave her the Heimlich maneuver. The mint was dislodged and expelled but damage was done in the process, and as often happens, one of Roberta's ribs got either broken or cracked.

The next morning, still somewhat dazed from the experience, she stumbled and fell in the hotel bathroom, breaking several bones in her face and causing other internal injuries. Saturday she wound up in the Marin County Hospital instead of flying home. She was treated and released and came to visit in Clarence's suite that night.

"I've been treating pain my whole life," she said. "Now I get to live with it for a while. This is another accident that could have been avoided by wearing my William Holden Drinking Helmet."

She was in good spirits and on good drugs, which may be one and the same, but she scared herself and the rest of us.

"I've always wanted to outlive my doctors," said Clarence. "But this is ridiculous."

Clarence

"I had a heart attack," I said.

Don had just called after receiving a message from me that something was wrong.

"Where are you?" he asked.

"At the hotel," I said. "I had a physical today in preparation for the knee operations. I had an EKG and a stress test, the whole thing. When I was done the doctor told me that I suffered a mild heart attack sometime in the last two to three weeks."

"Do you remember feeling it?"

"Yeah. Remember the day I called you, I think you were sick with food poisoning or something, and I told you I'd been feeling weird? My chest was tight and I got chills and then real tired?"

"Yes, I do," he said. "But you say shit like that every day."

I laughed. Don has a way of always cheering me up.

"Well, on that day I think I was having a heart attack. They said the damage was minimal, but this is a real warning, man. I have had my last cigar and my last tequila."

"Well, if you look at this as dodging a bullet," he said, "which is how you have to look at it, you are very, very lucky."

"I know," I said. "God damn, this has me freaked out."

"Is Victoria with you?"

"Yes, thank God she's here to take care of me," I said. "But when somebody tells you that you've had a heart attack, it scares you so much that it could give you a heart attack."

"True," he said. "But besides lifestyle changes, is there anything you have to do?"

"No," I said. "Just lose weight, eat right, exercise, don't drink, and don't smoke."

"Are you sure you want to go on living?"

"Yeah, but only 'cause they didn't tell me to stop fucking."

"So what's next?" he asked.

"After this last gig I'll go to Florida for a few weeks, go up to Georgia to record my stuff for the new album, then I'm going to have the surgery done here in Manhattan."

"Are you going to rehab there, too?"

"Yeah, I'm going to stay in a hotel across the street from the hospital for a month. Nils is going to have his hips done at the same time. Half the fucking band is going to be in this joint."

"Wow," he said. "This has been quite a week."

"I think it'll be good from now on," I said. "I'm also on a health kick. I quit drinking. I only started drinking so much to kill the pain in my knees. Once this operation is done I won't need anything. Hopefully."

I hung up and looked out the window in the dark New York night. And I thought about death. Don is always saying, "Life is a movie with a bad ending," and I always chastise him and tell him he's being too negative. But as that day gets closer for me, I can see where he's right. I don't want to talk about religion here too much, but I do believe in Heaven and life after death. I'm just not in a hurry to get there. I've been blessed so much in this life that it's too sweet to leave. It's too sweet to leave. Too sweet.

Don

Clarence loves jokes.

If there is a quick answer to the "What is he like?" question, it's that he's funny.

If even I know a joke that he's telling I wouldn't stop him, because even unfunny jokes become funny when Clarence tells them. Often it's better if the joke he's telling is old just to hear the spin he puts on it. As we say in the comedy business, he's got a good joke axe.

One night Jimmy Vallely, perhaps the funniest man in the world, invited us both out to dinner. At one point during the evening I had to crawl out of the room in fear that I would injure myself laughing if I stayed. I was laughing so hard I couldn't stand up. There have been more than a few nights like that.

Once we were sitting on the G5 taking the band to Foxborough for the Gillette Stadium show. We were moving around in the sky dodging thunderstorms, so the flight was longer than usual. There was time to kill. Clarence kills time by telling jokes.

"This paratrooper comes back from his first jump," said Clarence. "His roommate is waiting for him. 'How did it go?' asks the roommate. 'I was the last one in line,' says the paratrooper. 'I got to the door and I froze. The sergeant says to me, "Either you jump or I'm going to shove my cock up your ass!"' 'So did you jump?' asks the roommate. The guy says, 'Well, a little at first.'"

This was one of the "in and out" shows. The band drops out of the sky, kicks ass in your town for three-plus hours, and then they're gone. They're in a hotel in another city while you're still in the parking lot. (The first example I remember of this was watching Frank Sinatra lift off in a helicopter at the Newport Jazz Festival in the '60s. He lifted off while we in the crowd were still cheering for him to come back onstage. Jilly Rizzo later told me they landed at the Sixty-third Street heliport and were in his club drinking in under an hour.)

This does not happen after every show. In fact, Bruce likes to hang out after the shows and talk and review and continue to entertain. If the venue provides, he'll take a shower and begin the long process of unwinding after a show. On fast outs that's not possible, and the postshow plane rides often start out with a lot of high energy.

It must be difficult to return to normal after one of these marathon shows. How can anything feel normal after hearing eighty thousand people singing your name? What is normal about being paid a king's ransom to have people worship you? Bruce, Clarence, and the guys in the band all breathe rarified air. I don't know how you can keep your head straight in this lifestyle. I don't feel like I'm telling tales out of school when I say that Clarence is used to being treated like a star. Hell, *I'm* used to being treated like a star, and all I do is hang out with him. But, after being on the road, I will admit to having a reduced amount of patience when going to the airport to take a commercial flight. It is a humbling experience. I find myself expecting the best table and all the other preferential treatment you get out on the road. Clarence is used to having things his way and can show irritation when they aren't. But it's rare, and he does maintain a sense of humor that helps him get through these situations.

"These things only happen to live people," he's fond of saying when he finds himself in the pat-down line at the airport.

He'll sulk for a moment or two and then often will tell a joke.

We went out to dinner in New York the night after the Boston show, and although he'd called ahead to check, the restaurant was out of his favorite dish. (Which in this case was liver.) He got quiet for a minute or two then ordered something else. He sipped his wine. He took a deep breath and closed his eyes for ten or fifteen seconds. Then he opened them and turned to me.

"This bank robber's mask slips. He pulls it back up and says to this guy, 'Did you see my face?' and the guy says, 'Just for a second'—and the robber shoots him dead. He then walks over to this couple and says to the husband, 'Did you see my face?' and the guy says, 'No, but my wife did.'"

On the jet back to New York from Foxborough, Clarence sat back in one of the big leather chairs and sipped his drink. I was sitting across the aisle from him, thrilled to be in this privileged environment. It really did feel dreamlike.

"I heard the worst joke," he said.

"Oh, yeah?"

"Terrible joke," he said.

"Is that right?"

"In fact, it's the worst joke I've ever heard."

"Worst as in not funny?" I asked.

"No, no," he said. "It's funny, all right. But it's nasty. It's offensive."

"I don't believe that I can be offended by a joke," I said.

"This joke will test that opinion," he said, smiling.

"Let's hear it," I said.

He took another sip and put his drink down. Bruce was sitting up front, as usual. He was talking to Jon Landau. Steven and Nils were listening to iPods. Garry was reading a magazine. Max had his eyes closed and appeared to be sleeping. Roy and his wife were huddled together in deep conversation about real estate. They were considering selling the Malibu house. Charles was looking out the window at the dark sky. Soozie was flying with Patti and a few others on a separate plane.

"This guy's wife gets into a terrible automobile accident," he began. "He goes to the hospital and the doctor says, 'I've got bad news. Her back was broken in three places, and the blood supply was cut off to her brain. She's a vegetable. She'll never regain consciousness. Plus, your insurance has run out, so you're going to have to care for her at home. I'm going to give you some salves and creams to use on her body, because she's going to develop these weeping bedsores, and she's completely incontinent. That means you're going to have to change her diapers several times a day....' And at that point the guy breaks down crying and says, 'Oh, my God, why did this happen? Why? Why? Why?' And the doctor smiles and laughs and says, 'I'm just fucking with you. She's dead!'"

Several days after the wedding it was back to New York, where the band would be based for the next two and a half weeks. For most of the remaining eight shows they would fly in and fly out. Clarence had spent a good part of the year in the Trump Hotel overlooking the park. He liked it here. New York is a good city for celebrities. It understands and rewards fame.

He called me when he got settled.

"Long day, my brother," he said. "Getting to the airport and flying across the country with your whole family is stressful. But everybody got home safe and sound, and Victoria and I have a few days before we hit the road again."

"Can you smell the barn?" I asked.

"I can smell the hay in the barn," he replied.

"When do you go into the studio?"

"Sometime in September," he said. "I'm waiting on firm dates so I can schedule my knee replacement surgery."

"Are you dreading that?"

"No, I want to get it over with. Get this pain behind me. Plus I'm anxious to start rehab so I'm in shape for the tour next year," he said.

"You'll be fine," I said, crossing my fingers.

"Heard a joke," he said.

"Go ahead."

"This guy goes up to a pharmacist and says, 'I need contraceptives for my twelve-year-old daughter,' and the pharmacist says, 'Is she sexually active?' and the guy says 'No, she just lays there like her mother.'"

* * *

During the last weeks of August the show schedule became intense. There were a bunch of shows in a short time frame. There was a lot of flying and a lot of stage time, which for Clarence meant a lot of discomfort. He took Victoria and his new in-laws on the road for the first two shows. Victoria's folks are simple blue-collar, salt of the earth type people from Siberia. They suddenly found themselves in the world of police escorts, private jets, and sold out stadiums filled with people screaming for their new son-in-law.

"They can't stop smiling," said Clarence.

"Wait till they have to fly back to Russia in coach," I said. "They'll stop."

"I think their coach days are over," he said.

"I have a joke," said Victoria.

Clarence and I were both startled.

"Really?" he said.

"It's a Russian joke," she said, smiling.

"Let's hear it," I said.

"Putin and Medvedev go into a restaurant. The waitress comes over and Putin says, 'I'll have a steak and a baked potato,' and the waitress says, 'What about your vegetable?' and Putin says, 'He'll have the same thing.'"

Clarence called from New York the day before back-to-back shows in Virginia and Pennsylvania.

"The end is near," I said.

"That's what I'm afraid of," he laughed. "Actually, this week will be a little easier. Victoria is going back to San Francisco with her folks, and they're going home in a few days. She's going to meet me in Florida after the last show on the thirtieth. So all I have to worry about is me."

"You'll feel better when the surgery is behind you," I said.

"Yeah, I will," he said. "I'm just tired."

There was a brief pause then he spoke again. "What's the difference between a girls' track team and a group of clever pygmies?"

"I don't know," I said honestly.

"The pygmies are a group of cunning runts," he said.

Clarence

I sat outside tonight looking at the water as the sun went down, and I made some random notes I hoped might turn into stories for the book. They didn't, but taken together they have a kind of lyrical quality. —C.C.

There's a song that I love. It's called "Christo Redentor," or "Christ the Redeemer." It's by Donald Byrd from his *New Perspective* album. He's leaning on the hood of an XKE on the cover. It's everything I love about horns. Donald plays trumpet but it's all the same. He wrote that song after flying into Rio and seeing the huge statue of Christ on top of Corcovado. It appeared out of the clouds. And the tune is like that. It floats like it's weightless. But when I hear it I see a wet street somewhere in Manhattan with a guy standing under a streetlight playing a horn.

At the end of the movie *Titanic,* when they're looking for survivors, you hear this guy yell, "Is there anybody alive out there!" and it's with the same urgency, the same passion, that Bruce says it with. He's been doing that since the beginning. I wonder if they got it from him.

Black folks know me more from *Diff'rent Strokes* than from being with Bruce. Or that movie I did with Keanu Reeves, *Bill and Ted's Excellent Adventure*. For some reason black people loved that movie.

Touring is like seeing a big valley stretched out in front of you and you descend into it.

And then all you can do is keep going forward.

I was at this stone crab restaurant one night and Bo Diddley was in there. Everybody's got the mallets, you know, for cracking the crabs. Bo Diddley starts tapping out the Bo Diddley beat. Pretty soon the whole place is doing it and Bo starts singing. It was fucking great. I miss Bo.

I used to work for this fishmonger when I was a kid. Big racist. He was always amazed when I knew shit. He used to call his daughter out, she worked in the office. She was fat and dumb. He'd give us these quizzes. Like he'd say, "What's the capital of England?" and she wouldn't know, and I'd say "London," and he'd shake his head and say, "Isn't that the goddamndest thing?"

He couldn't have been more amazed if I had risen up into the air and flown around the room. It was as if he'd just seen an orangutan run out of the jungle and start to play the piano.

Bruce wrote "Hungry Heart" in ten minutes. He wasn't happy with something the record company was doing. I don't remember exactly what it was, but I know he was pissed off about something. We'd been in the studio all day with nothing much to show for it. In fact, we had started to pack up for the day. Bruce goes to take a piss and when he comes back he says, "Back in the studio, guys, I think I've got something." And he sits down and writes the whole thing out without pausing. Boom! Just like that. I think it's still our biggest hit. One of them, anyway. "Got a wife and kids in Baltimore Jack." I loved that it was *Baltimore* and *Jack*. Good sounds. The perfect words. "I went out for a ride and I never went back." Who hasn't been there? Ten minutes. Amazing.

*   *   *

I was talking to somebody the other day, I can't remember who . . . Shit, I can't remember anything anymore. This getting old stuff is a lot of fun. You know what the best advice is about getting old? Bring money.

Anyway, I was talking to somebody and for some reason they said, "Tramps like us," and I said, "And vice versa." Then I find out somebody said that in a song. The Hold Steady. Maybe I heard it somewhere. I can't remember.

Don

Clarence's world is different from the world in which you and I live. Like the very rich, his life is very different. I've been around famous people my entire adult life and I've never seen anything like it. Everyone tries to make his life easier.

Waiters, drivers, golf pros—everyone seems to have genuine love for the Big Man. They want to help him in any way possible. All would overlook bad behavior on his part, but there isn't any.

It's not only like this here in south Florida. It's the same wherever he goes. People who have never met him feel affection for C. Not even Bruce elicits this response. There is a warmth that radiates from Clarence, and it touches everybody who comes into contact with him.

It is extraordinary.

It makes you feel good to be in his company. Today was my birthday. Having spent it with Clarence was a very good present.

A writer I knew named Ron Leavitt died. I'd read it in the news that morning. Lung cancer. It's usually cancer or heart disease that takes us. I never knew Ron well, in fact we'd only spoken a few times, but I know he was a bright and talented guy. He cocreated *Married...with Children* and put the Fox network in business. It was a home run and made him rich, and now he's dead.

It feels that fast to me now. A lifetime can be summed up in one sentence.

Clarence and I talk about death a lot, but with the dark humor that binds us. Death may be a motherfucker, but life has been a hell of a ride so far, and all you can do is keep riding until the end.

"Don't look back," Clarence has said to me many times, and I know it's good advice.

So now we bid farewell to fallen comrades and look ahead.

The road beckons, and the E Street nation is ready to take that long walk from the front porch to the front seat.

It was a blustery and rainy morning in south Florida. The weather forecast was calling for lightning and thunder and isolated tornados. It was a good time to throw some things into a suitcase and head west toward home. It was a good time to hasten down the wind.

Clarence

There are three pictures on my saxophone stand onstage. I look at them every night. One is of my spiritual guide, Sri Chinmoy, shaking hands with Terry Magovern. The second is of Danny, and the third is of my friend Dick Moroso. All of them are gone now, but they live in my heart every single day.

I met Dick in the mid-'70s, and we had some high and wild times together. I mean that literally. We were high most of the time and we were wild. I had a friend in Jersey named Bob Duffy who was into racing cars, and he invited me out to the drag strip in Englishtown one weekend. Dick was also a race car driver, and we met and hit it off right away. We had similar views of the world, and we both liked girls and booze.

Dick went on to build a hugely successful business in the racing world called Moroso Performance. His company manufactured aftermarket parts to make cars go faster. At the same time he got rich and I got famous. This proved to be quite a combination. I could attract lots of women, and Dick was there to charm the ones I wasn't with.

He moved to Connecticut and bought a big house there that became party central for a while. There was a period of time in the early '80s where we got into serious recreational drug use. I remember one night when we'd gotten deep into it. We had some girls visiting, and it was about midnight when Bruce called and said he wanted me in the studio right away.

It's amazing that I didn't kill myself or some innocent strangers driving down the turnpike doing lines to stay awake. One of the girls I was seeing at the time came from a family who traced their roots back to the *Mayflower*. Needless to say, she was white and her folks were not happy about her seeing me. It had snowed earlier in the day, and as I approached the exit that led to their house I got an idea. It was the kind of idea that only occurs to you when you're loaded. Despite the fact that Bruce was waiting for me in the studio I decided to make a short detour. I pulled up in front of her parents' house, got out of the car, and spelled my name in the snow on the lawn in a lovely shade of yellow.

I got back on the road and somehow made it to the studio in Manhattan. When I got there Bruce said it was a false alarm and he didn't need me after all.

The next year Dick moved to Florida. He's really the reason I went down there and why I still live there to this day. He called and said he'd bought a boat and invited me down. He said it would be fun. When Dick said something would be fun, he was usually right. And this time was no exception.

The boat was a fifty-two-foot Bertram, and Dick was living on it in the marina on Singer Island. When I arrived the boat was filled with beautiful women. A party took place. I'm not sure of any details, but I do remember lots of naked bodies and booze and loud music. And I do remember the harbormaster stepping over passed out girls to tell Dick to get the hell out of the marina and to never come back.

Dick bought a house a short distance away on the intercoastal waterway. He tied the boat up to his dock, and we continued to enjoy everything there was to enjoy—and there was a lot.

We started taking boat trips. Dick loved being out at sea on the boat. It was the great joy of his life. We'd go out for weeks at a time and island hop. There are still people on the island of Bimini who know me as Calypso Joe.

Of course it wasn't all debauchery. Dick was a great friend, and we shared a lot of ups and downs. We'd seek out country-and-western bars and I'd sit in with those bands—something I had done when I first started out. And he introduced me to fishing.

He started going down to the Keys and entering these competitions. He invited me to go with him to try to catch bonefish. My first time out I caught the biggest fish and won the contest. I was hooked more than the fish were.

Dick and I were alike in so many ways. I bought a red Cadillac Eldorado convertible one day and drove it over to his house to show off. He was just pulling into his driveway in the new car he'd just bought: an identical red Cadillac Eldorado convertible.

Of course over the years we stopped the drugs, except for the occasional joint, and settled down. Our lives became almost semi-normal. During that time our friendship deepened, and we talked about more important things than cars and girls.

Dick got sick and died in the late '90s. I went to visit him in the hospital near the end. The cancer was obviously going to win the battle, and his doctor gave him the option of going home. He said he wanted to take his boat out one last time. So the doctor and I took him to the boat, and we went out for one last ride.

And that's how I remember him. Standing there in the sun laughing as we flew through the waves for the sheer joy of it. That's why we were there . . . for the sheer joy of it.

The Ride Home

Don

For me all the discussions about the best show ever ended (temporarily, I would guess), on August 30, 2008, at the Ride Home in Milwaukee, Wisconsin. That night I saw *the* best show by Bruce Springsteen and the E Street Band that I have ever seen.

It was a performance that had all the things that make any concert great and more. It lasted three and a half hours and contained thirty-one songs. And it was an emotional roller coaster. You come to expect the hard-driving anthems and the sing-alongs, and those were present and accounted for. But this one had more humor—and more bittersweet sadness—than most shows.

Partly because it was the last show. As mentioned earlier, every time this band ends a tour, there are no guarantees that they will ever take the stage together again. So that feeling was there on that Saturday night in the middle of America. Danny's son, Jason, who looks so much like his dad, came out onstage with his father's accordion, stood between Roy and Bruce, and played "Sandy." There were not a lot of dry eyes in the huge crowd of bikers.

It was a beautiful night on the edge of the lake, and the band was in a playful mood. The great photographer Danny Clinch was along for the ride, covering the whole thing and doing a formal photo shoot before the show in front of a scrim set up between the trailers. He took pictures of Bruce alone, Bruce with his son Sam. Then Bruce and Clarence, Clarence alone and then with the core members of the band, finally joined by Jon Landau. I watched the whole thing from just a few feet away with Victoria, and I couldn't shake the feeling that I was watching something special — that these photographs would take a special place in the huge photo album that's part of the band's history. The whole shoot didn't last a lot longer than fifteen minutes because Bruce was chomping at the bit the whole time to get the show started. Alejandro Escovedo had finished his set about fifteen minutes earlier, and we could all hear the big crowd getting restless, ready to start the celebration that is Bruce and this band.

At one point Bruce spoke to his assistant, Wayne Lebeaux.

"I just had an idea," he said. "Download 'Born to Be Wild' and play it on the sound system when we get off the stage."

This was a nod to the occasion, the 105th anniversary of Harley-Davidson. There were hundreds of thousands of bikes in town, all having completed the ride home. The ride back to Milwaukee, where the company started and where every engine for every bike is still built.

"Fuck it," said Steven. "Let's just play it ourselves."

I had started the day before in Los Angeles. Clarence had called me late Thursday night and invited me to ride with him to the gig on the chartered jet. As jaded as I am at this point in time, the opportunity to take that ride was thrilling. I flew into New York on Friday night and made my way to the Trump International Hotel the next afternoon at one. I met C in his suite. Victoria had rejoined him after getting her folks on their way back to Russia. His fantastic assistant, Lani Richmond, was busily packing the five bags they take to every show. These are filled with clothing, specific foods, medical equipment, computers, and music. Clarence was feeling good after his recent heart scare. The tequila and the cigars were gone, and his eyes were clear.

"I'm so ready for this show." He smiled. "After tonight I get to go home and get ready for these knee operations. I am sick of being in pain."

This show was almost like a reward to the people in the band. They got to do it one more time, but since they knew there was a long break following it they could cut loose a little. There was a festive feeling about the whole experience. The only thing that kept it from being complete was Patti's absence.

About 1:45 we headed downstairs and piled into the big stretch limo and headed for Jersey.

"I've been in a haze for so long, it feels totally different to be going to a show with a clear head," said Clarence.

"Do you feel better?" I asked.

"*Better* is a relative term," he said. "I'd like to have a buzz going, but on the other hand I'm kind of enjoying the feeling of being...I don't know what the right word is...*present*. Yeah, that's it."

We looked at a wedding video on Victoria's computer on the ride to some far corner of the Newark airport.

Jon Landau greeted us when we walked into the lounge. We sat down and told a few show-business stories and laughed at a few of Clarence's latest jokes.

The guys from the band began to arrive. Garry came in first, wearing a spiffy Panama hat with a black band. Max followed with his son Jay and signed a few autographs for Clarence, and vice versa. The guys in the band do this a lot. They are like fans of each other and go around getting autographs on drumheads and album covers and magazines and books just like everybody else. They like to collect along with the rest of us.

Bruce came in and hung out. He's a good guy to be stuck with when the plane breaks down and you have to sit around somewhere and kill time.

Which is exactly what happened.

The planes being chartered for the last part of the tour were standard Midwest Airlines Boeing 717s. They're designed to carry eighty-eight passengers. Our group that day was under thirty, so although these were not fancy Gulfstreams there was a lot of room to stretch out. These planes get you where you want to go. Except for today.

There was some mechanical problem with the plane sitting out on the tarmac, and it would be about an hour and a half before the replacement plane would arrive. This came as no surprise to anybody in the band.

"Something always happens on the last show," said Bruce. "One time in Boston our plane got struck by lightning. Put a big hole in the fuselage."

To save time, and since all the catering was already on board the aircraft that wasn't going anywhere, it was decided that we would get on the first plane, have lunch, then switch later. So, with Bruce in the lead, we walked out to the plane and went through an abbreviated security check. Somebody looks at your bags, checks your name off the manifest, runs a metal detector over you, and off you go. This is a good example of the phrase, "Rules is rules." What happens if Bruce's name gets left off the list?

"Sorry, sir, I can't let you on board. The rest of these folks can go, but you'll have to stay here."

So after this bit of silliness we all got on the plane (except for Nils, who was already in Milwaukee, having gone directly from his Arizona home), and had lunch.

For about an hour this plane was the most unusual diner on the planet. But the food was good, and the sense of anticipation about the show was high. Milwaukee is an hour earlier, so even with the delay we'd still arrive in town at about five thirty in the afternoon. Next time I'm stuck in a delay at JFK, I'm going to remember that even if you're the biggest rock star in the world, this kind of shit happens when you travel.

Eventually a plane identical to the one we were sitting on pulled up alongside. We all deplaned, walked thirty yards, and climbed the stairs into the new one. (It should be noted that Clarence actually rode the thirty yards in a van, as he did to the first plane. The idea being that the less he has to walk the better off he'll be. In this case, the thirty-yard case, I think he expended more energy and took a greater risk of injury getting in and out of the van.)

After all this we took off and flew west for an hour and forty-five minutes into the heart of America.

Flying with Bruce and the band is the same as flying with any-body else, only it's a thousand fucking times better. Maybe ten thou-sand. The cool factor alone is almost incalculable. I don't care who you are; you'd enjoy the experience. Other rock stars would enjoy it. Why? Because you're flying with Bruce Springsteen and the E Street Band, that's why.

We landed in Milwaukee and they rolled the stairs up to the door of the plane. At the bottom of the stairs was a fleet of vehicles: SUVs, vans, and the Big Man's limo. Bruce hopped into the shotgun seat of the lead SUV, a black Escalade. I've never seen Bruce get into the backseat of any of the cars or trucks that take him to and from the gigs. He's always in the front, and more often than not he has the window open so that he can wave to people as we pass.

We climbed into the limo, and as soon as the cops arrived (two cars and eight motorcycles) we took off.

"How far is it to the venue?" I asked the driver.

"Twenty minutes," said Clarence. "It's always twenty minutes."

"Twenty minutes," said the driver.

It was an interesting drive. During the last two or three miles the streets were lined with Harleys. There were bikes of all shapes, sizes, and vintages. I saw one with New Zealand plates.

On the hill just before we dropped down to the site, the lead police car had to stop for a bike that was in the road. Within seconds a huge crowd gathered around Bruce's car, taking pictures and asking for auto-graphs. Bruce smiled and waved and accommodated everybody he could. Clarence kept the window in the limo closed.

"These situations still scare me," he said.

"Doesn't bother Bruce," I said, as I watched the Boss lean out the window and put his arm around some biker chick while the guy she was with snapped pictures with an iPhone.

"Bruce," said Clarence, "can move a lot faster than I can."

After a few minutes we got rolling again and finally pulled into a fenced area behind the stage where the trucks were parked. The catering tents were up and the "dressing rooms," a cluster of trailers way behind some temporary fencing, were ready, with guards posted at the entrance to the area.

"You need to call this one the Tin Can of Soul," I said, as we entered the trailer.

Jennifer Jacobs had once again worked her considerable magic, and inside it looked like home. (Jennifer herself was running a fever with no other signs of distress. Several doctors had looked at her, and their best guess was West Nile virus.) Clarence had his doctor visit and began a now-abbreviated get-ready ritual. This one involved heat, ice, and a nap, in addition to the numbing shot at the base of his back.

"The idea is that once the knees are fixed, the back will stop hurting 'cause I'll be able to move properly again," he told me.

I left him with Victoria and set out to check out the crowd.

The police estimate I got on the size of the crowd was slightly over one hundred thousand people. I walked up on the stage before Alejandro Escovedo went on and looked out at a sea of people. There were concession tents in the far distance, and all the space in between was filled with people. It was an amazing sight. They were mostly bikers but this crowd, at least near the front, was noticeably younger than, say, the Giants Stadium crowd. This group looked vibrant, happy, and more than a little tipsy. But there was none of that Hells Angels/Altamont feeling here. This felt more like a Middle America Fourth of July picnic than anything else. The one thing that was clear was that these were rabid Bruce fans and they were expecting a great show.

Nobody was disappointed.

I'd been in the habit of looking around at the shows for African Americans. Clarence likes to know if they're his fans, and he likes to make sure they've got good seats or access to the pit if that's what they want. They were few and far between, though. Rock music has never been big with black folks, and that's just the way it is. However, many of the security people at the venues were black, and some of them claimed to be fans.

I walked out of the catering tent and saw a young black woman in a security shirt sitting alone by the perimeter fence. I went over and said hello.

"What are you doing over here?" I asked.

"Oh, I'm just watching the fence here in case anybody tries to climb over," she said.

"Does that happen a lot?" I said.

"It did for Elton John," she said, laughing.

"I don't think you're going to get much action tonight," I said.

"That's fine," she said.

I introduced myself and told her that we had just flown in from New York.

"My name is Clarissa," she said. "I was born and raised here, but someday before I die I'm going to see New York City. It's one of my dreams."

"Good for you," I said.

I had a brief fantasy of bringing her with us to the jet and taking her to New York that night, but I quickly dismissed it. There are some things that just don't work no matter how cool they sound.

"Are you a Springsteen fan?" I asked.

Nine times out of ten the answer to this question from African Americans is an "Are you insane?" expression.

"I sure am," said Clarissa. "Since I was a little girl."

"Wow," I said. "What's your favorite song?"

She answered immediately.

"'Jesse's Girl,'" she said.

I had a few words with my idol, George Travis. "What's next, George?" I asked.

He laughed. "Oh, I don't know, something will come up."

"Do you have any idea what the next thing will be?"

"Yankee Stadium," he said. "There's going to be a big celebration for the closing of the old stadium and the opening of the new one. I'm going to do that."

"You couldn't find anything big to work on, huh?"

"No, that'll have to do," he said.

It was beginning to get dark when he finished, and I made my way back to the Temple of Soul.

"Ask Danny if he wants me to wear black and gold or black and silver," Clarence said to Lani, referring to Danny Clinch, the photographer.

"I already did," she said.

"This woman is incredible," said Clarence, turning to me.

"You can never leave us," Victoria said to Lani. "Even if we can't afford you."

"In that case you'll have to adopt me," said Lani. "And put me in the will."

"Deal," said Clarence. "So which is it? Black and gold or black and silver?"

"He said he's shooting black and white, so it doesn't matter," she said.

"I know Danny," said Clarence. "He'll do some color, too. Let's go with black and gold."

"Sold," said Lani.

Clarence was right. Danny did shoot several rolls of color.

After the photo shoot I made my way out into the crowd to watch the opening of the show. There is such an adrenaline rush when the band hits the stage that you can feel it in the crowd. Tonight it felt like nitro as the guys took the stage in the gathering darkness to the sounds of roaring motorcycle engines and went into "Gypsy Biker" to start the show.

There was a gigantic roar that seemed to come from another zip code when they recognized the first notes of the tragic biker song. It felt to me like the crowd was at the level other crowds don't get to until three or four songs into the encore.

There was a lot more to come, and by the time we got to the fifth song of the encore we were all in another place.

Hours later aboard the plane home, Clarence was stretched out across three seats trying to relax his back. Bruce walked down the aisle and stopped.

"C," he said. "Come sit up front with me in one of the big seats."

"You've got big seats?" said Clarence, who was wrapped in a cream-colored terry-cloth robe that Jennifer Jacobs had made for him.

Bruce shrugged.

"Of course I do," he said. "I'm Bruce Springsteen."

Everyone within earshot laughed along with Bruce.

"They're wider but they don't recline," said Barbara Carr, who was sitting in front.

"But they don't recline," said Bruce.

"I'll stay here," said Clarence.

"Good show, huh?" said Bruce.

"Yeah," said Clarence. "Was there any fucking song you didn't play? We could go back and do another one if you want to."

Bruce laughed.

"It's funny," he said. "After the third song I was exhausted. I was thinking, *I'm not going to make it through the night.*"

"Wrong," said Clarence.

Wrong indeed.

This felt like the show that would never end. For everybody but Clarence this was good news.

Bruce got into a groove and simply didn't want it to end. He was framed by huge photographs of himself riding Harleys over the years. He seemed to channel that biker spirit in a hell-bent-for-daylight performance that was actually awesome. He was on fire, intense and energetic like some kind of supersonic gypsy.

"Out in the Street" followed "Gypsy Biker," and the third song, the one that exhausted Bruce, was "Radio Nowhere." "Promised Land" followed, and I looked up at my friend as he stepped forward to play the solo, and I listened as the crowd roared in recognition and the joy of sharing the experience with Clarence. This happens over and over when he saunters forward, looking like the coolest man in the world, and steps into the spotlight. I think that in those moments he actually *is* the coolest man in the world. The connection that these massive crowds around the world feel with him is directly attributable to who he is as much as what he does.

Then came one of those turning points that happens in all the shows. This was the moment when everything got shifted into a higher gear. Bruce picked a sign out of the crowd, held a brief conference with the band, and with a Spanish countdown, launched into Sam the Sham and the Pharaohs' barn burner, "Wooly Bully."

From there on out it was a big, freewheeling rock and roll festival. Bruce and Steve communicated with guitars on "Murder Incorporated" in a secret language that everybody understood. Steve had a great night. His singing on "Long Walk Home" was deeply felt and soulful. The show was great. All the way through to "Seven Nights to Rock," the old nugget from Moon Mullican, the man who inspired Jerry Lee Lewis.

Then the encore began. It started with Bruce asking for Jason to come backstage. I figured every guy and some ladies in the building named Jason would charge forward. But there was only one Jason whom Bruce was looking for—Danny's son, Jason Federici.

"This is the first time we're closing a tour without Danny," said Bruce. "So I'm pleased to be joined by his son Jason."

Then they played "Sandy," the song most closely associated with Danny. It was a touching moment that found a lot of people with tears in their eyes.

After that they charged through a musical juggernaut. "Tenth Avenue

Freeze-Out," with all the little pretties raising their hands once again, followed by "Glory Days," "Born to Run," and "Rosalita." I thought the show was over and took a few steps toward the back of the stage.

"When he went into 'Bobby Jean,'" said Clarence later, "I wanted to kill him."

After that they did "American Land," and once again I headed for the limo. Once again I came back to see Bruce now do a change of pace song: "Thunder Road." His eighth song of the encore is a slow song. (It took me back again to the Santa Monica Civic Auditorium in 1974, when they opened for Dr. John and played a ballad, "New York City Serenade," as their encore.) Then another shift of gears into "Dancing in the Dark," and I felt certain the show was over. It had to be over.

It was not.

Apparently Bruce had taken Steve's suggestion to heart, and they closed the night with the biker anthem "Born to Be Wild."

We left quickly. With a hundred thousand recently fueled bikers surrounding us, it seemed like a good idea.

"When skating over thin ice," Clarence likes to say, "our safety is in our speed."

I waited for him backstage and helped him down the stairs. He put on the big white robe that Jennifer had made for him and paused only to greet the woman who sat guarding the ramp to the stage. She was a big fan but could only listen to the show from a folding metal chair.

"Next time come to see me," said Clarence.

Then we were in the limo again, surrounded by motorcycle cops zooming out of the parking lot and coming dangerously close to the cheering fans who were lining the road. There were people waving all the way to the airport.

We got on the plane and were airborne in minutes.

All of this produced an adrenaline rush that made me feel like I could've flown without the plane.

On board there was fried chicken and hot dogs and Milwaukee brats and lollipops and ice cream and cookies. I am not making this up. It was the menu from every kid's birthday party in the history of time. I found myself wishing the flight were longer. I would've been perfectly content if we had just continued to fly all around the world forever.

Sometime during the flight Bruce wandered back through the plane like he always does, and I got to tell him the story of Damon Wayans and Steve Van Zandt in Spain, where Damon had no idea who Steve was. And when he saw Steve onstage said, "Wow, Bruce must be a big *Sopranos* fan." Bruce laughed and shook his head.

"That's funny," he said. "I just sit around watching TV, and if I see somebody I like I say, 'Find out if this guy plays an instrument. I'm thinking of putting him in the band.'"

We flew on through the night while most of America slept. Sometimes when I'm at home and I awaken during the night, I wonder if the band is on a jet somewhere in the world going to or coming from a show somewhere. Clarence calls the people who tag along on these trips cling-ons, and I guess I'd been one of them. I was reporting on what was happening and I could tell myself that I had a higher purpose, but in fact I was just lucky to be Clarence's friend.

"We have just exploded into the air," said Bruce over the plane's intercom, just after touchdown in Newark.

"I just want to thank everybody, starting with the captain and crew here, and everybody on board for a fantastic show and a fantastic tour. I want all of you to get a lot of rest 'cause I know you're all exhausted. Plus, I've booked us another show in two days."

He got off first, then stood at the bottom of the stairs to greet and thank everybody on the plane for taking this journey with him. I was with C, and I watched as he and Bruce hugged.

"You were there for me night after night after night," said Bruce.

"And I'll be there again," said Clarence.

It was four o'clock in the morning in New Jersey. It was the end of the ride home. The scene was surreal, with the lights from a nearby hangar illuminating the tarmac where this truly motley crew milled about next to the plane surrounded by more trucks and vans and the one big limo.

It was the end of a long, long trip. This, the most recent segment of it, started a year ago, but the journey itself was much older. This was the culmination of decades of travel and music and friendship and money and fame and joy and pain. This was one of those points in time where you stop to catch your breath and maybe look around to see how far you've come. Maybe even risk looking back a little and then, if you're not too scared, ahead.

Clarence

I sat on the back deck of my house and looked out over the Gulf of Mexico. Victoria was in the house getting ready to go out for the evening. The plan was to eat and then find a little bar somewhere with live music where I could sit in and play. The horn was in its case by the front door. I always sat here between tours and surgeries and hurricanes. I had just returned from Atlanta where I laid down the horn tracks for the new album, to be called *Working on a Dream*.

When I walked into the studio Bruce seemed thrilled to see me, and you could sense his excitement about the new music.

It was like the old days. Just the two of us in the studio. Of course, we've had a lot of practice and it didn't take as long.

In fact, I completed my part on six songs in one day. Bruce sat in the booth behind Brendan O'Brien and listened and smiled. Somehow we communicated once again in our unique way through music.

I loved the new stuff. It was amazing...fantastic. It was still rock and roll but so much more complex musically. He'd done it again.

In two days, I was going to leave for New York and the first of the knee replacement operations. I wouldn't be back here until sometime near the end of November. The rehab process would be slow and difficult. It would be good to look at this knee shit in my rearview mirror. I knew that it would eventually make my life better.

I miss Danny. I miss him every day.

Back in the day, we were on the road in Boston. Bruce, Danny, and I were sleeping in an attic that had some beds in it. It was a house that belonged to Jim Cretecos's mother. We were working a place called Paul's Mall, opening for David Bromberg. He had this song called "Red Haired Boy," and we had this red-haired roadie named Danny Gallagher who was convinced that David was making fun of him. Danny was going to kick his ass. Bruce had to calm him down and tell him that the song wasn't about him.

Anyway, Mad Dog started out sleeping in the room, too, but his feet stank so much that we threw him out. He went downstairs and slept on the couch. He snored like a motherfucker, too.

So we were up there and Danny was asleep. Side note: nobody could sleep like Danny. We had this tour bus once with bunks in it. We went around a corner, and Danny fell out of the upper bunk and landed on the floor—and didn't wake up. He just lay on the floor, snoring.

Back to the story. Bruce and I lay there bullshitting. As I said before, Bruce could tell these amazing stories. Ghost stories and shit like that. He was really, really good at it. So he was telling some story, when all of a sudden Danny bolted upright like he was possessed. His eyes were wide open like saucers. We were terrified. Then he said, "Chevy coma soma doma!!" and fell back down, out like a light. Bruce and I just looked at him. We were scared shitless. And then we started laughing.

Throughout all the years since then, we'd repeat that phrase. It became like a secret language. I'd be talking to Bruce and before he'd hang up, he'd say, "chevy coma soma doma" and laugh. Danny always claimed that he knew what it meant. That some secret had been revealed to him in his sleep.

I went to Danny near the end. It was the last time I saw him alive. I was hoping that I could make him laugh, so I asked him what it meant. I told him that this was his last chance to share the secret. He just smiled. He didn't tell me.

I plan to ask him again when I see him.

Clarence

A book?" said Jimmy Buffett. "You can't write a book. You're a musician!"

We were in the bookstore on the side of the road in the Keys, where Jimmy was signing copies of his latest book.

"Oh, right," I said. "I forgot."

"Stick to what you know," said Jimmy, signing another copy. "Play the horn and keep your mouth shut. Don't make waves."

"That's good advice," I said.

"Damn right it's good advice," said Jimmy.

"How come you didn't follow it?"

"I'm exceptional," said Jimmy. "See, I can do the whole music thing but I also have a literary bent. So much so that I say things like 'literary bent' in casual conversation."

I had wandered in here after having lunch at Manny and Ida's, which was practically next door. I had a Cuban sandwich and conch fritters. I felt good after lunch, and I thought I'd go buy a new book and spend the afternoon reading. I walked in to find a line of parrot-heads lined up waiting to meet the author, who was sitting at a book laden table wearing shorts, flip-flops, and a Hawaiian shirt that looked like it was a thousand years old. I walked up to the head of the line and waited for Jimmy to notice me. It's very hard not to notice me. Especially in a tiny Florida bookstore a few feet off the highway.

"You'll have to get in line with everybody else, sir," said Jimmy, when he finally looked up.

"I don't think so," I said.

"I don't think so, either," said Jimmy, smiling. "Big Man! Look, everybody, it's Clarence Clemons!"

The folks in line smiled. Two big stars for the price of one in a very unlikely setting. Well, one big star and me. They applauded.

"What are you up to?" said Jimmy. "Are you guys on the road?"

"Yeah," I said. "We'll be out till next fall."

"Ka-ching!" said Jimmy.

"Amen," I said. "Plus I'm working on this book."

Now we were sitting on one of the beach couches across the road at Pierre's. I had a signed copy of Jimmy's new book. The sun was beginning to sink into the Gulf. I was sipping a beer; Jimmy was drinking iced tea.

"It's all about stories," said Jimmy. "A good book is a good story. Or, from what you're describing, a series of stories."

"Right," I said.

"Shit, I'll buy a copy," said Jimmy.

"Reason enough to do it right there," I said.

"So tell me one," said Jimmy.

"One what?"

"One story. If you're going to do a whole book of them, you ought to be able to tell me one."

I picked up my beer and sipped it. The couches were set in deep, soft beach sand behind the restaurant, and I felt very comfortable. I'd run into Jimmy down here many times over the years. We'd even taken a fishing trip together down into the islands on Jimmy's seaplane. I feel at home with the guy. We have a lot in common.

"Rosa Davis," I said.

"Who's Rosa Davis?" asked Jimmy.

"I'm thirteen, maybe fourteen years old. Rosa was about the same age. I started going to this new school, and she was in the school. I used to walk, and I had to come over this hill just before I got to the school. I used to carry my horn with me 'cause I took band class. You know, music class. I had found music by that time. Anyway, I've been going to the school for about a week and I'd seen her around a few times. She was tough. Good looking but kind of a tomboy. Everybody was afraid of her. Anyway, I come up over the hill one morning and she's standing there waiting for me. I say, 'How you doing?' or something and she walks up to me, looks me in the eyes, and pushes me with both hands. She's a little thing and she's pushing me. I just laughed.

" 'You think that's funny?' she says.

" 'Yeah,' I say. 'I do.'

"And she hauls off and punches me in the stomach with all her might. She knocked the wind right out of me and I went down like a tree! Boom! I'm on the ground.

" 'See you tomorrow,' she says, and walks away.

"So there I am the next morning, and there she is, waiting.

" 'You planning on hitting me again?' I say.

" 'Yup,' she says.

" 'I'll have to hit you back,' I say.

"She steps towards me.

" 'You do what you have to do,' she says, and she punches me again.

"This time I'm ready, though, so I turn out of the way and I reach out and shove her. She punches me right in the mouth. Boom! My lip is split and I'm bleeding.

" 'See you tomorrow,' she says.

"Sure enough, she's there the next morning. This time I put the horn down and I face off with her. Now I'm a big dude, right? And at the time I was in great shape. She's a tiny little girl. And she proceeds to beat the shit out of me! I just couldn't bring myself to really hit her back with a closed fist 'cause I'm afraid I might kill her. So I try to defend myself and just push her away but she keeps coming back and she can hit! Finally I just cover up, and she doesn't even stop then. She kicks me!

"'See you tomorrow,' she says.

"So now I can't sleep thinking about what the hell I'm going to do about this. I could walk a couple of miles out of the way and avoid her but shit, I'm not going to run from some tiny chick. That's nuts! So I figure I've got to fight back. I still don't think I can actually hit her, but I can use my size and my weight to fight back. That was the plan, anyway. I dreaded getting up in the morning. I felt like I was walking into rat city wearing cheese pants.

"There she is the next morning. I put the horn down and we face off. She tries to kick me in the balls, but I grab her foot and spin her to the ground. She gets up quick and dusts herself off. She looks at me and laughs. She actually laughs. Then she attacks me like an insane person. This time I grab her before she can do any damage, but she stomps on my foot and we fall on the ground. We're rolling around in the dirt now, and she's scratching and punching and biting, and I finally roll over on top of her and pin her hands back. It was like trying to hold a cat down. Finally she stops twisting and turning and she looks up at me.

"'Why are you doing this?' I say.

"And she lifts her head up and kisses me.

"At first I'm too surprised to even realize what's happening. But after a few seconds it becomes pretty clear what's happening. Thing is I've never been kissed like that before. She was a hell of a kisser. So I start kissing her back. Then she starts ripping at my clothes, and well...

"Anyway, that's the story of my first real love."

Jimmy wiped tears of laughter from his eyes and finally composed himself. He let out a big sigh and picked up his glass of iced tea. He raised the glass in my direction.

"Big Man," he said.

Don

Clarence was being rebuilt in New York that week. He had his first knee-replacement surgery on Monday and was looking at an autumn filled with hospitals and rehabilitation. But the alternative became intolerable.

"My knees are the worst they've ever been," he said on Sunday. "Maybe it's because I'm so close to the operations, but the pain this week has been off the charts. I'll call you as soon as I can. I might not know what I'm saying and I probably won't remember it, but I'll call."

The Big Man moved forward into the adventure of advancing years with the same positive attitude and optimistic outlook I have always known him to possess. That attitude rubs off on you and explains why hanging with Clarence is such a good experience.

"I hate traveling now without the band," he said before leaving for the airport to head up to New York. "I've got so much metal in my body I set off all the alarms. And they always pull me out of line and wand me. It's a royal pain in the ass."

Then he had the operations.

I was back in Los Angeles. I got a call from Bruce's "body man," Wayne Lebeaux, who had a weekend break from being with Bruce in

Atlanta, where he was continuing work on the album. Wayne's mom was hospitalized in Boston, and he was headed there to see her before going back to Atlanta on Monday.

"I talked to Clarence briefly," he said. "He's in a lot of pain. He has to go on this machine that flexes the new knee, and it sounds like it's a bitch. He's out of it on painkillers right now. There's not much point in calling him yet."

He went on to say that he agreed with Clarence that the new music was great. He also confirmed what Clarence had told me weeks before—that the rumored appearance of Bruce and the Band at the Super Bowl in Tampa had been confirmed.

I put in a call and sent an e-mail and waited for news. Waiting never gets any easier.

A few days later I got the following e-mail from Victoria:

Hi Don and Judy,
C is getting better and better every day (better and better good looking every day too;)) the surgery went fantastic. His right knee was replaced with a black implant (not because he is black) The wound looks dry and sealed. His doctor is pleasured with the result. His knee has not been bothering him too much. He takes pain medication every three hours. I am with him all the time. We spent two days in a nice room on the 8th floor overlooking the East river. Then he was brought downstairs to a recovery room where they bring patients right after surgeries to monitor their blood pressure, oxygen level etc....He was in the same room right after surgery. We're stuck here for several reasons; low blood pressure, low sodium level, slow kidney function, dehydration. He is on an IV. He got a blood transfusion yesterday. A lot is going on in his body. Doctors are trying to get everything back to normal. Everything is getting back to where it was before the surgery. His doctor didn't know that he had a chronic kidney disease. Neither did C. His doctor in Florida never mentioned it to him. The blood work C did in Florida showed a mild kidney problem as we found out. His doctor didn't take it seriously enough to point it out even knowing that C is undergoing a big surgery.

Now we know.

C's condition is stable now but the kidneys need to be followed up by his doctor later. His right ankle is swollen and has some redness on it. It seems like this is normal after a knee replacement surgery.

He is just very tired. It is hard to get some rest in a hospital. Every 10 minutes different doctors, their assistants and nurses come to ask him questions, check on him etc.

I heard Don had some health problems too. I don't know the details. I hope everything is fine. I wish you all the best.

V.

I called him later that day and assured them both that I was fine other than a mild case of food poisoning a month ago. It turned out that he was in intensive care and would remain there until things stabilized.

"The list of things that are working inside you is shorter than the list of things that aren't," I told him.

"Sad but true," he laughed. "I hate this shit but I really had no choice. I wore out the old knees totally. It was this or a wheelchair. This is better. The new knee is going to be great. It's just that the rest of my shit is fucked up."

A week later I sat with him in his hospital room and found him in incredible pain. His spirits were as low as I'd ever seen them. I was very worried for my old friend.

A week after that disturbing visit in the hospital, he had moved across the street into a suite at the Bel Air Hotel. He was feeling a little better and the doctors had cut back on the painkillers. He was learning to walk again.

"Ain't this a bitch?" he said.

"I've seen you better," I said.

"This is the hardest shit I've ever done in my life," he said. "They put me on this machine that bends my knee for hours at a time. This is what they do to terrorists when waterboarding doesn't work."

He was propped up on the bed. Victoria had gone out to pick up some movies for him to watch. He put his head back and closed his eyes. He sighed deeply then looked at me.

"There's this guy in Florida named Big Dick. He works a strip joint in Islamorada called Woody's, and he's got his own band and they play there every night. They're called Big Dick and the Extenders, and when I'm down there I sit in with them. I've known Dick since he first got to town. He's one of the funniest motherfuckers I've ever met in my entire life. He insults the audience. I've seen him get into fistfights with the audience. He's a huge guy, maybe six four, and he's well over three hundred pounds. He's fast for a guy that size and he's tough. Anybody gives him shit and he says, 'I don't come over and fuck up your job at Wal-Mart, do I?'

"He calls the girls who work there 'cheap whores' to their faces and they all love him. In fact the whole town loves him. He's actually a super-nice guy and does a lot of charity work. He says he has to or they'll shut down his pussy palace. Anyway, when I first met him back in the early days, it wasn't that common to see a black man in a nightclub. Especially a club filled with naked white women. But Dick invited me to sit in with the band, and I'll never forget that. It was a bold thing to do at the time. He didn't much give a shit what people said because he was my friend. But when I showed up there and started playing, somebody got nervous and called the cops.

"Well, this lady cop shows up. She was Cuban and she was smoking hot and we hit it off. When the club closed, Dick stayed behind to count money, and she drove me to his house. I was staying in his guest room.

"When Dick got home he sees this cop car parked in his yard. He goes into the house and finds this trail of clothes going from the front door all the way up the stairs to the door of my room. It was her uniform and all of my clothes. I made her keep her gun on, though."

He rubbed his hands over his face and laughed.

"He had some bad-looking women working there," he said.

"Bad as in good or bad as in bad?"

"Bad as in they looked like they'd been smacked in the face by a thousand cocks," he said.

"That's bad."

He sat for a while and touched his knees. He winced and sighed.

"One night we were doing a show someplace and...you know how Jo used to toss me my fedora halfway through the show? Well this one night, I'm pretty sure we were in Manchester, England, I turn to get the hat and it's already in the air and it lands perfectly on my head."

"I was there," I said. "Jo turned and looked at me. We were both in shock."

"Me, too."

"He said, 'Did you see that?' and I could only nod."

"I have no idea why I thought of that," he said.

"Who cares? A good story is a good story," I said.

"Yeah," he said. "Did I ever tell you how I used to run five miles in the morning before school? I did it every day. I used to pass this guy who was loading a produce truck in the morning, and he stops me one day and says he'll give me five bucks to load the truck for him when I passed by. So I said great. I'm getting exercise and I'm making money.

"Then about a week later another guy stops me and asks me if I'd like to make a few bucks every day by feeding his turkeys. He had a turkey farm that I ran past. So I did that, too. Then after school I worked a few hours for a fishmonger and a few hours for the racist butcher. I had four fucking jobs while I went to high school.

"I made more money a week than I did during the first three years with Bruce. We were broke. We'd sleep on the floor in these cheap motels, the whole band in one room, 'cause that's all we could afford. We were doing that even after the second album! Can you imagine that shit? We've got two albums out and nobody has any money. We didn't start making real money till after *Born to Run,* but then things started looking up. And they haven't looked down since. That's why I'm always careful with money...I never had any.

"It was fun, though, you know? We didn't realize that we were poor 'cause we had the music. Plus we developed a following and there were always girls around. It was a wild time. I hung out with Danny most of the time. We shared an apartment eventually. We got to be like brothers.

"He always did everything first. And then he'd turn me on to whatever he'd just discovered. That was true of my first joint, my first drink, and my first time hearing classical music. He could play all the classics. He always led the way. He was also one crazy son of a bitch. I really miss him. I really do."

Later we sat in the living room and watched *Blade Runner,* which Victoria had never seen. Then we ordered dinner from room service and talked some more. Once you get Clarence going it's like an iPod on shuffle. The stories and lines come out in random order but they're always entertaining.

"Twice in my life I've gotten great deals on real estate 'cause people wanted to spite their racist neighbors. Once in Sausalito and once in Sea Bright," he said.

"You told me that before," I said.

"Bears repeating," he replied. "Besides, how am I supposed to remember what stories I've told and what I haven't told? I'm on drugs and I'm old. I can't remember shit anymore. I can't even remember what I can't remember."

"Let's forget it," I said.

"You know what's fun? Melting urinal ice. I wish there was a way to turn that into a game or a sport or something. I'm having a urinal put in the new house so I can melt ice whenever I feel like it. There's something very satisfying about the whole process."

"All right," I said.

"You're not supposed to bring bananas on a boat, you know."

"Why not?"

"It's like no peanuts in the pit at the races. No bananas on a boat. It's 'cause bananas are heavy, and when they started shipping them from Hawaii a bunch of boats sank, so they started to fly them out. True story. It's also true that when business is up at the racetrack the stock market goes down. When the market goes up the take goes down. Basic economics."

"No kidding?" I said.

"Nope," he said, smiling slightly. "These are all facts that most people don't know. The Who were originally going to call that song 'The Kids Are All White,' but they thought better of it."

"You should put all this stuff in a book," I said. "*Little-Known Semifacts,* by Clarence Clemons."

"Albert Einstein got tons of pussy," he said. I could see him changing gears. "People need to spank their kids. And they should go to church."

"Who? The kids or just people in general?"

"Everybody," he said. "And you should listen to your heart 'cause your heart will never lie to you."

There are times when I've been in Clarence's company when he uses words and thoughts like musical notes. He riffs, letting one thought flow into the next no matter how far they're separated by content. It's fun when he gets like this. It's like turning the dial on the world's hippest radio and listening to the voices.

"If I ever open another club, and I'm thinking about doing that down in the Keys, I'm going to call it the Salt Lick, because you keep coming back to a salt lick," he said.

Victoria went and got another movie. This one was called *Venus* and starred Peter O'Toole. Clarence loved it. He said it was his favorite movie of all time. He also said that after *Blade Runner,* and I suspect he says it after every movie he watches.

The next day after his morning exercise, which to my eye was indeed like torture, we sat in the living room and talked story.

"You're going to be incredibly healthy when you get out of here," I said. "You can't drink, you can't smoke dope, and you can't eat any bad shit. I hope it doesn't kill you."

"Me, too," he laughed. "Actually I stopped smoking dope a while ago, and I stopped drinking while I was getting ready for this."

"You keep this up and we'll have to change the name of the book to *Middle-Sized Man,*" I said.

He laughed again and sat back in the chair. I thought he had fallen asleep but he was just thinking.

"Nobody wins a war," he said, apropos of nothing. "Somebody just loses less."

"You have a tendency to speak in T-shirt captions," I said.

"Missed my calling," he said.

"I don't think so."

"I could go for an Italian beef sandwich," he said. "There's this place in Chicago called Al's on Taylor Street that has the best ones."

"Be cold by the time it gets here," I said.

"We could heat it up but it wouldn't be the same," he said.

Victoria went online, found a Chicago themed restaurant nearby, and ordered three Italian beef sandwiches to be delivered.

"Cell phones have gotten stupid," said Clarence. "I was in an airport men's room last week and heard a guy talking to his wife while he was taking a shit. How much respect do you think he has for this woman? How much esteem does he hold her in when he's grunting and farting his way through 'Yeah, I love you, too.' Sweet Jesus. You should be allowed to shoot a motherfucker like that. You should be allowed to do it in the name of preserving mankind."

"There'd be too many dead people," I said.

I went into the kitchen and got myself a beer. When I came back he had switched into a more reflective mood.

"I think about death a lot more lately," he said. "Course that makes sense, given my age and my medical condition. I'm thinking of reading the Bible more often. I think of it as cramming for my finals."

Like a lot of people, Clarence has deep religious beliefs but needs to be forgiven a lot.

"Yeah," I agreed. "The death thing fucks everything up."

Outside we could hear the sounds of New York City. The horns and the sirens. People coming and going, some for the first time and some for the last. It was getting darker out.

"I thought *Magic* was a great title for the last album," he said. "Course I happen to love magic. I think people need to be amazed, and magic is one of the few things left that can do that. We've lost our capacity to wonder, and that's just sad. But when you watch somebody do sleight-of-hand—I'm talking about somebody good—you become a participant in the trick. The magician uses your instincts against you. I read this fascinating article about it in the *New York Times*. It said that 'magic exposes the inseams, the neural stitching in the perceptual curtain.' Isn't that fantastic? Isn't that magical?"

He didn't really want an answer. His face was filled with the wonder he found missing in others. He shines from within and radiates a kind of...goodness. You don't really care if Albert Einstein got laid a lot (he did); you just want to hear the Big Man tell the story. He has the ability to distract you from the bitcheries of life. He can do it with music and he can do it with words. He creates something out of nothing. If that's not magic, then what is?

About a week later he was back in the hospital with more complications. I went there and sat with him one afternoon. He was on a lot of painkillers and was in and out of it the whole time. But still we talked and laughed the way we usually do. It started to get late and I was about to leave.

"I was going to say something," he said.

"About what?"

"I don't know, it's gone," he said. "I forget everything nowadays."

He was quiet for a few seconds and I thought he'd drifted off again.

"But the things I remember," he said with his eyes closed.

I'm not at all sure that he was talking to me or if he even knew that I was still there. A smile spread across his face and he spoke again.

"The things I remember...," he said.

The Legend of Clarence's Last Visit with Norman Mailer, Paradise Island, Bahamas, 2001

Of all the stories in the book this is my favorite. It feels so real that sometimes I think it actually happened. If I close my eyes I can feel the sun on my face and I can hear the ocean. But that might be due to the fact that I'm writing this at the beach. —C.C.

Clarence and Norman Mailer sat on the beach in front of the One and Only Ocean Club. They were in low beach chairs, which had been draped with thick, white towels from the hotel. Although it was January, the beach wasn't crowded with snowbirds. It was a beautiful day, albeit a little windy. It was an onshore wind.

Clarence wore white shorts, a gauzy, loose-fitting white shirt, and the Panama hat he got in Puerto Rico a long time ago.

Norman wore only cargo shorts and blue-tinted sunglasses.

Both men had their eyes closed and were facing the ocean. They kept their eyes closed as they spoke.

"I'm going to tell you something I've never told another human being," said Norman.

"Why?" said Clarence.

"Why? What do you mean, 'why'?" said Norman.

"*Why* shouldn't be a difficult question for a literary giant," said Clarence.

Norman opened his eyes and looked at the big man, who remained motionless. Buddha-like.

"You believe in God, right?" said Norman.

"Is this the thing you've never told anybody before?" asked Clarence, eyes still closed.

"No, I'll get back to that," said Norman. "This is something else."

"Yes," said Clarence. "I believe in God."

"Okay," said Norman. "And I would assume you subscribe to the theory that God can do anything."

"Yes," said Clarence.

"Good," said Norman, sitting forward in the chair, shoulders hunched, rounded...a fighter's position. "So, could He create a rock that was so heavy that He couldn't lift it?" He smiled, his face flooding with amusement but showing no teeth.

"Freshman philosophy," said Clarence.

"So what?" said Norman. "We're not doing anything else, and it's a perfectly good question. So what's your answer, smart guy? Mr. Smarty Pants."

"Yes," said Clarence.

"Yes what?" said Norman.

"Yes, He could," said Clarence.

"It's not a yes or no question," said Norman.

"Yes, it is," said Clarence, opening his eyes for the first time. He took his sunglasses from his shirt pocket and put them on. "You said, 'Could He do it?' and I said yes."

"Yes, but the question is a conundrum. If your answer is really yes, then there's a rock out there someplace that your God, who can do anything, I remind you, can't lift. The two things are inconsistent, you see. You can't be able to do everything but be unable to do something at the same time. Even a musician has to see that," said Norman.

"He would change physics," said Clarence.

"How?" said Norman.

"You wouldn't understand," said Clarence.

"Try me," said Norman.

"Nobody would understand," said Clarence. "God would do something only God could do and he would change the laws of physics, which I remind you are man-made laws, so that He could lift a rock that He couldn't lift."

"That defies logic," said Norman.

"He'd change logic, too," said Clarence.

A beach boy wearing shorts and a hotel shirt approached them and they ordered beers. He was the same color as Clarence.

Time passed and they listened to the waves. They listened to the beach sounds. Finally, after what seemed like a long time, Norman spoke.

"Three guys get stuck in the city," he said.

"What city?" asked Clarence.

"Doesn't matter," said Norman. "New York City."

"If it doesn't matter why did you pick New York?" said Clarence.

"Because I love New York," said Norman.

"Okay," said Clarence.

"There's a snowstorm or something and they can't get home, so they go to a hotel," said Norman.

"Three guys go to a hotel," said Clarence.

"Right," said Norman. "The desk clerk says, 'There's only one room left. It's thirty bucks a night,' and the guys say, 'Okay, we'll take it,' and they give the desk clerk ten bucks apiece."

"Stop right there," said Clarence, turning to him. "A hotel room in New York City for thirty bucks a night? Is that what you're telling me?"

"For the sake of this story, yes. It's a thirty-dollar hotel room in New York City," said Norman.

"But that defies logic," said Clarence, smiling.

"I know," said Norman. "I'm changing logic."

"Go ahead," said Clarence.

"So they each give the guy a sawbuck and go up to the room," said Norman.

"Three guys together. Are they gay?" Clarence asked.

"They could be," said Norman. "Is that important?"

"I don't know, it's your story," said Clarence.

"No, they're straight but curious," said Norman.

"Okay, they go up to the room," said Clarence. "Then what happens?"

"Then the desk clerk realizes he made a mistake; the room is only twenty-five dollars," said Norman.

"This gets better and better," said Clarence.

"So he gives the bellboy five singles and tells him to bring them up to the guys," said Norman.

"Why not a five-dollar bill?" asked Clarence. "Why singles?"

"'Cause if it's not singles there's no fucking story," said Norman.

"Tell me more," said Clarence.

"On the way to the room the bellboy says, 'Why should I give them all five dollars? I'll give them three and keep two for myself,'" said Norman.

"Who does he say that to?" asked Clarence.

"Himself," said Norman. "Do you want to hear the rest of this or do you want to ask another stupid question?"

"I object to the word *stupid*, but, yes, I can't wait to hear the rest of this," said Clarence.

"So." Norman half turned so he was facing Clarence, who was facing the sea. "That's what he does. He gives each guy a one-dollar refund. Therefore each guy has now paid nine dollars for the room, right?"

"Right," said Clarence.

"Three times nine is twenty-seven," Norman began. "The bellboy has two dollars, which makes twenty-nine. What happened to the other dollar?"

Norman smiled, sat back in his chair, and closed his eyes. "Take your time," he said.

Clarence didn't move. He looked like a statue. A full minute passed. Norman opened his eyes and looked over at Clarence.

"Well?" he said.

"Well what?" said Clarence.

"What happened to the dollar?" said Norman.

"Who gives a fuck?" said Clarence.

"You don't know, do you?" said Norman.

"I know that I don't give a fuck," said Clarence. "It's just a dollar."

"So then where is it?" said Norman.

Clarence turned slowly and looked at him. "You're like a child," he said. "You get these little things, these games and these puzzles, and they delight you as they would a five-year-old."

Norman smiled his cherub smile. "Where's the dollar?" he said.

"I've got it," said Clarence.

"No, you don't," said Norman, who was filled with joy. It was all he could do to keep from laughing out loud.

"Look," said Clarence sighing. "There's twenty-five dollars downstairs with the desk clerk, the bellboy has two, each guy has one, so that's thirty. You only 'lose' a dollar when you verbally combine an addition problem with a multiplication problem. It's a linguistic trick and it's stupid." Clarence sat back and closed his eyes. Norman continued to stare at him.

"I hate you," Norman said.

"Fine," said Clarence.

"Fine," said Norman, sitting back and closing his eyes.

The waiter approached, trudging through the sand holding two silver buckets, each containing bottles of beer and crushed ice. One bucket held Heinekens, the other Budweisers.

"You sign for the beer," said Norman.

Three beers later:

"You ever seen Eddie Izzard's act?" asked Clarence.

"Never heard of him," said Norman.

"He's a part-time transvestite comedian and actor," said Clarence. "He's good."

"I'll check him out," said Norman. "He sounds interesting."

"He is," said Clarence.

They each opened another beer.

"Engelbert Humperdinck got killed today in a car crash," said Clarence.

"No," said Norman. "Where?"

"Pacific Coast Highway in Malibu," said Clarence. "I saw it on CNN just before I came down here."

"That's a shame," said Norman. "How old was he?"

"I don't know," said Clarence.

"Too bad," said Norman. He sipped from the fourth bottle of Bud and thirty seconds passed.

"I'm kidding," said Clarence. "He didn't die."

"He didn't?" said Norman.

"No, I made it up," said Clarence.

"You asshole," said Norman, smiling.

"No, actually he did die. I was just fucking around, I'm sorry. He is dead," said Clarence seriously.

"Is he dead or not?" said Norman.

"Yes," said Clarence. "He was killed in a car crash on the Pacific Coast Highway in Malibu."

"Shit," said Norman.

Clarence took the bottle of Heineken out of the melting ice and took a pull. "He's not dead," he said.

Norman looked at him.

"Yes, he is," said Clarence, looking out to sea.

Norman continued to stare at him.

"No, he's not," said Clarence.

Norman waited.

"Yes," said Clarence. "No," said Clarence. "Yes," said Clarence.

Norman stared at him.

Clarence shook his head no, then nodded yes.

"Fuck you," said Norman, turning away.

"You sail, don't you?" asked Clarence.

"I do," Norman answered.

"How come you don't own a boat?" said Clarence.

"That would violate one of my four rules for a happy life," said Norman.

"Which rule would it violate?" asked Clarence.

"Number four," said Norman.

"Which is what?" said Clarence.

"If it floats, flies, or fucks, rent it, don't buy it."

Clarence laughed. "What's number three?" he asked.

"Try jiggling the handle," said Norman.

"And number two?" asked Clarence.

"One should never be where one does not belong," said Norman.

Clarence laughed and shook his head. "You are the funniest white man I know," he said. "People have no idea how funny you are."

"I know," said Norman. "I'm stealth funny."

"Okay, I'll ask," said Clarence. "I'll play straight man. What is your number one rule for living a happy life?"

"Never eat fish from a truck," said Norman.

Later they moved up to the beautiful, open-air bar above the beach and ordered conch fritters and more beer. Everything in the world felt right. They sat at one of the tables along the far side of the place next to the sea. There were huge white clouds on the horizon.

"The thing I've never told anybody before —," began Norman.

"I was wondering if you'd get back to that," said Clarence.

"— is that I'm a compulsive liar," said Norman.

"Is that true?" asked Clarence.

"Good question," said Norman. "Yes, it's true that virtually nothing I say is true. I've been this way all my life. Even as a child I'd just make shit up. I turned it into a career. Now I make shit up for money. But I do it even when there's no reason to do it. I'd simply rather lie. Maybe *rather* is the wrong word, because it implies choice and I have no choice. As I said at the outset, it's a compulsion. It makes me quite unique. A rara avis, a squonk's tears, a trumpeter swan sandwich."

"*Outset*," said Clarence. "Good word."

The fritters came in a small basket lined with a linen napkin. They each ate one. A woman with two children entered and sat on the other side of the bar. She wore some kind of sheer cover-up over a blue, one-piece bathing suit, which was not flattering. The kids, both boys around six or seven each, sported Prince Valiant haircuts.

"That's it?" asked Norman. "I tell you my deepest, darkest secret, and you have no comment?"

"Is it really your deepest, darkest, secret?" asked Clarence.

"Maybe," said Norman, popping another fritter into his mouth and wiping his fingers on the napkin. He smiled.

Clarence took off his sunglasses, tilted his Panama hat back, and leaned toward Norman. He reminded Norman of a lion.

"You're an interesting man, all right," said Clarence.

"I think so," said Norman. "Or maybe I don't. It's hard to say given the facts, isn't it?"

"And what makes you so interesting," Clarence continued, "is the fact that you're so much like me."

"How's that?" asked Norman.

"Well, I, too, am a compulsive liar," said Clarence.

"You are, huh?" said Norman.

"Lie all the time," said Clarence.

"Well if what you're saying is true," said Norman, "and I have no reason to doubt your veracity, and what I'm saying is true, which I've already indicated is virtually impossible, then neither of us can believe anything the other one says about anything at any time. Because, all things being equal, the truth is that nobody really knows what the truth is."

Clarence ate a fritter.

"True," he said.

That night after dinner they sat in the comfortable lobby lounge and smoked Cuban cigars. Clarence smoked a Hoyo de Monterrey double corona and Norman smoked a Montecristo #2. They were sipping cognac from crystal snifters. They sat in adjacent chenille covered chairs facing the lawn, which in turn faced the sea.

"Do you think anyone, and mind you I'm not restricting this to

Franklin, do you think anyone ever went down on Eleanor Roosevelt?" said Norman.

"I hope so," said Clarence. "She was a fine woman."

"That she was," said Norman. "I worry about this."

"That's what you worry about, huh?" said Clarence.

"Among other things," said Norman. "I always thought it would be nice to be a drummer."

"Is this in any way connected to Eleanor Roosevelt?" asked Clarence.

"No," said Norman. "I was just thinking how much fun it would be to own something called a trap kit."

"Sure," said Clarence.

They drank and smoked for a while.

"I walked by the pool before breakfast this morning, and there was a guy laying on a chaise lounge in the sun. After breakfast I passed by again and he was still there in the same position. And I thought of the first line of my next book," said Norman.

"I'd love to hear it," said Clarence.

Norman closed his eyes and tilted his head back slightly.

"He died on a chaise lounge by the hotel pool just after eight a.m., but laid there all day until he was discovered that night with a sunburn so bad it would have killed him had he not been dead already," he said.

"That's good," said Clarence. "Then what happens?"

"I have no idea," said Norman.

A soft breeze blew into the room through the open doors and windows. It ruffled Norman's thin hair.

"Why don't you write about us?" said Clarence.

"You and me?" said Norman.

"No," said Clarence. "Although that might be interesting, too. I was thinking about me and Bruce and the band. The whole thing. Show bidness. Sex, drugs, and rock and roll."

Norman drew on his cigar and blew smoke in a slow, steady stream.

"Nah," he said. "It's been done to death."

"There must be a fresh angle," said Clarence. "C'mon, you're a fucking genius, aren't you?"

"Yes, I am, which is why I'm saying no," said Norman. "Your fans, Bruce's fans, the band's fans, are true fanatics. At least some of them are. They've chronicled every shit you've taken for the last thirty years. I've seen the Web sites. These poor fuckers have no lives of their own, so they pore over the minutia of everything E Street like demented archaeologists. Bruce sings a song he hasn't done for a while, and they all go fucking nuts like he cured cancer or something. I can't write for people like that. They're crazy, rabid fuckheads who would crucify me if I said anything that didn't conform to the God like status they've endowed upon you. Pass." He sipped the cognac.

"Maybe you're right," said Clarence.

"Oh, I'm right," said Norman.

Clarence nodded. The woman with the two kids from the bar walked into the room with a short, bespeckled balding man. He wore a Tommy Bahama shirt with palm trees on it. She wore a black dress and some kind of transparent shawl, which looked similar to the cover-up she wore earlier. She looked at Clarence and Norman and then at their cigars. She wrinkled her nose and said something to the man, and they left. Clarence smiled.

"Unless...," said Norman.

"Unless what?" said Clarence.

"Unless it was partially bullshit," said Norman.

"What was bullshit?" said Clarence.

"The book," said Norman. "What if it was bullshit? What if we just made things up? I mean, I could write some real stuff about you, but then I'd say you also invented the cardiac stent. Not the medicated one, the original."

Clarence laughed out loud. It was a big sound and made the bartender look up from all the way across the room.

"You're funny," he said.

"It could be good," said Norman. "Remember that book Guy Peellaert and Nik Cohn did? It was called *Rock Dreams* or something."

"I don't think so," said Clarence.

"I'm going back thirty years," said Norman. "They were paintings and stories. They imagined rock stars in fantasy situations but real at the same time. Like the Drifters were under the boardwalk and the Beach Boys were on the beach and Dylan was in the back of a limo wearing Wayfarers and a big fur coat with a cat on his lap."

"I'll check it out," said Clarence.

"Yeah," said Norman. "But I'm talking about a journalistic equivalent of that. Just let my mind go and see where it takes me."

"And I'd be in it?" asked Clarence.

"Yeah," said Norman. "Ostensibly, it would be about you. You, Bruce, Queen Elizabeth, Englebert Humperdinck, Rodney Dangerfield, whoever. Maybe I'll put myself in there."

"I like it," said Clarence.

"So do I," said Norman. He smiled. He looked pleased with himself. "The possibilities are limited only by the imagination."

"That could be a problem," said Clarence.

They smoked their cigars. It occurred to Clarence that he hadn't heard a dog bark since he'd arrived here.

"Course I'd have to tell real stories, too," said Norman. "That's where it gets difficult."

"Why?" said Clarence.

"Well," said Norman, "the problem is that it's all been said. You've been so covered, so interviewed, so photographed, and so mythologized that there's nothing left to say."

"You could talk about what a good dancer I am," said Clarence.

"Always an option," smiled Norman.

"So do you want to do it?" asked the Big Man.

Norman thought for a minute.

"Nah," he said finally. "You can have the idea, though. Give it to one of your hack writer friends. I just don't have the time."

An hour later Norman had gone to his room, and Clarence sat on a bench at the edge of the low bluff, looking at the night sea and feeling the warm tropical wind on his face. There were storm cells out over the ocean, and he could see them backlit by moonlight. Individual clouds drifted by with curtains of dark rain trailing from them like the tendrils of a jellyfish. Heat lightning burned the sky. Clarence thought about a girl he knew in high school, then about a song he used to play, then about the house he grew up in back in Virginia, then about a street in Paris, then about a room he stayed in once in San Francisco, then about a painting of a child and a dog sitting on a pier, then about a bottle of wine he especially enjoyed at a restaurant in New York or maybe Boston with its gardens and grown-up houses and trees along the river and the pizza in the North End and a car, his first car, a '62 Chevy, a burgundy convertible; and he thought about all the people who had died and he thought about death itself and how his was coming someday and about how scared he would be to stop living and lose it all and slip into that great blackness and would it hurt and for how long; and he thought about the endless rush of time and color and sound as he moved down some corridor like at the end of *2001: A Space Odyssey*, where that guy is in that room where you're young and you're old and you're young and you're old again; and he thought about his mother and his father and his children and his concept of God and about Heaven and who would be there and would there be awkward moments like when Jackie O runs into Marilyn, and he wondered why ghosts are always wearing clothes and did that mean that shirts and pants existed after death, too; and he thought about all the things he didn't do that he said he would, the broken promises, the broken hearts, the broken glass, the fragments of regret scattered around all his rooms, all his days; and he thought about the rain, the soft, steady kind, the deep, soaking rain that strangely brought him comfort on the days that said the sun would never come out again, and the rain would wash him clean if he stood in it and opened his arms to it and turned his face to the dark, weeping sky and allowed it to soak into his soul and make him one with the rain, part of it, lost in it where there was no pain and no memory and no regret, a place of peace and quiet, a place beyond hope, beyond repentance, beyond redemption, and beyond death.

*   *   *

If you had looked from the hotel you would've seen the Big Man sitting on the bench put his hands over his face and breathe deeply. You would have seen him stand slowly, feeling all the pain his body carried, and turn slowly, from the sea and begin to walk away. You would have seen him gradually fade from view and finally disappear into the darkness.

Clarence

I've never felt this bad in my life," I said.

It was Thanksgiving week. Don and I had been talking and texting for a few days about the horrible depression that had descended on me in the days after I got home from the hospital. The operations and the constant pain were taking a psychological toll as well as a physical one.

"They didn't tell me this was going to happen," I said.

"Of course not," he replied. "If they did you might not have the operations and the doctors couldn't buy new BMWs."

But even Don couldn't make me smile today.

"I can't talk anymore, Don," I said. "Call me tomorrow."

The next day brought a slightly more hopeful attitude.

Had a good day, I texted to Don. *Hard workouts. Same tomorrow. I will get through this.*

The previous week I had described myself as an emotional mess. "I am really losing it," I said.

These operations and the attendant rehab process would be a bitch for someone who was in good shape when they went into it. I was not, so my recovery was all that much harder. Postsurgical depression is a very real thing, and it hit me hard. Today I read of a new study of heart patients with depression. The rate of another "event" occurring was 50 percent greater among the group who were the most depressed. This happened because they were less likely to continue their exercise programs and watch their diets. Basically they were more likely to just say, "Fuck it." The fact that I'm working out hard is a good thing. The question is, can I keep it up before this dark cloud descends on me again?

Last week the release of the new album was announced. Five days later Bruce and the Band will be playing at halftime in the Super Bowl game in Tampa. Right now it seems impossible that I will be able to walk out on that stage and perform with them. If I do, it will take some kind of miracle. And I'm afraid that I might be all out of them.

Don

I saw Clarence in person tonight for the first time in months and he looks great. Following his double knee-replacement surgery he's lost forty pounds. He's working out daily and watching his diet. He has stopped drinking and smoking, and his eyes are clear and bright and he looks fantastic.

Except for the wheelchair.

I wasn't prepared for the wheelchair.

A little earlier, I was standing outside the world's most bizarre night-club/restaurant, Tatiana's, located in a dying strip mall in Hallandale, Florida, between the senior health-care center and a credit dentist. I was there to meet Clarence and Victoria and her twin sister, Julia, who were celebrating their thirtieth birthday. I was with Damon Wayans and his date for the evening. Damon and I had come to Florida to attend Clarence's charity golf tournament, to be held the two days before we headed to Tampa for Super Bowl week. Clarence's limo pulled up and Lani Richmond got out, followed by Victoria and Julia and her husband. Clarence leaned out of the back door and smiled.

"Daddy-o!" he said.

Perfect Tommy Kline, Clarence's driver and facilitator extraordinaire, got out of the car, said hello, and took the chair out of the trunk.

The Super Bowl show was eight days away. In fact, Clarence had flown to New York for the first rehearsal. We would all be driving up to Tampa after golf, and there were more rehearsals scheduled for Tuesday through Friday at the site.

Clarence got out of the car with help from Tommy and Victoria, and stood. Tommy handed him a cane.

"Getting old is fucked," said Clarence, smiling.

"Can you walk?" I asked.

"A little," he said. "It's getting better every day. This has been a bitch on wheels."

"What about the Super Bowl?" I asked. "Are you going to make it?"

"We'll see," he said. Then something shifted in his eyes and he spoke again. "Hell yes, I'm going to make it. And then we're going back out on the road for the best part of the next year. I'm going to make all of it," he said.

"Are you in a lot of pain?"

"Yeah, but it's not my knees or my hips," he said. "Now it's my back."

"You're not thinking about more surgery, are you?" I said.

"Yeah, I am," he said. "I have to. I'll do it after this tour because there's going to be a long, long recovery period after this one. But then I'll be perfect and pain free. Then I'll probably drop dead."

We had a fun time in the deeply weird Russian restaurant. Words actually fail to convey what the evening was like. Suffice to say it included lots of food I couldn't identify, lots of Russian music and conversations in Russian, festive and unbelievable costumes, giant Fabergé eggs lowered from the ceiling by exposed wires, lots of traditional dancing, a snake charmer, artificial smoke and holograms, a girl who flew around the room suspended by pieces of cloth, the old Santo and Johnny hit "Sleep Walk" played by a Siberian trio, and a fire-eater. And that barely scratches the surface.

The next night, Damon and I attended the charity auction back at the Hard Rock in Hollywood, Florida. Then Damon headed down to South Beach, and I went northwest to Tampa to begin the countdown to halftime, when the horns would kick in and "Tenth Avenue Freeze-Out" would begin. I still could not imagine that my old friend would be able to walk to the front of that stage and stand next to Bruce when it was time for "the Big Man to join the band."

Clarence

Tuesday afternoon is the first time the band gets to practice on the stage. Everyone is in high spirits. The new album, *Working on a Dream*, has just been released, and the new tour dates are being announced. We'll be touring the States for a couple of months starting in April, then spending most of the summer in Europe. When we return home we'll continue to play into the fall. It's a heady time, and we all feel lucky and blessed.

But first there is the Super Bowl gig. We have been given twelve minutes onstage. Bruce quickly decided on the edited four song set list of "Tenth Avenue Freeze-Out," "Born to Run," "Working on a Dream," and "Glory Days." He also added other horns and the choir to beef up the sound and the spectacle.

This morning I sat with Don and listened to a CD of those four songs that Bruce had sent over, with crowd noises added so that it was as close as possible to how it would sound onstage. It is this attention to detail that continues to amaze me.

But that obsession with perfection becomes even clearer inside the big tent, where the stage is set up. We rehearse those four songs for more than three hours. Three hours would be a long time to rehearse four songs even if they were new, but when you consider the fact that we have played three of these songs thousands of times before, and that there are potentially four more days of rehearsal, the dedication to getting it right becomes somewhat astounding.

I ride home exhausted.

Don is staying near Victoria and me at the Saddlebrook Resort outside of Tampa. I have stayed here before and liked it. Bruce and the rest of the band are staying in Sarasota at the Ritz Carlton. Nobody is staying anywhere near the event itself.

We go out to an early dinner, and I know everyone could see the exhaustion in my face. This is, after all, the first time I have tested my energy level since the operations.

"I can't sleep," I say. "I keep waking up, and then I just lay there thinking."

"What do you think about?" Don asks me.

"The show," I say. "Performing onstage. Getting it right. You'd think I'd have it down by now, but every show is like the first time. And I'm worried about falling down in front of a billion people."

After dinner we go back to the house where Victoria and I are staying and I put the rehearsal CD on again. I chat with Don a little more, make plans for tomorrow and he starts to leave. Before he closes the door, he looks back and tells me that what he sees right now is the definition of who I am. I agree. It is a summation of my life: after playing the song for hours that day, after playing the song thousands and thousands of times over the last thirty-five years, I am sitting in a room somewhere in Western Florida listening to "Born to Run."

Don

It is my birthday again. I'm not one to spend any time looking back, and I'm not going to start now. I'm looking forward to the show on Sunday, and all my hopes and prayers are with my friend. I hope he can do this. I hope he can walk out on the stage and stand up at the front for all his solos like he's always done.

Today is another trying day of rehearsal, lasting almost four and a half hours. Again they play the same four songs over and over and over again. At one point in the show (and in all the shows for the last ten years or so), Bruce asks Steve, "What time is it?" and Steve (and most of the crowd) answers, "It's Boss time!" When they reach that point during the third hour of today's rehearsal, and that point comes during the fourth song, "Glory Days," Bruce decides to change the answer to "It's Super Bowl time!" After making that word change, Bruce feels compelled to start the entire set again from the top. It is exhausting just to watch. But that's why these guys are who they are. (After making that change the Boss decides to put it back the way it was.) Clarence spends most of the day sitting on a stool on the stage.

Later that night, Clarence, Victoria, and Lani throw an impromptu birthday party for me. We laugh, tell jokes, and make plans for the future that none of us know if we'll be able to keep.

It is a nice night. What Sunday will bring is still very much in doubt. As I said, Clarence has spent all of today seated and has not tested his new knees. I don't ask him if he thinks he'll be able to stand on the stage Sunday and play, because I already know the answer.

Clarence

It is another long and busy day. We drive into town for the first Bruce Springsteen press conference since 1987. It's hard to say why he waited so long, because he is loose and entertaining and very, very funny.

When he is asked the secret of the band's longevity he says, "We stayed alive."

Afterward we drive to the stadium for a run-through on the stage inside the arena. This would be tough enough on me if it weren't raining, but it is.

"That fucking stage is like glass," I say to Don after the first of three full performances.

In fact, when Bruce does his patented knee slide he goes right off the edge of the stage into the cameraman who is shooting from that angle. (An "accident" he would repeat during the actual performance.)

I try to be a trooper and stand for part of the performance. The pain is intense. I am shuttled back and forth to the stage in a golf cart driven by George Travis, who apparently does everything well. He backs an extended golf cart out of the stadium and through the crowd of extras as if he's been doing it all his life. (George says, "Once a truck driver...")

Earlier in the mobile Temple of Soul, Don asked me about my youngest son, Jarod, who is now eleven years old. Jarod's mother is White Jackie, whom Don had never met.

"He's a great kid," I told him. "He looks exactly like me. He can pick up an instrument and five minutes later he's playing it. He flew down from Connecticut on his own and stayed with us last Thanksgiving. I didn't know he existed until he was three years old."

"What?" said Don. He thought by this time he had heard all of my significant stories, but he was wrong.

"We were playing a gig in Hartford, and these cops show up backstage just before the show to arrest me for unpaid child support," I said. "So George Travis comes over and asks them to at least wait until after the show but they said no. Then George says, 'Okay, handcuff him and take him out through the audience of sixty-five thousand people who are out there waiting to see him.'

"The cops backed off, and I got in touch with Jackie and everything got worked out.

"To this day I have no idea why she didn't tell me about him," I said. "I took the DNA test, but I knew for sure he was my son just by looking at him. He's a great kid and he's added so much to my life. They just moved down here."

Later Don asks George to confirm the story. I'm standing backstage with Victoria when Don asks George if he remembers the police showing up to arrest me before a show. George paused, absorbing the question. He looks at me, then at Victoria, then back at Don. His face never changes. He continues to look at Don with the slightest twinkle in his eye until it became apparent that he has no intention of answering the question.

"You'll have to narrow it down for him," I laughed. "To which arrest you're talking about."

George finally confirms the story, sort of, but only with a nod and a smile. The man is a genius. If I were given the choice to come back as another entity I would choose to come back as George Travis.

The halftime production looks fantastic. After the third pass, this one in full wardrobe (I'll be in a stunning black and silver frock coat), with the moving stage and the fireworks, everyone is exhausted. The guy playing the referee takes an almost comic pratfall on the slippery stage. He isn't hurt, but it scares me. I don't want to fall, it would be brutal. We head home with the prospect of two days off. The next test will be the final one on Sunday evening, when I roll out of the golf cart in the darkness of the stadium, climb the stairs to the stage supported by Lani and Jo Lopez, and get transported out onto the field and am left to stand there alone. The challenge will be to once again become larger than life, transcend this constant pain and transform myself into the Big Man. They tell me a billion people will be watching. A handful of those people, the ones who know me best, will be watching with their fingers crossed.

Don

After two days of rest, during which two of Clarence's sons, Charles and Jarod, join us, Super Bowl Sunday finally arrives. Many years and different mothers separate Jarod and Charles, but they're both similar to Clarence in spirit. Jarod now lives here. In fact, yesterday we drove to the lovely house where he lives with his mother in an Ozzie and Harriet neighborhood, and we sat in their small living room and watched him play drums with his eleven-year-old guitar player friend, Kyler. They were great, and it was sweet to see Clarence watch his youngest son take the first steps on the same journey he himself had taken so many years ago.

"How are you feeling?" I ask Clarence this morning.

"I'm feeling good," he says. "Except for the coughing-up-blood thing."

"What?" I say.

"It's just a bronchitis thing," he says. "An upper-respiratory deal. It fucking freaks me out, though."

"No shit," I say. "Shouldn't you talk to a doctor?"

"I will," he says. "After the show."

"Why wait?"

"'Cause a doctor might tell me that I can't do it," he says.

We get our credentials and leave for the stadium at about one o'clock. We actually have a doctor with us. Dr. Mark Rubenstein flew up from Palm Beach to help the Big Man with his back.

This is my first time attending a Super Bowl, and there is an electricity in the air. Famous faces are everywhere, and everybody tries to out-cool each other. "I was at Derek Jeter's poker party" or "Snoop's shindig" or whatever. Everything is "exclusive." But on this day there is nothing cooler or more exclusive than rolling into the stadium with Bruce Springsteen and the E Street Band. Nobody can get back to the E Street compound of RVs without special credentials.

Times being what they are, and this event being what it is, security is beyond the beyond, and we are almost prisoners back here in the section of the field behind Raymond James Stadium. However, it suits Bruce and the Big Man perfectly. Everybody knows that they're right over there, but you just can't get to them.

Clarence is at peace in the limo on the way to the gig. He feels as good as he can feel, and if determination was lightning he'd be a thunderstorm.

"You up for this?" I ask.

"Watch me," he says.

An hour before halftime Bruce comes into Clarence's trailer just to check on him and to say hello. He comes back fifteen minutes later. Clarence and I are the only ones in the RV.

"I want to make a little contact with you at the top," he says. "Let's stand back to back."

Clarence stands and Bruce backs up to him.

"Now when Max starts and you hear the first piano notes we turn and touch hands," he says. He then starts to hum the concert intro to "Tenth Avenue Freeze-Out," and they each half-turn, face an imaginary audience, touch hands, and separate.

"Once more," says Bruce. "Turn a little slower."

Again he sings the tune and again they turn. This time Bruce squeezes the Big Man's hand.

"Good," he says. "That's good. Then I'm going to do something else. I don't know what yet. Probably put my hand on your shoulder."

"Got it," says Clarence.

"You all right?" Bruce asks.

"Feeling strong," says Clarence.

"Good," says Bruce. "Now on 'Born to Run,' after the camera does that big sweep across the stage you can sit down for the rest of it."

"No," says Clarence. "I want to stand for the whole song."

Bruce looks at him for a long moment.

"Good," he says again, then amends it. "Excellent."

The halftime show is spectacular. A billion people see Clarence standing on the stage and playing his horn loud and clear and strong. He looks like the Big Man in full sail in his black fedora and amazing silver spangled coat. I am up in the stands across the field, and after "Born to Run" I finally exhale.

Afterward in the E Street tent, everyone is on a tremendous high. Bruce is hugging anybody who gets close to him and posing for pictures. Jon Landau is running around like a kid. Clarence is the last to arrive, having been shuttled in after the crowd. When he walks into the tent there is a round of spontaneous applause from the other members of the band.

Bruce opens his arms, crosses to Clarence, and hugs him like a long-lost brother. It is a sweet and touching sight. I am standing next to Clarence and slightly behind him, so I am able to overhear the words that Bruce speaks.

"Big Man," he says.

The Legend of Pozo, 2009

And so here we are again. Bruce and I together somewhere just being who we are. These stories have been set in odd locations or in cars or saloons, because those are the places where we've spent our lives. My friendship with Bruce has defined my life. I can't imagine what would have happened to me if we had never met. I'd still be making music, but not his music. His music feels like it's my music. But not having those songs to play wouldn't be the greatest loss. The greatest loss would have been the friendship we have enjoyed over the decades. Through it all Bruce and I remain a constant. He is my anchor and my friend. He is my brother. —C.C.

Bruce Springsteen walked into the Pozo Saloon, took his sunglasses off, waited for his eyes to adjust, and decided it was good. He was in the right place. It wasn't easy to find. It was miles past Santa Margarita and not on any tourist map.

He hooked his glasses into the collar of his black T-shirt, took a seat at the bar, and ordered a beer. He didn't see any sign of recognition in the bartender's eyes. He was just a kid, maybe twenty-five years old. This pleased Bruce. Sometimes nobody knew who he was and he got to float.

Earlier that day he had lunch in a great place called the Wild Horse Café up near King City, and the same thing had happened. Nobody in the joint had any idea who he was. It made him feel invisible. He'd ordered and enjoyed the Trucker Burger, which was the house specialty. It was delicious.

While he was there an odd thing happened. The waitress behind the counter where he sat on a stool flirted with him. Not in an overt way, but she was flirting without a doubt. She looked to be about forty but it was hard to tell. She was no beauty but she was well, you know. She was a waitress in a truck stop café. But she liked him and she had no idea who he was. No idea. But she liked him. It was clear that if he wanted to hang around King City till she got off work they could have dinner together and maybe something more. For some reason this pleased him more than all the groupies in the world could have. Well, maybe not all of them, but most of them. This woman's response to him was a simple, sexual thing at the most basic level. "You look good to me." Yes. How nice that was every once in a while.

He left a big tip and got back on the highway. He was heading south. He almost took the exit to Jolon just out of curiosity. He had made this drive before and that sign had always intrigued him. It brought the song "Jole Blon" to his mind, and that was a good memory. He'd recorded it years ago with Gary U.S. Bonds, and it was still one of his favorites.

But he continued on. He got off the freeway in the town of Templeton and bought a diet soda from a small deli located in a frontier style strip mall. As he was walking back to his car, he saw the actor Josh Brolin walking toward him. He thought to himself that Bruce Springsteen and Josh Brolin were about to meet. But Josh, sensing someone coming out of the deli who might recognize him and give him some kind of shit, lowered his head and walked right past Bruce. Bruce found poetry in this. Some kind of satisfying beauty. Something about being alone and remaining intact and unto yourself, or some shit like that. All he knew for sure was that he got a kick out of it and wondered if someday down the road he'd run into Josh Brolin and tell him that they had passed within a yard of each other one day in Templeton, California.

Back in the car Bruce looked at the old text message and programmed the exit into the navigation system of the rented Mercedes he was driving.

When the woman's voice told him to take the next exit he did. He drove through the tiny town of Santa Margarita and continued on toward Pozo.

This time of year everything was brown. There was a unique quality to Southern California in the summer, when it was dry and beautiful and vulnerable. The entire place felt fragile to Bruce, and he could relate. Time moved for him at the same speed that it moved for others, and the end of the highway was now closer than the beginning. This place, here and now, was a metaphor for life its ownself, as Dan Jenkins might say.

Bruce was a few beers deep when Clarence walked in. Almost immediately everything changed. There were four women in the room. Two in their forties sitting together and two others sitting with guys. When Clarence walked in they all stopped what they were doing or saying and looked at him. Bruce laughed out loud. Clarence, recognizing the laugh, turned and crossed to the bar. He took the stool next to Bruce, sat down, and smiled. Bruce was having none of this polite shit so he stood and embraced the now seated Big Man.

"Brother" was all he said.

Clarence didn't have to say anything.

Clarence had begun his day in La Jolla. He was staying in a beachfront hotel, and he was feeling good about almost everything. Of course nobody ever felt good about everything, but he was close. He had been to the Pozo Saloon years earlier with this girl from Texas who wanted to be a veterinarian and have a chicken-fried steak, and he remembered the place fondly, so when it became clear that he and Bruce would be crossing paths somewhere in central California, he had suggested meeting there.

Clarence had spent the previous week attempting to sell ideas for TV shows to people in Hollywood who wanted to say that they knew him and could hit him up for tickets when the band came to LA. He had not been successful, but he had found the process to be interesting. But now he and Bruce were sitting here on another of these little islands they had found during their lifetimes. Both of them had the same reaction to these places, these seams in the world where they could actually behave like everyone else. The reaction was relief.

They moved to a table. The eyes of all the women (and one of the men) followed Clarence as he walked.

"Where are you headed?" asked Clarence.

"The LA house for a night, then back to Jersey," said Bruce. "You?"

"My wife's family in San Francisco," said Clarence.

"Good for you," said Bruce. "I really mean that, C. Good for you."

"Thank you, Bruce," said Clarence.

They sat for a while and enjoyed their surroundings.

"Something's been bothering me," said Bruce after a while. "I wanna clear the air, so to speak."

"All right," said Clarence. "Commence clearing."

Bruce used his right thumbnail to remove the label from his beer bottle. Then he looked at Clarence for a moment then back at the bottle.

"One night before a show, I can't remember where we were," he began.

"Philly," said Clarence.

Bruce looked up. "Ahhh," he said. "I'm not alone here."

"As long as I'm breathing you're never going to be alone." Clarence smiled.

"We argued about something that night," said Bruce. "I don't even remember what it was, but I said some things that I didn't mean."

"Forget it," said Clarence. "I did."

"Yeah, but the thing is—"

"Bruce," Clarence interrupted. "I love you."

Then Clarence smiled and Bruce nodded and that was the end of that.

Cows could be seen walking around through the back windows of the place. Three of the women kept stealing glances at Clarence. The fourth one was standing by their table.

"You're that saxophone player, aren't you?" she said.

"Guilty," said Clarence.

"I love you guys," she said.

"What's your favorite song?" asked Clarence.

"The dancing one, I guess," she said. "The one with Courteney Cox in it from a long time ago. Before *Friends*, even."

"Yeah, that was fun," said Clarence.

Bruce sipped his beer.

"Would you do me a favor?" she asked Bruce.

"Me?" said Bruce.

"Would you take our picture?"

She took a cell phone out of her purse and handed it to Bruce.

"Well, sure. Be glad to," he said, as he stood.

"You just look through there and then push this button," she said.

"Got it," he replied.

She then sat next to Clarence, who put his big arm around her, leaned toward her, and smiled at the camera. "Make me look good," he said to Bruce.

"I can only do so much," said Bruce, as he took the picture. "One more for luck," he added, and he took another.

"Thank you so much," she said to Clarence while extending her open hand toward Bruce. Bruce put the camera in her hand and sat again.

"My pleasure," said Clarence.

"What are you doing here in Pozo?" she asked.

"Just came to see my buddy here," he said, nodding toward Bruce.

"Are you going to be doing any more shows?" she said to Clarence.

"That's up to Bruce," said Clarence. "He's the Boss."

"Well, you can tell him that I think you should be the boss," she said.

"I will," said Clarence.

"Okay, then...thanks again," she said.

"You're very welcome," said Clarence.

She gave him a little finger wave then walked away.

"She thinks I should be the boss," said Clarence.

"She might be right," said Bruce.

They hung out and talked for a while about nothing in particular, but if you broke the conversation down you'd find that it covered incidents from more than four decades. They also talked about the future for a while. The bar thinned out, and they switched to soda and then coffee.

They split a chicken-fried steak and a piece of apple pie with a scoop of vanilla ice cream.

Then they had another cup of coffee and talked about music.

Some new people came into the place, and one guy at the bar kept turning around and looking at Bruce with that surprised smile of recognition. The guy was trying to position his cell phone to take a picture. Bruce didn't really mind. He was used to it. In fact, this was closer to normal than the rest of the day had been.

"Maybe he'll ask me to take a picture of the two of you," said Clarence, smiling.

"I don't think so," said Bruce.

The swinging door leading to the kitchen opened, and a Hispanic kid wearing an apron and a hairnet walked out. When the door was open voices could be heard speaking Spanish.

The kid went over to the jukebox in the corner. It was an old Wurlitzer model and had the words Mi Cabana written on the front. He dropped a coin into the slot and began to look at the choices.

"I say Freddie Fender," said Clarence.

"Nah," said Bruce. "That thing has forty-fives, so it'll be something old. Willie Nelson, maybe, or something like Canned Heat."

The kid pushed a couple of buttons and went back into the kitchen.

"If it's 'Born to Run' you're picking up the check," said Clarence.

Within thirty seconds a song began to play. It was "The Girl from Ipanema" from the summer of 1964. Stan Getz's honey-coated sax filled the room, followed by Astrud Gilberto's breathy voice.

"This is from the soundtrack to my life," said Clarence.

"Me, too," said Bruce. "Me, too."

They listened quietly, each with their own thoughts, until the song ended. Nothing else came on afterward.

Outside the day began to pale toward that thin California twilight.

"Well," said Bruce. "Shall we hit the road?"

Clarence

Marathon Key, Florida

And so we did hit the road. A month after the Super Bowl we began rehearsals for the "Working on a Dream" tour that would take us all over America and Europe. We went out on the road and pretty much stayed out for the next nine months. The band was better than it's ever been. I wish I could say the same for myself.

Once again my bad back kept me in almost constant pain. I was still recovering from my knee replacement surgery, but the biggest problem was the disks in my back, which were pretty much shot. But the operation I needed was a motherfucker and would put me out of commission for many months. Since I fully intended to keep my record intact of never missing a show, the back situation would have to wait.

I had a lot of help out on the road. Bruce got a cart for me to get back and forth to the stage and had an elevator installed so I didn't have to face the stairs. Plus I had what he called "The C Team." It consisted of the three beautiful women who took care of my every need: my beautiful wife, Victoria; my incredible assistant, Lani Richmond; and my physical therapist, Krista Simon. Krista traveled around backstage on roller blades and Lani had a scooter. They all took to wearing these big purple hats. It was quite a sight to see them hovering around me onstage. I could not have done it without them.

My youngest son, Jarod, joined me in Europe for a good part of the summer. He was ten years old and a pretty good drummer so this glimpse into the world of big-time rock and roll was a real eye-opener for him. He was with us from Brussels to Spain. When he got home he had a new attitude and started doing really well in school. I hope I was able to provide a bit of inspiration.

There were some great shows on this tour. The band was now performing at the highest level. We played with the combined experience of forty years together. There was no song we couldn't do and do well. We played Bob Dylan's "Like a Rolling Stone" one night and I swear it felt like we'd been doing it for years. In Philly, Bruce added the old Jackie Wilson tune "Higher and Higher" and it ROCKED! We kept it in the show for the rest of the tour.

We played some memorable shows at Madison Square Garden where we duplicated the early albums. It was a joy for us as much as it was for the fans. To do those songs in order and in their original arrangements was a real kick. If I had to pick, I guess "The Wild and the Innocent" was my favorite. Although "The River" was a blast too. Shit, I like them all. I've been playing this music most of my life and I swear to you every time is like the first time. When we're not on the road and I'm home in Florida, I listen to Bruce Springsteen music. Thank God for E Street Radio. It's an essential part of my life.

It was fun to do the book tour when the hardcover version was released. I met a lot of old friends and I'd like to thank everybody who waited in line for a signed copy. It was humbling and a bit overwhelming to see and meet so many people who love me.

We got some wonderful reviews and some really nasty ones too. You can't please everybody. I think some people wanted one of those tell-all books and that's not what I wanted to do. The book was meant to be like a show, and by that I mean I wanted it to be entertaining. Don and I love to sit around and tell lies and we've collected a lot of them in this book. I really hope it gave you a few laughs. We certainly had a few writing it.

I want to talk about the Rock and Roll Hall of Fame show we played in New York last fall. I played that show under protest. I'm not pleased with the Hall of Fame because, although Bruce is in it, the E Street Band is not. Under their rules we don't qualify. It hurts my heart that Danny will never be in the Hall of Fame. I contend that this band is a lot more than a collection of sidemen or backup musicians. We are a family. It's just wrong that we're not recognized as such in Cleveland, of all places.

We finished the tour in Buffalo. It was a great show. Bruce even pulled out one of the old "It was a dark and stormy night" stories when he introduced me like he used to do back in the day. We all woke up from a forty-year-long dream and found ourselves in Buffalo.

I believe we will tour again. I would never say never when it comes to Bruce and this band. We are simply too good to stop now.

After the last show I went to New York and had my back repaired at the Hospital for Special Surgery. In a thirteen-hour surgery my spine was fused from L2 to L5. I now have a lot of metal in my back. Actually I've got metal all over my body now. It's in my hips, knees, chest, and back. Don't come to the airport with me unless you've got a lot of time.

While hospitalized I met one of the most inspiring people in the world. I call her Mama. Her real name is Geri Rivero. She works in the accounting department at the hospital and she was a fan of mine before we met. Now I am a fan of hers. Every morning since we met she sends me an inspirational message. She is filled with more love than anybody I've ever met. Every day in the hospital began with a big smile, a hug, and muffins. Mama is pure positive energy and a very important person in my life. She was there for both Victoria and me during a very difficult time and we both love her. She is proof that angels do exist.

By the time you read this I will be known as Dr. Clarence Clemons due to my honorary degree from the University of Maryland Eastern Shore. At their spring commencement exercises I was made a Doctor of Humane Letters. That's right, Bruce will now have to introduce me as "bestselling author Doctor Clarence Clemons." My Father, God rest his soul, is saying, "I didn't know the boy could read." Trust me, I'm a doctor.

Most of my time lately has been spent in Florida healing. It's a slow process but I'm doing well. I feel stronger every day and look forward to dancing across the stage again on the next tour.

As I write this I'm sitting on my porch looking out at the Bay toward the horizon where the ocean meets the sky. I intend to keep on keeping on until the day the music swells and giant letters rise out of the sea and spell the words "The End."

Dr. Clarence Clemons
Marathon, Florida
May 19, 2010

Don

I went back to my "normal" life after the book was done and produced a couple of television shows. I dropped in on the "Working on a Dream" tour in Philly and New York City but for the most part have spent my time in California.

I am currently in Florida to go fishing with the good Doctor. He remains my favorite person in the world to hang out and tell lies with.

I think the best thing I've ever heard said about my friend was part of Bruce's band introduction one night in England. He said, "I have seen the future of the whole fucking thing and it's Big Man Clarence Clemons!"

Don Reo
The Moorings
May 19, 2010

Acknowledgments

The authors would like to thank the following people: Bruce Springsteen and the entire E Street family. Jon, Barbara, and George for their class and graciousness. Brian, Maria, Scott, Perfect Tommy Kline, and the amazing, amazing Lani Richmond. Darlene DeLano, Wayne Lebeaux, Jo Lopez, Jacob Clemons, Christopher Clemons, Charles Clemons, Jarod Clemons, Nick Clemons; Victoria Clemons for all her help and charm and spirit and love. Judith Allison for all of it. Damon Wayans, Dean Lorey, Rodney Barnes, Chris Rock, and Erik Reo. Jimmy Vallely, who opened the door to all of this. Lydia Wills, who brings grace into the world of agents; the ridiculously talented Ben Greenberg, Mark Long, and all the men and women at Grand Central Publishing. Debbee Klein, Sam Gores, and Ralph Weiss. Cele Cooper. Kinky Friedman, who is an inspiration and example to all.

To Sandy Goldfarb and Bob Mitzman, thanks for the jet.

To all the people who appear on the pages of this book in truth or in fiction. And finally, thanks to all the writers who continue to throw something that glows into the darkness.

With Big Love to all of you,

Don and Clarence.